THEN & NOW

BOONE COUNTY

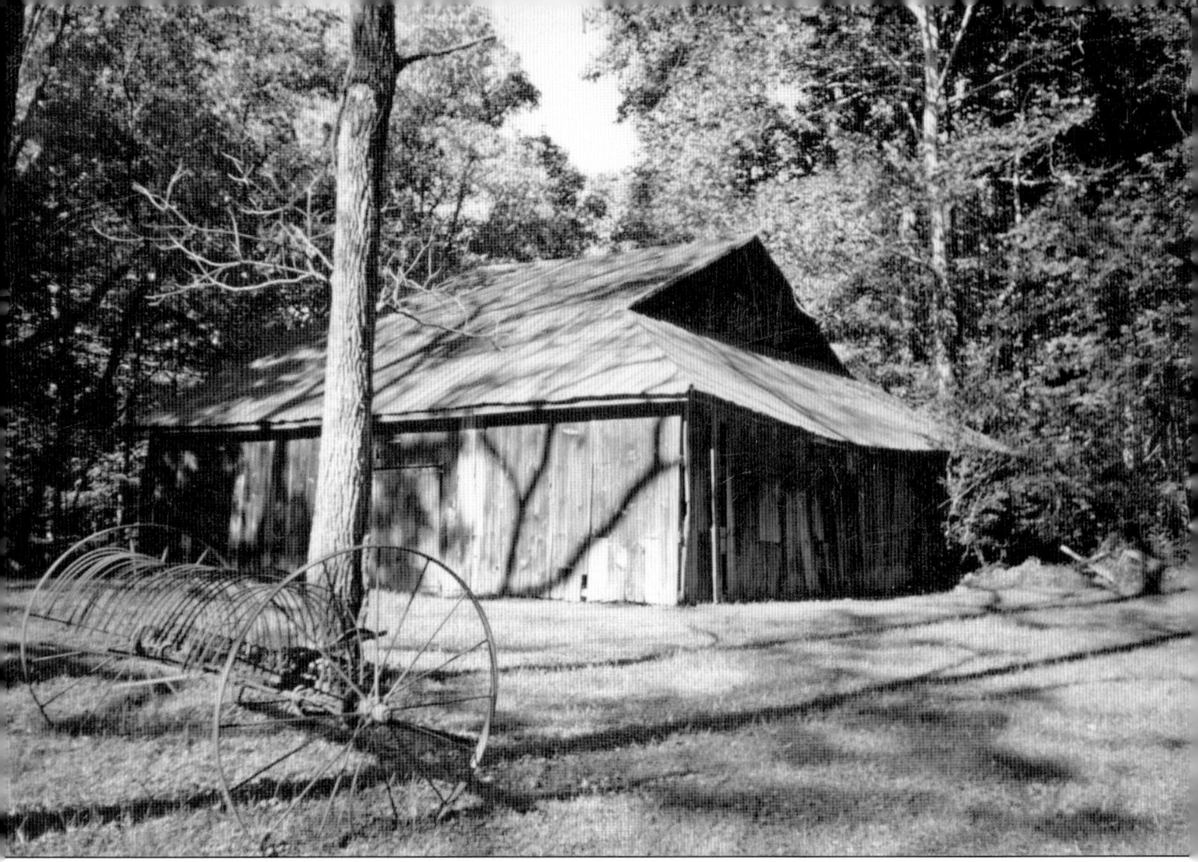

RIGHT BEFORE YOUR EYES. Driving, walking, or biking around the county, one is hard-pressed not to see Boone County history displayed right before their eyes. One great way is to notice the historic barns that appear all around the county. Many are over 100 years old and are a testament to the agricultural past and present. The barn located across from the historic Dinsmore Homestead on Route 18 is a perfect example. Next time you are traveling around the county, take a look.

THEN & NOW

BOONE COUNTY

Robert Schrage

ARCADIA PUBLISHING

ISBN 978-0-7385-4227-0

Published by Arcadia Publishing
Charleston, South Carolina

Printed in the United States of America

Library of Congress Catalog Card Number: 2005933688

For all general information contact Arcadia Publishing at:
Telephone 843-853-2070
Fax 843-853-0044
E-mail sales@arcadiapublishing.com
For customer service and orders:
Toll-Free 1-888-313-2665

Visit us on the Internet at www.arcadiapublishing.com

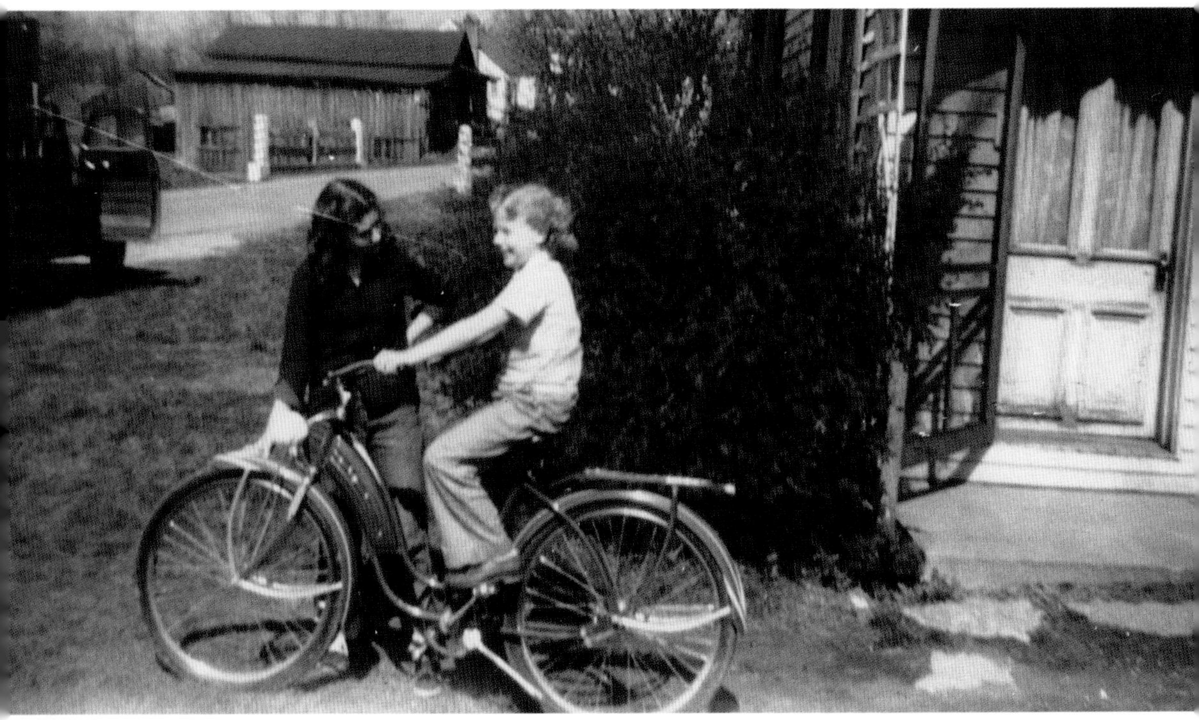

HEART OF BULLITTSVILLE. Doris and Wilma Engle pose with a bicycle in Bullittsville in 1947. A truck holding fruits and vegetables for sale sits on Kentucky Route 20. Behind the Engles and down the road is the old Bullittsville Bridge and the blacksmith shop operated by Theodore Birkle. Doris and Wilma are longtime citizens and have attended Bullittsville Christian Church for many years.

CONTENTS

ACKNOWLEDGMENTS

Putting together any book could not be done without the help of many people. The author wishes to express gratitude to the following individuals and organizations: Matt Becher, Boone County Planning Commission, Boone County Public Library, Layne Cheesman, Donald Clare, Dorothy Coyle, Ralph Denham, M. Keith Dykes, Wilma Engle, Bruce Ferguson, Friends of Big Bone, Mark Jacobs, *The Kentucky Post*, Pat Lense, Betsy Maurer Ligon, Bob Maurer, Margaret Maurer, Doris Newland, Earl Newland, David A. Osborne, Sherry Pinson, Roger Rolfes, Jack Rouse, Michael Rouse, Ann Schrage, Hugh Skees, Bridget Striker, Turfway Park, Mayor Phil Trzop, John Vissman, and Harold Williams.

Although mentioned above, a very special thank you goes out to Bridget Striker of the Boone County Public Library and Matt Becher of the Boone County Planning Commission and the Historic Preservation Review Board. Their contributions to this book were tremendous. These two individuals are truly dedicated to preserving the history of Boone County and are making a difference.

Thank you to Richard J. Schrage (1917–1984), who still lives within me.

Finally thank you to Ann Schrage for her love, indulgence, and great editing skills.

—Robert Schrage

INTRODUCTION

Boone County has continually evolved since its establishment in 1799. The people, churches, institutions, and communities making up this northernmost county of Kentucky have shaped its history through decades and then centuries of influence. However, even before this relatively modern history, Boone County was something special. Not long after its establishment, President Jefferson dispatched Meriwether Lewis to visit the Big Bone Lick section of Boone County for the purpose of collecting bones from the large prehistoric game that once roamed the salt licks. The first residents were prehistoric Paleo Indians and then much later Fort Ancient, Shawnee, and Miami Indians. The Paleo Indians found their way to Big Bone around 12,000 B.C. to hunt the large game. Fort Ancient Indians settled upon Big Bone as a village, and Shawnee and Miami Tribes would visit the salt licks. In later years, Big Bone served as a vacation resort for the citizens of the area and others who visited thinking the water was a cure for some illnesses.

The first settlement of the county by Americans of European descent was Petersburg in 1789. John Tanner, a Baptist preacher from North Carolina, brought a settlement party to the area, first called Tanner's Station. John James Flourney developed Petersburg in the second decade of the 1800s. He platted the town, and in 1818, the Kentucky Legislature officially recognized Petersburg. Prior to this time, Petersburg was the prehistoric site of two Fort Ancient Indian villages; it today lies as the burial sites of these early inhabitants of the county. The community of Burlington, originally called Craig's Camp and then Wilmington, was quickly settled as the seat of Boone County government. It was founded on 74 acres of land donated by Robert Johnson and John Hawkins Craig. Originally incorporated, Burlington's charter was annulled in 1924, and today it has the rare distinction of serving as a seat of county government that is not incorporated as a city. By the early 1800s, other settlements began to develop.

Boone County lies on the Ohio River, and many streams and creeks flow into the river from various places. Beautiful hills and excellent farmland led to an influx of new settlers. As communities developed, agriculture and religion played perhaps the most important roles to the citizens of the county. Described best by the Boone County Fiscal Court Web site, "some small communities, such as Devon, Landing, Hume, and Hamilton, were even official Post Office sites while towns such as Berkshire, Grand Hall, Gunpowder, and Gainesville are only names on the back of an old picture, part of family legends or simply a memory." However, many communities retain their strong sense of identity and community despite tremendous change, including loss of population and the closing of their businesses. Areas like Rabbit Hash, Belleview, Beaver, Big Bone, Constance, and Limaburg are well-established communities that today are recognized by their tremendous history and community. Today Boone County includes only three incorporated cities: Florence, Union, and Walton. Each of these cities developed along toll roads and/or railroad lines. Many of the communities of the county were established along the Ohio River, as will become evident throughout this book.

Religion was important in each of the communities of the county, and as an institution, its start must be recognized as Bullittsburg. The Bullittsburg Baptist Church was founded in 1794 as the first Baptist church in Boone County. This very historic church settled on a road toward Tanner's Station in a beautiful area that allowed for good trade. Hopeful Lutheran was created in 1806. According to the book *Historic Structures in Boone County* (published by the Historic Preservation Review Board), it was founded "by a group of German immigrant families from Madison County, Virginia" and "is said to be the first Lutheran Church organized west of the Alleghenies." In 1850, immigrants from Ireland founded St. Patrick's Church as the first Catholic church in the county. Other denominations, such as the Christian Church (Disciples of Christ), Methodist, and Presbyterian, were founded as well. By far, the prevalent churches were Baptist and

Presbyterian, being founded all over the county. A couple of churches were founded by African Americans such as Zion Baptist in Walton and First Baptist in Burlington.

Today change is everywhere in Boone County. It is easy for those living today to call this a recent event as seen by the constant development and almost daily construction of homes and businesses. However, change started as far back as the 19th century with a depression in agriculture and a steady decrease in population. People moved to the city; however, this did not change the county from its strong agricultural base. The decline in population continued until almost the mid-20th century. Perhaps the biggest impact on the county's development yesterday and today is the creation of the Greater Cincinnati/Northern Kentucky International Airport. Between 1940 and 1950, Boone County's population increased 20 percent. Following the airport was the creation of Interstates I-71/75 and I-275. It is very true the county has never seen such dramatic change in its history than it is experiencing today. Boone County is the fastest growing county in the state and one of the fastest in the nation. Between 2000 and 2004, the population increased by 14, 346 to 101,354, up 16.8 percent. This made Boone County one of only four counties in Kentucky with a population over 100,000. Business and residential development is everywhere.

The impact of all this development has presented many challenges to preserving the rich history of Boone County. This book is meant to help develop an appreciation for this past and show through historic and current images the profound change Boone County has seen. Many people in the county are new to the area, and this book should serve as exposure to the great history of their new home. For those long-term citizens, enjoy the trip down memory lane and relive the tremendous past that makes Boone County what it is today.

Chapter 1
SCENES

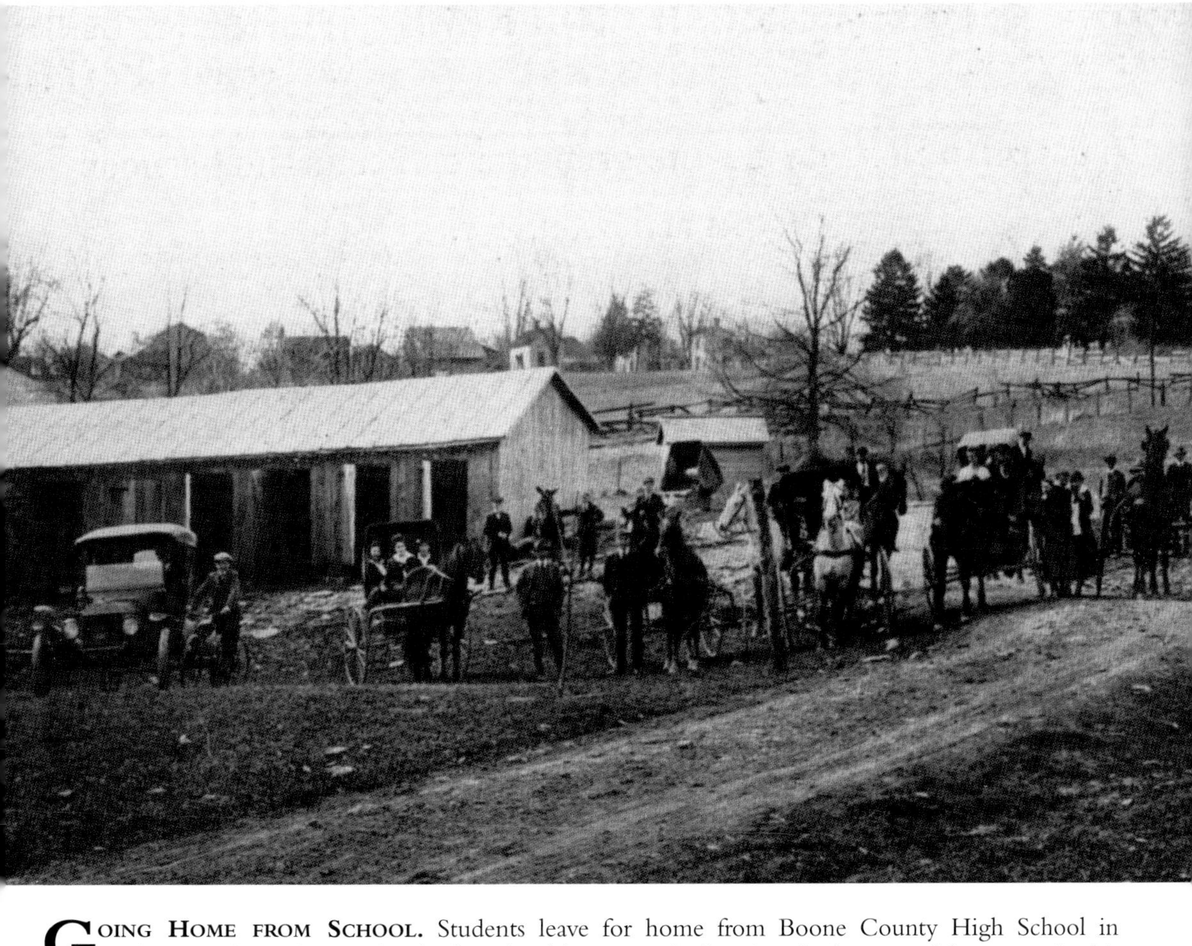

GOING HOME FROM SCHOOL. Students leave for home from Boone County High School in Burlington after a day at school. The school barn was for housing the horses and later cars. In this picture, it is a transition time between the use of horses and buggies and cars. This structure was located near the site of the current Burlington Elementary School.

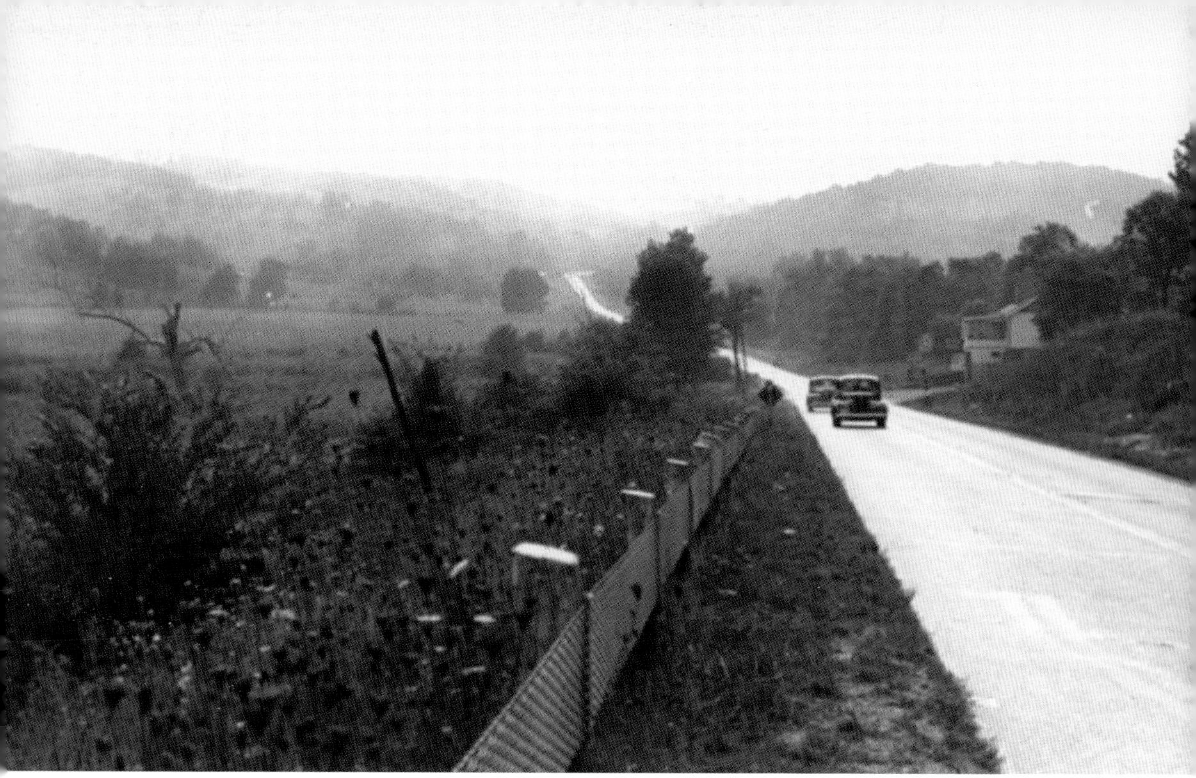

U.S. 42. This *c.* 1940 photograph was taken on U.S. 42 outside of the Beaver Lick area of Boone County. The old Duck Head Inn appears on the right of the vintage photograph, and what remains of it is in the new image. U.S. 42 at the time was the main route from Northern Kentucky to Louisville. Other than the paved Verona Mudlick Road seen on the left in the newer photograph, not much seems different.

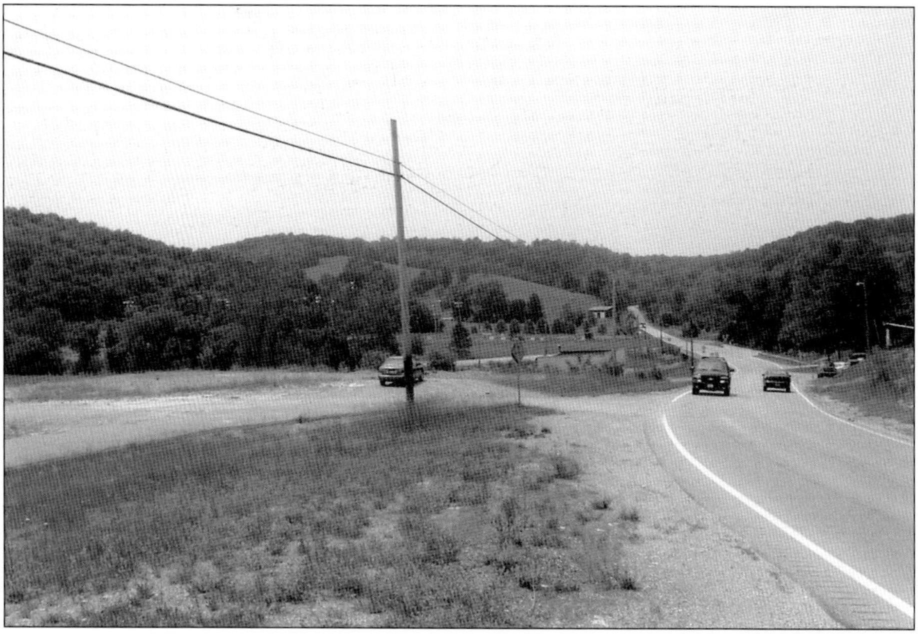

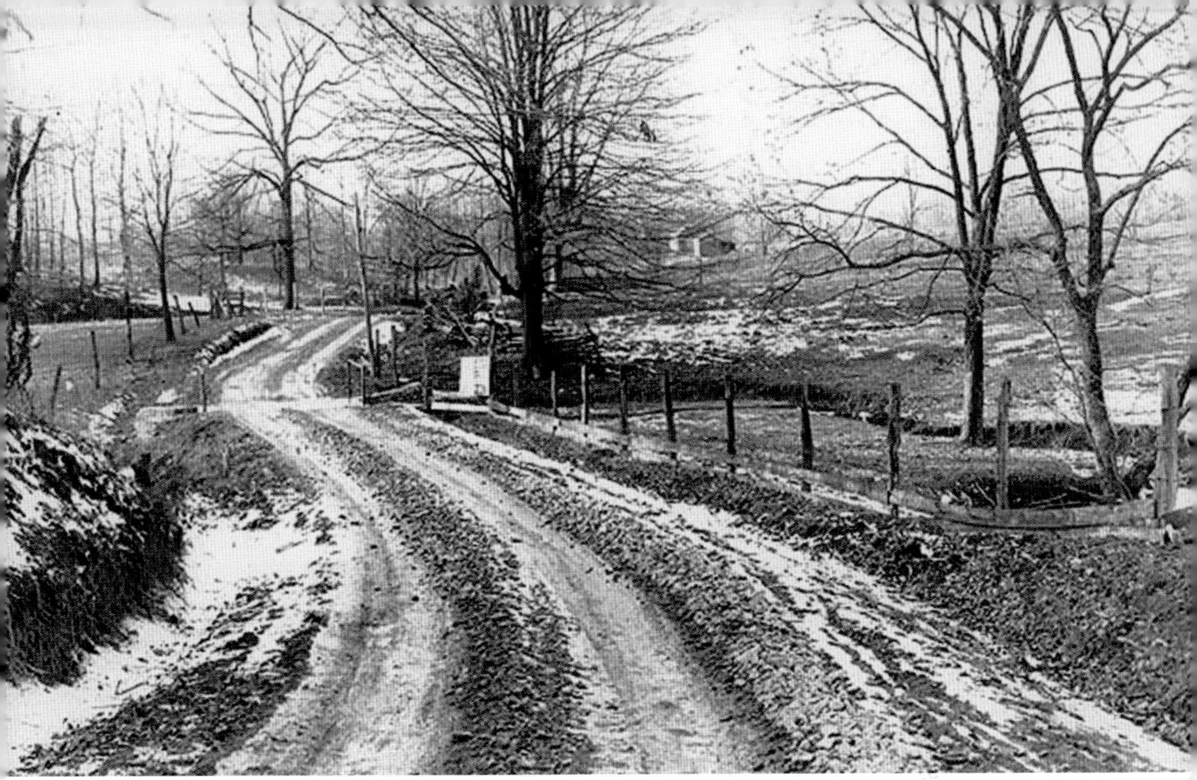

PRICE PIKE. Price Pike in Florence was a dirt road as seen in this photograph from the 1930s or early 1940s. Today it is a quiet paved street near busy Burlington Pike. In the late 1800s, when streets such as Girard, Shelby, and Main had many buildings, the future Price Pike was farmland on large lots. On the 1883 atlas, the part of Price Pike shown in these pictures, was on land owned by Barney Von Boken, and the lot went all the way to Main Street where the Florence Hotel sat.

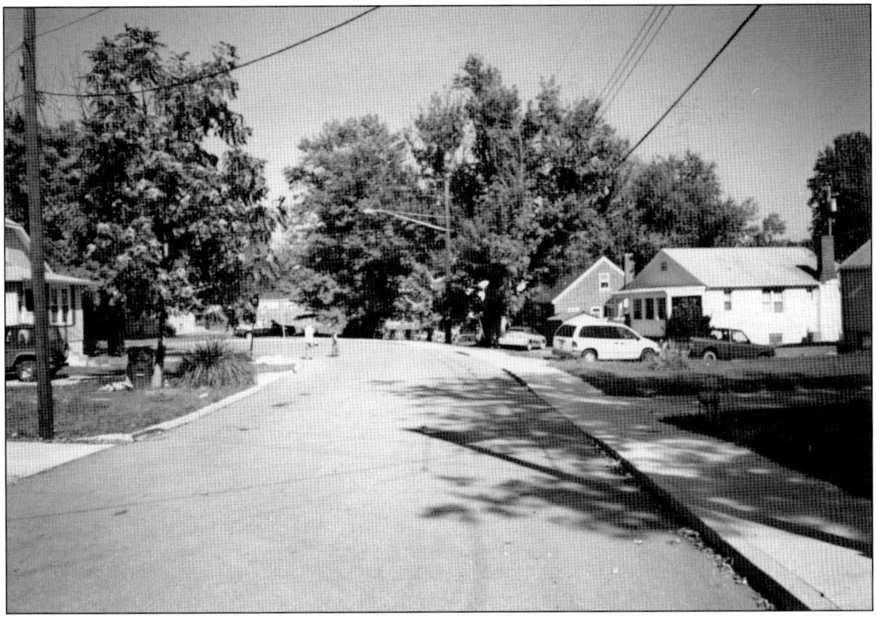

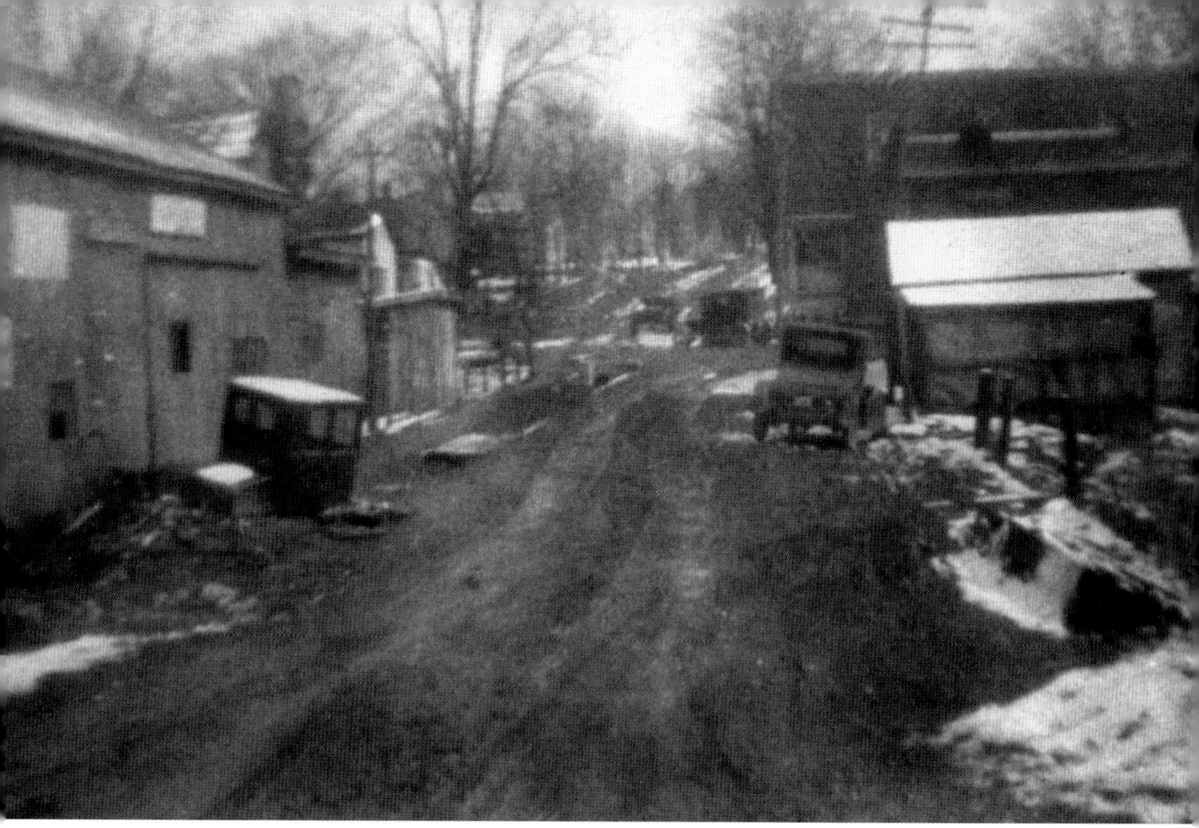

HATHAWAY IN UNION. This vintage picture shows Hathaway Road looking east toward Mt. Zion Road in Union. The taller building on the right side is the old Union Store, which had a central downtown presence until it was demolished in the 1990s. Its location was on the grassy area by the new Union Baptist Church. PNC Bank currently occupies the spot catty-corner from the old store.

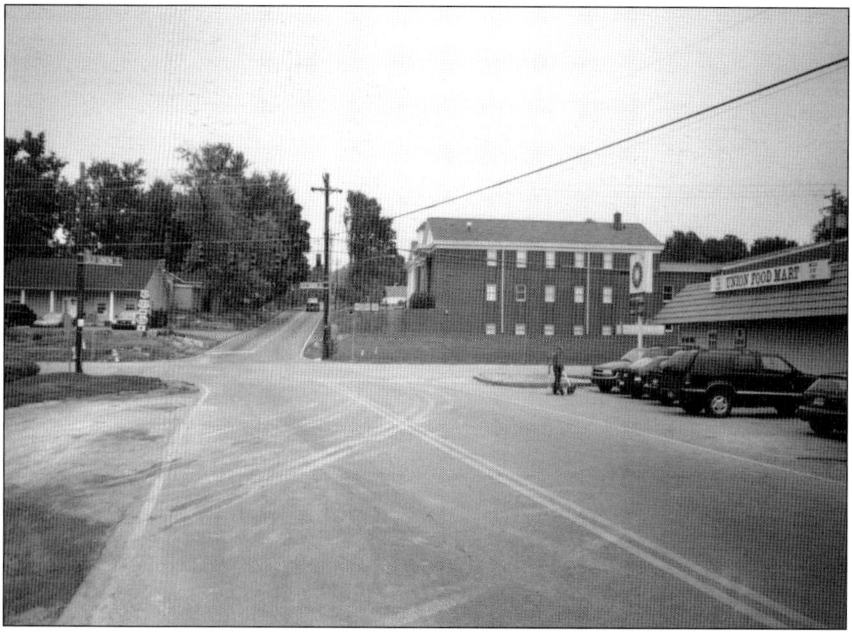

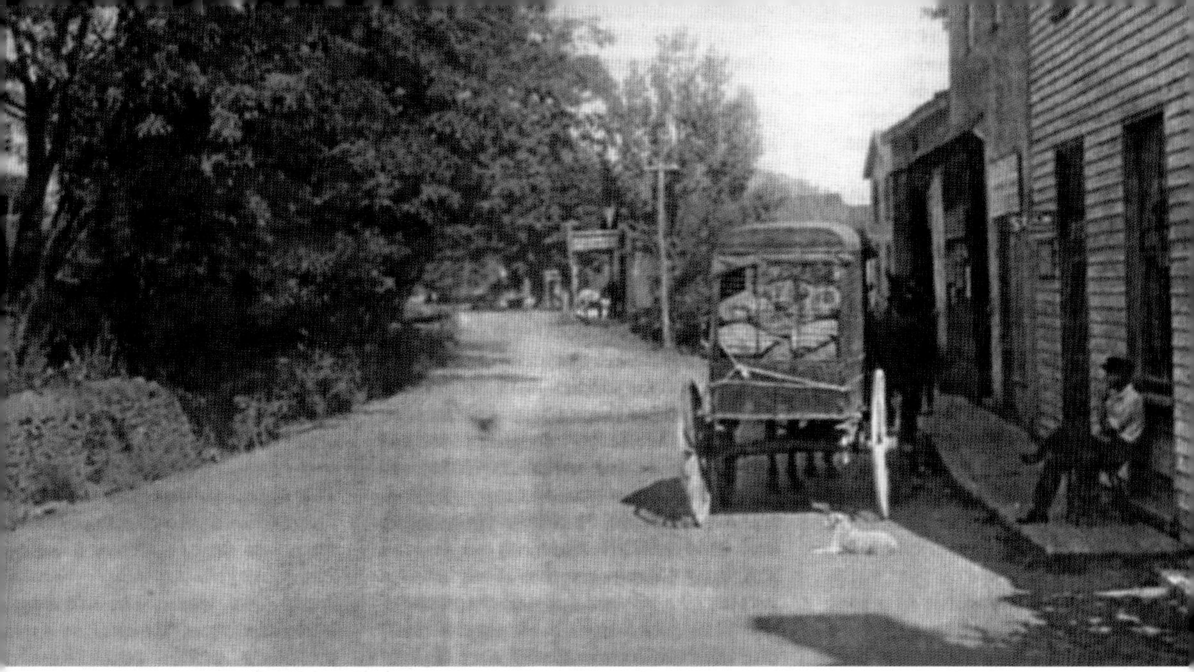

CONSTANCE RELAXATION. A man relaxes in front of a building in this photograph from the early 19th century. A wagon pulled by horses appears to be making deliveries. Constance, a small community along Route 8, sits below large hills that go up toward the Greater Cincinnati/Northern Kentucky International Airport. The building still stands in the heart of Constance, and a car sits in the same spot as the wagon, demonstrating the progress of the last 100 years.

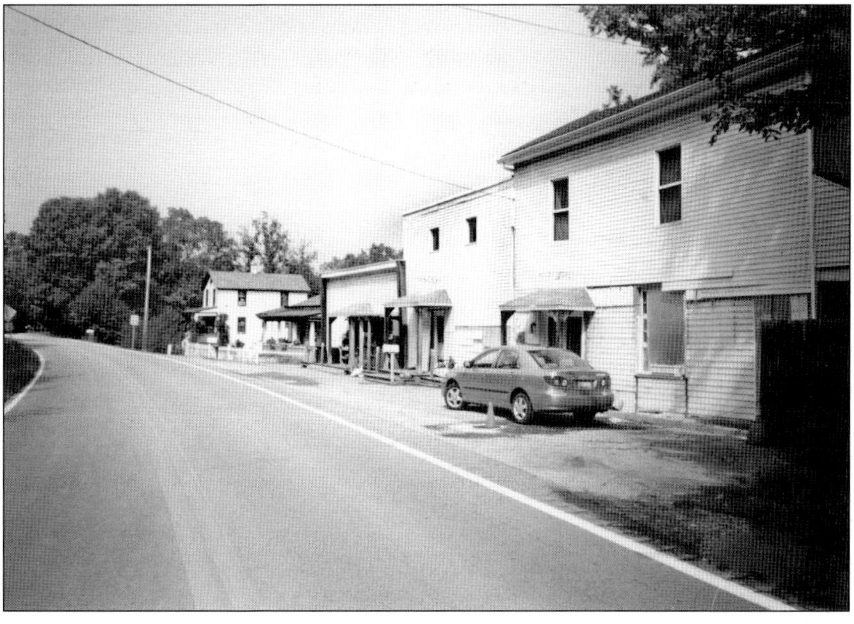

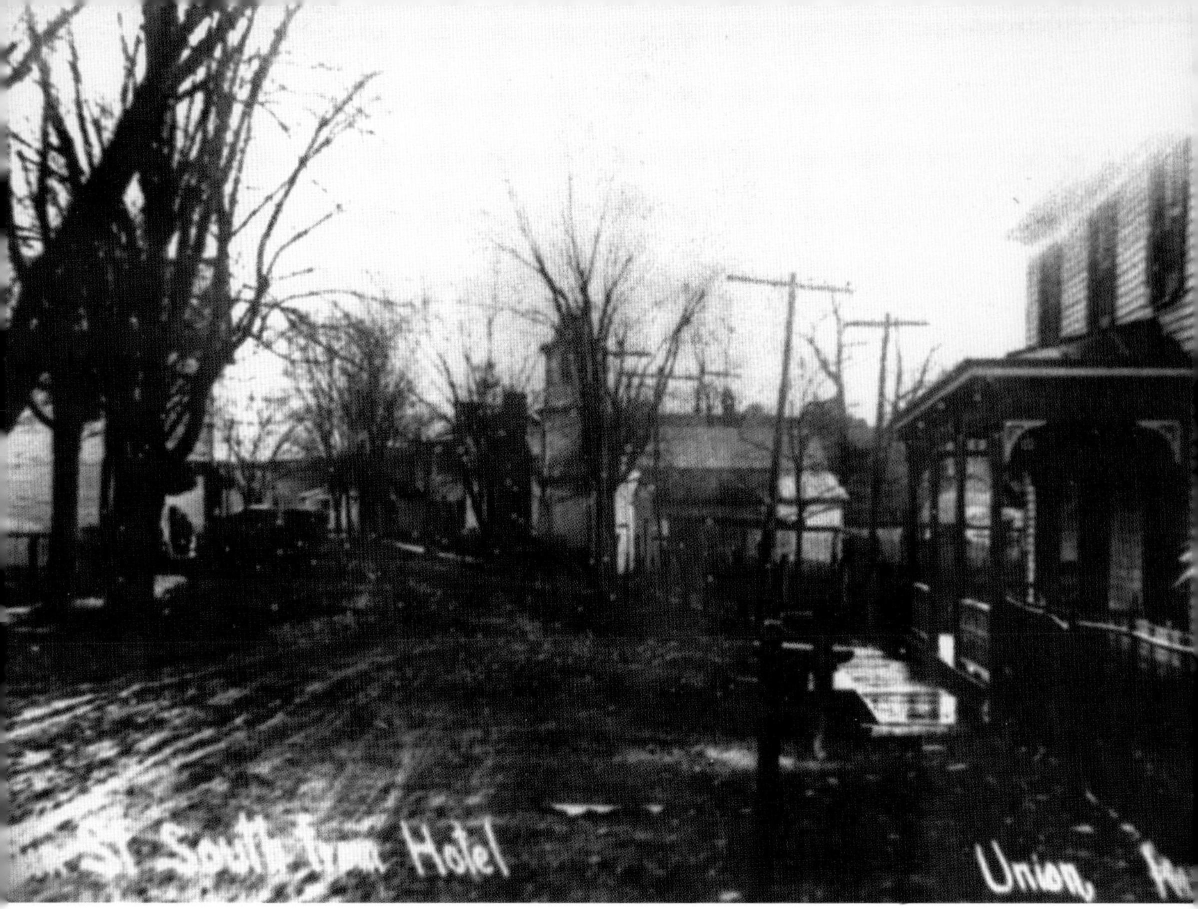

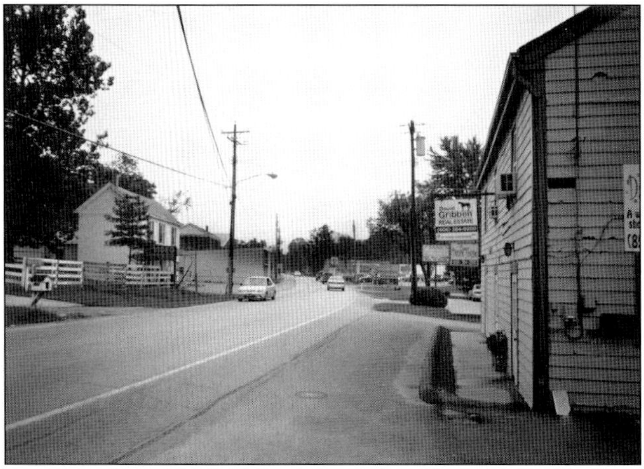

FROM THE UNION HOTEL. This undated photograph looks south on Route 42 in Union toward Mt. Zion Road from the old Union Station Hotel. Union grew as a community on the turnpike between Louisville and Cincinnati. The old Baptist church can be seen on the right side of the dirt road. The state recently built a bypass around this section of Union, and today it is much less traveled than at anytime in the recent past.

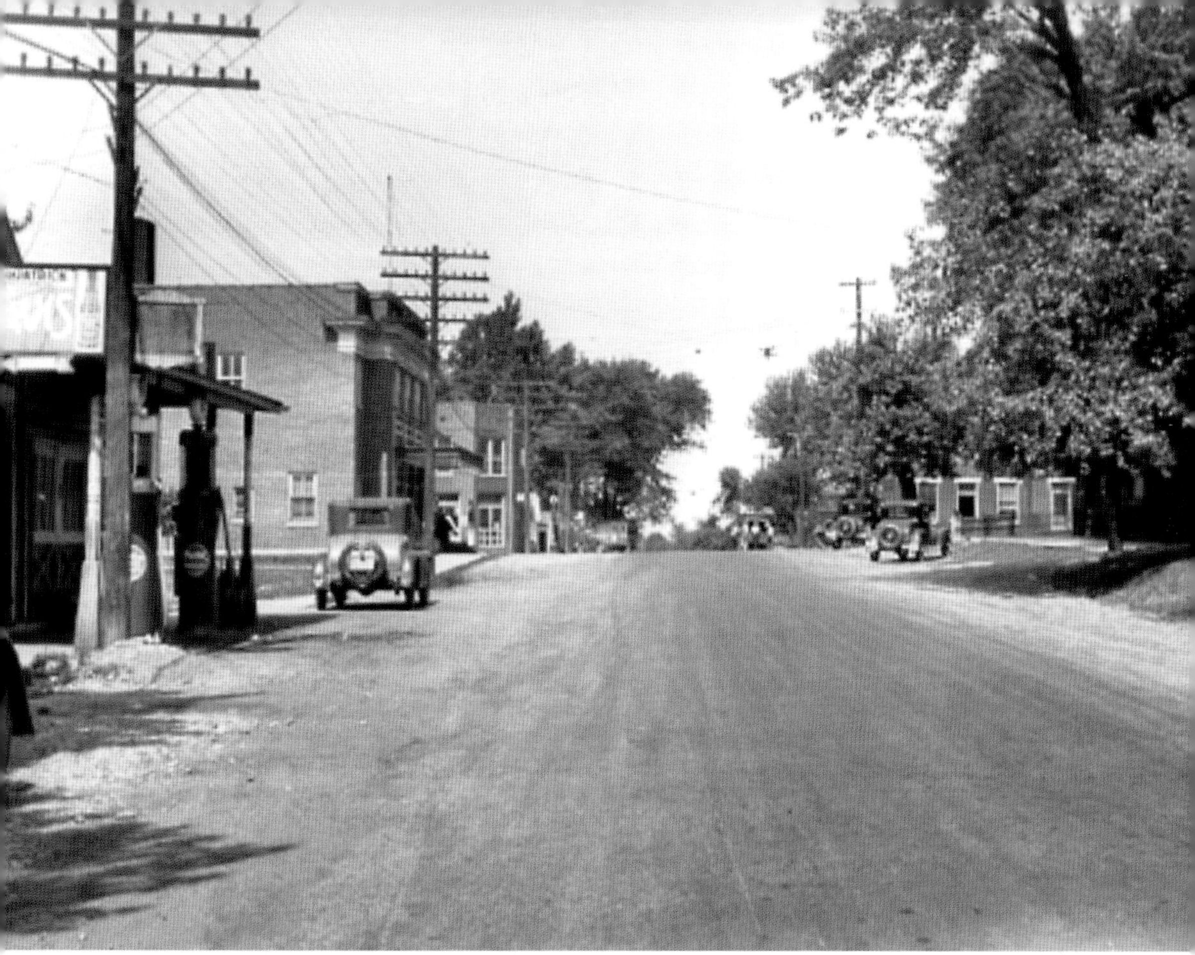

BURLINGTON, 1930S. A peaceful Burlington appears in this image from the 1930s. Today Burlington Pike is one of the most traveled roads in the county. The Boone County Deposit Bank building appears in both images, and the old courthouse is hidden by trees in one and is visible in the other. Surprisingly the dirt road of the 1930s is nearly as wide as the modern heavily traveled road of today.

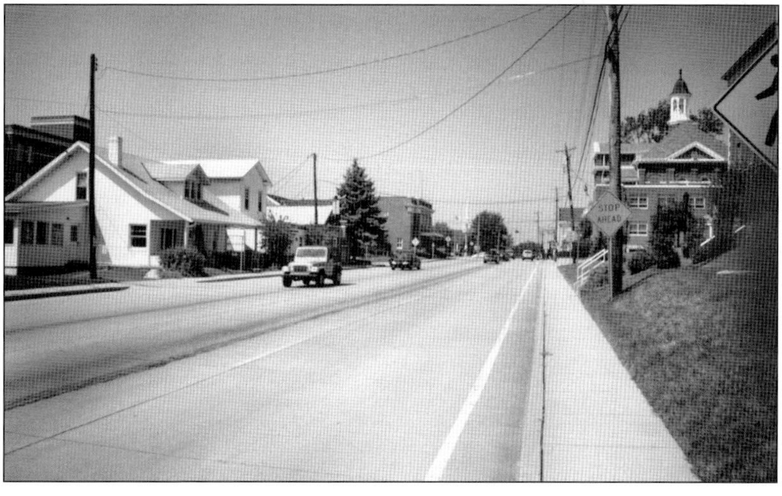

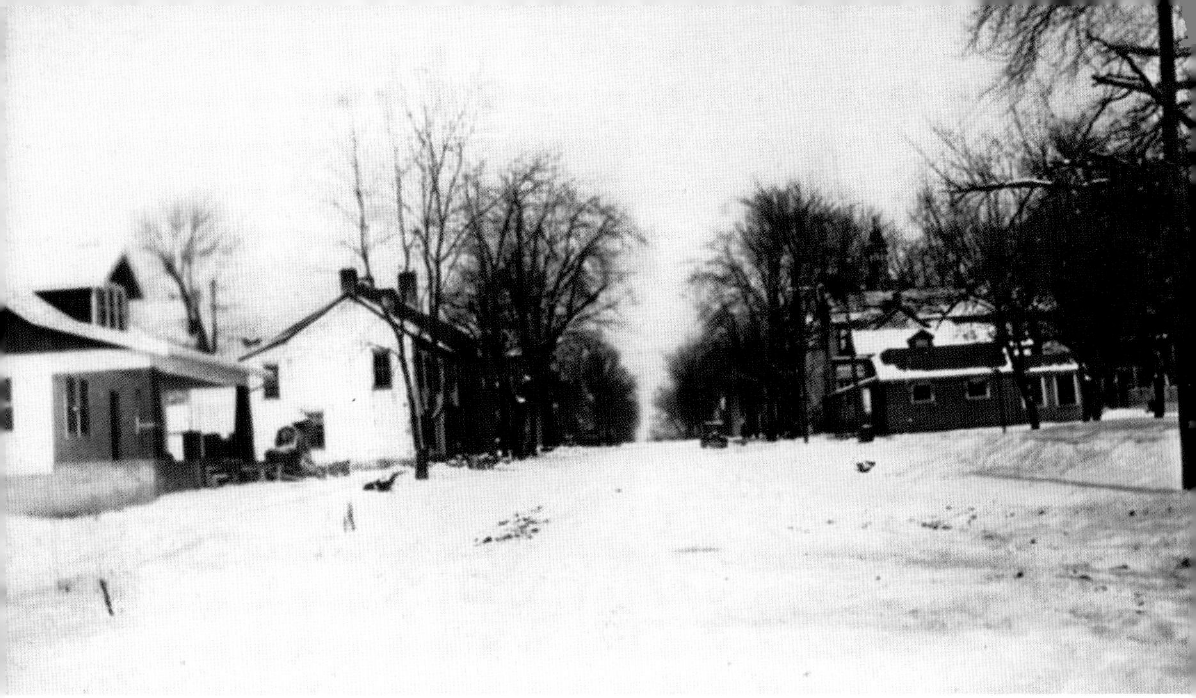

AND JUSTICE FOR ALL. This northern view of East Bend Road from Torrid Street shows both the old and new of justice in Boone County. The single-family residence on the left can be seen in both photographs. However, the new Justice Center dominates the east side of the street. The old courthouse, built in 1889, sits in the distance. The octagonal cupola of the old courthouse can be seen through the trees in the old photograph.

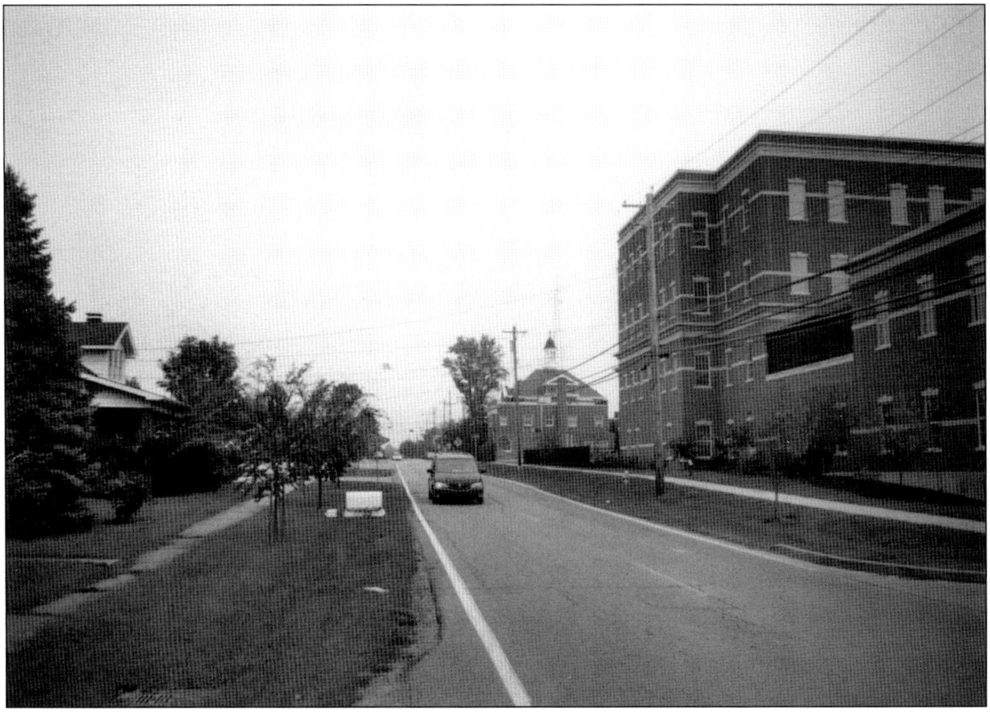

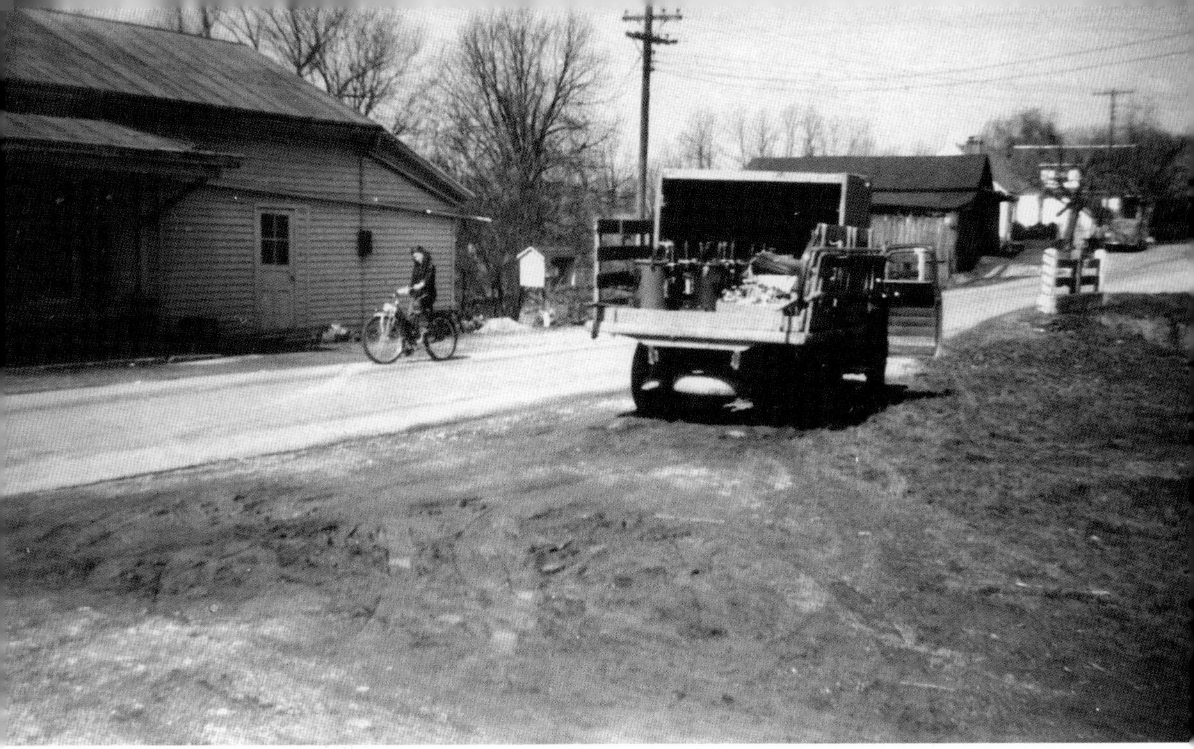

BULLITTSVILLE. The community of Bullittsville is located on Kentucky Route 20 and once had a school, grocery store, and blacksmith shop. This 1947 street scene shows the old bridge and the wooden blacksmith shop in the distance. The blacksmith's name was Theodore Birkle. His wife was Molly. Frank Battaglia sells fruits and vegetables out of his truck by the side of the road. The building to the immediate left in both pictures is the old general store. Doris Engle, longtime resident of the area, rides the bike.

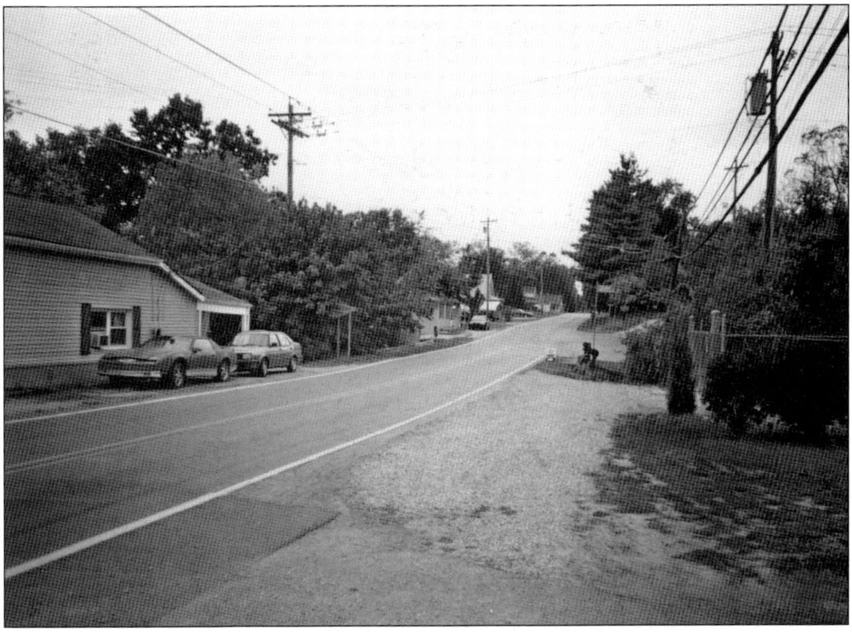

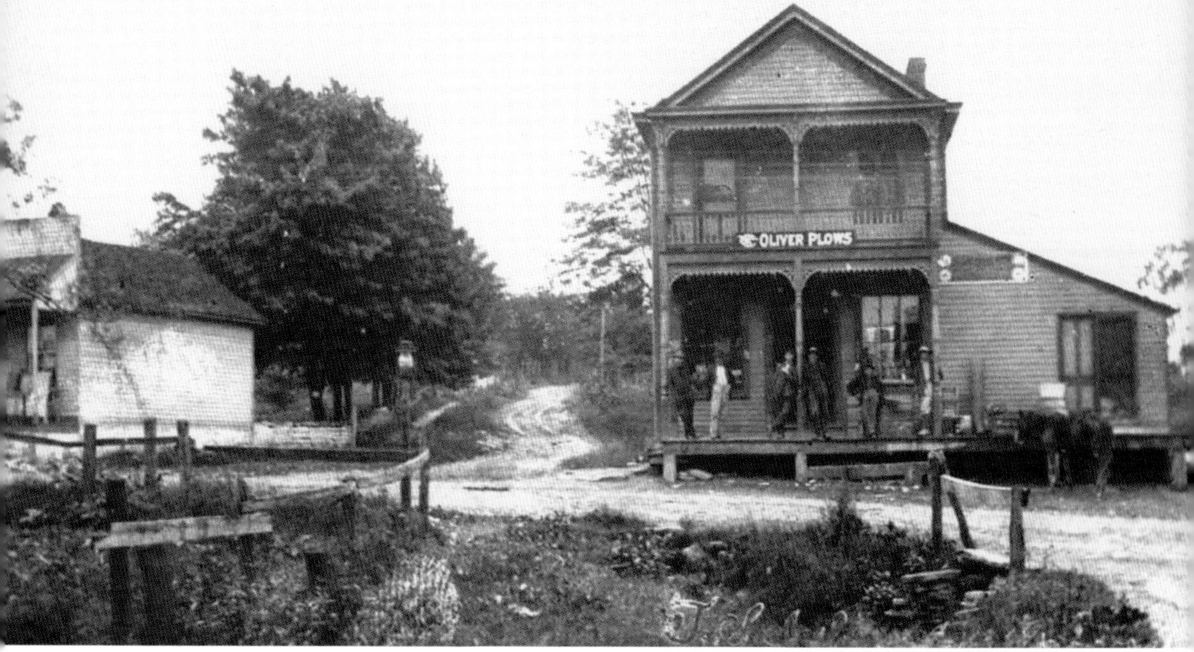

LOU KRUTCHER'S STORE. Located on Kentucky 20 in Hebron, the Krutcher's store advertises Oliver Plows. Oliver Plows became the most popular in the world after improving upon the old wooden models that dominated the frontier. In 1857, James Oliver received his first patent, called "Improvement in Chilling Plow Shares." Their new process resulted in a much hardened plow point. The Krutcher store sat on the Old Hebron Bank lot that is now a day care center.

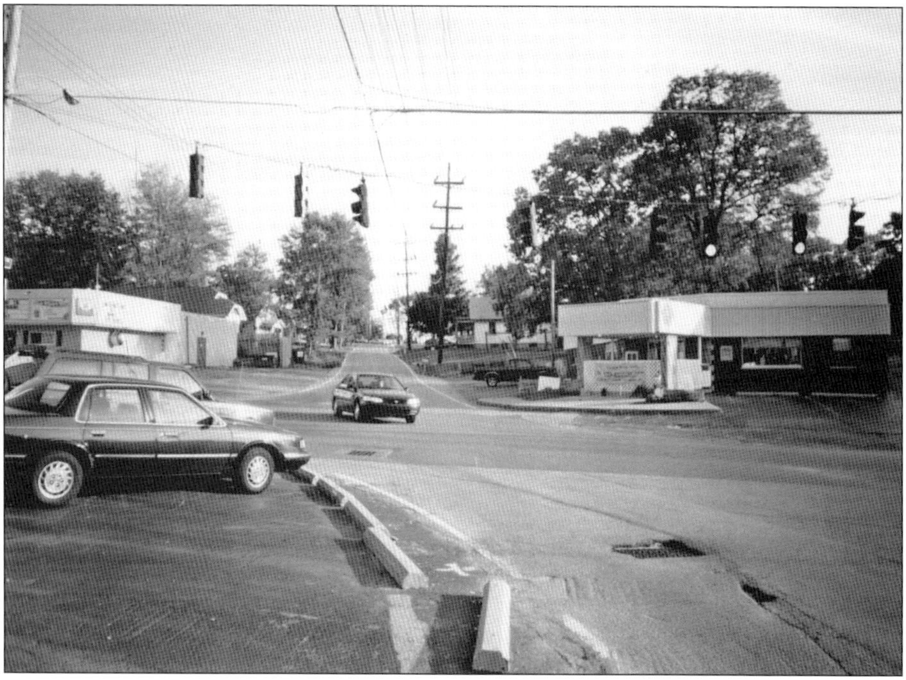

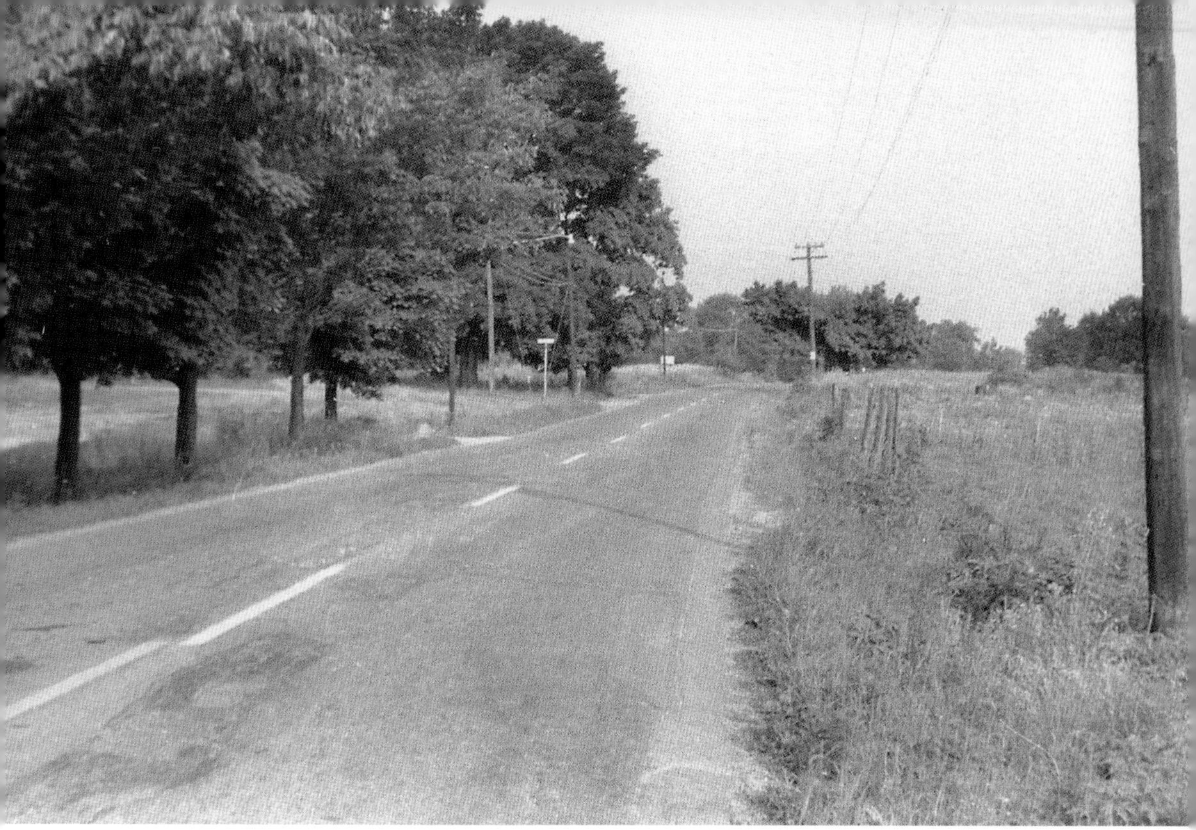

BURLINGTON PIKE AND TANNERS LANE. This 1959 photograph of Burlington Pike at Tanners Lane shows a real contrast between the new and old Florence. Taken before the construction of I-75, the rural charm of Boone County seems to even appear in Florence. Today this area is a major component of the road system that takes people in and out of Florence Mall and the surrounding commercial establishments.

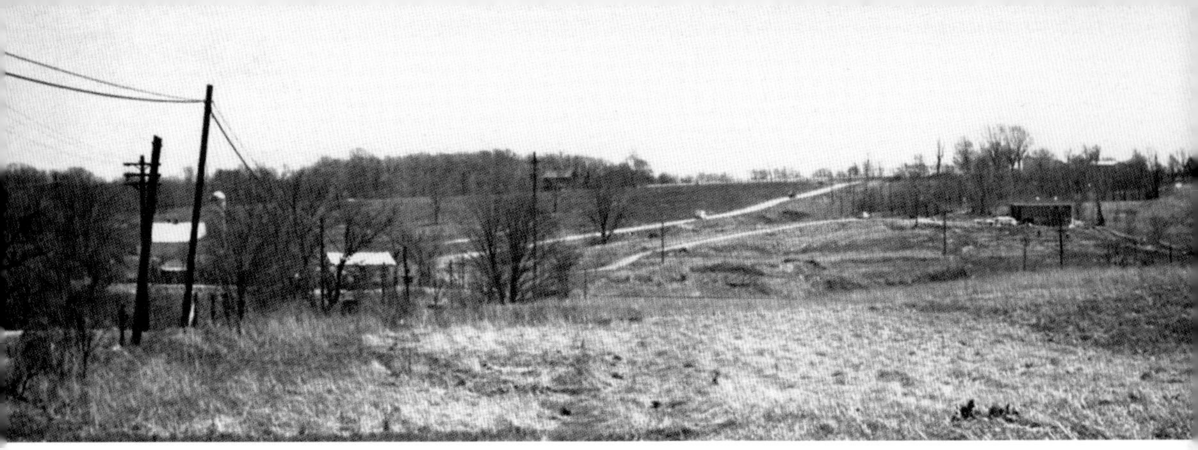

VIEW **D**OWN THE **P**IKE. This view down Burlington Pike has changed a lot over the years. The contrast can be seen between these two pictures. Note in the older photograph the silo and barn that still exist despite the development along this busy roadway. The silo is at the old "Florence Crossroads" area and near the old Limaburg Bridge and Mill.

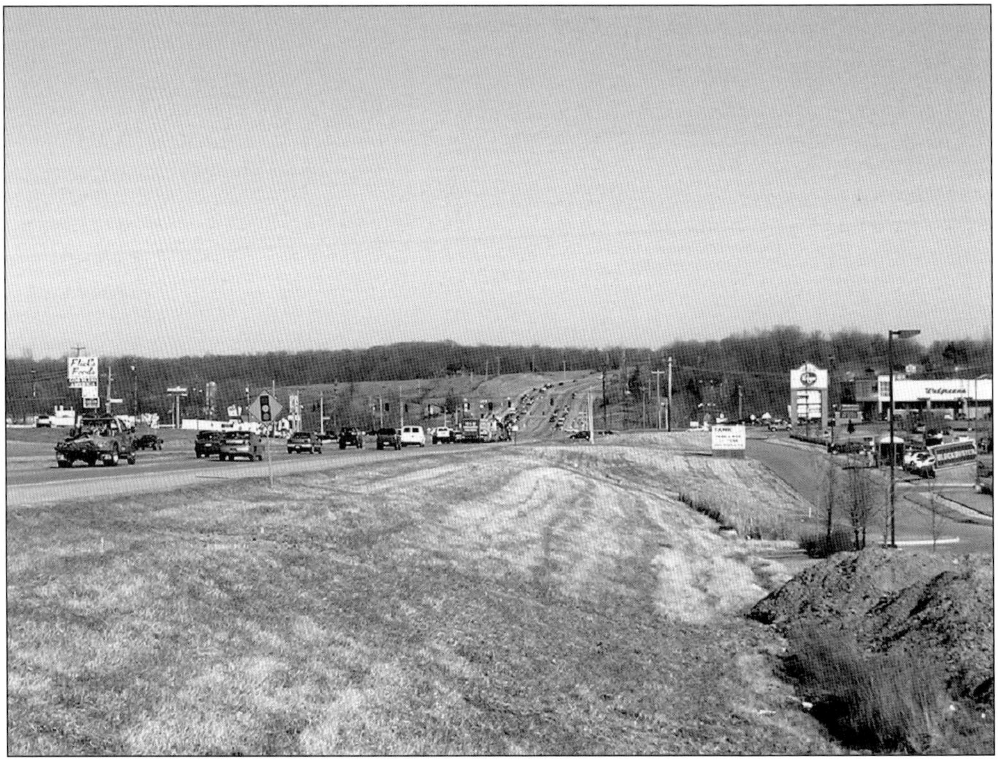

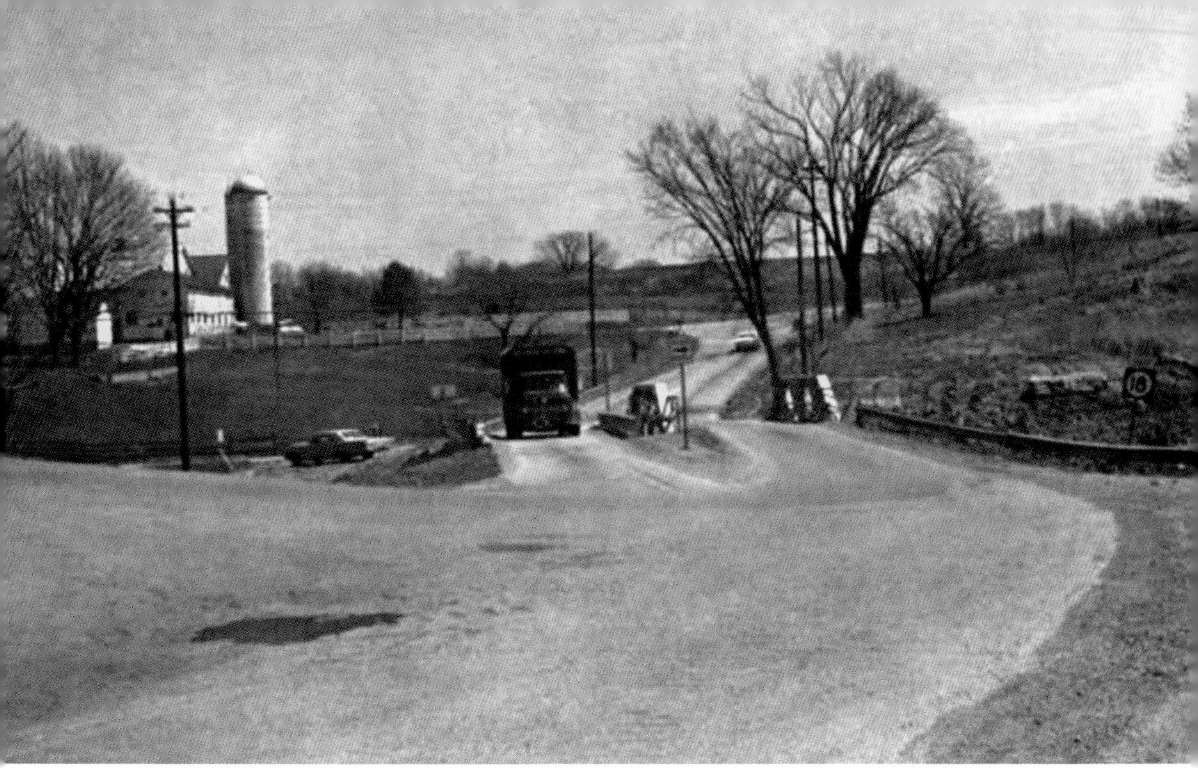

LIMABURG BRIDGE. The old Limaburg Bridge was a well-known part of Burlington Pike, located in an area called Florence Crossroads. Today the bridge location is on the old part of the Pike (Limaburg Creek Road). In this April 28, 1972, photograph, looking east, the area is wide open. The old mill was to the right of the bridge. This stretch of road now has many trees that block the farm buildings that still stand.

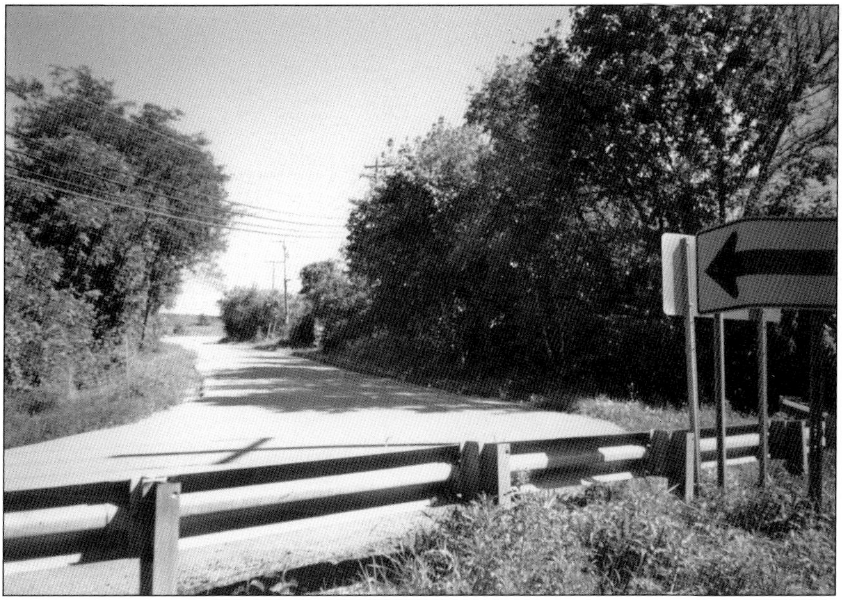

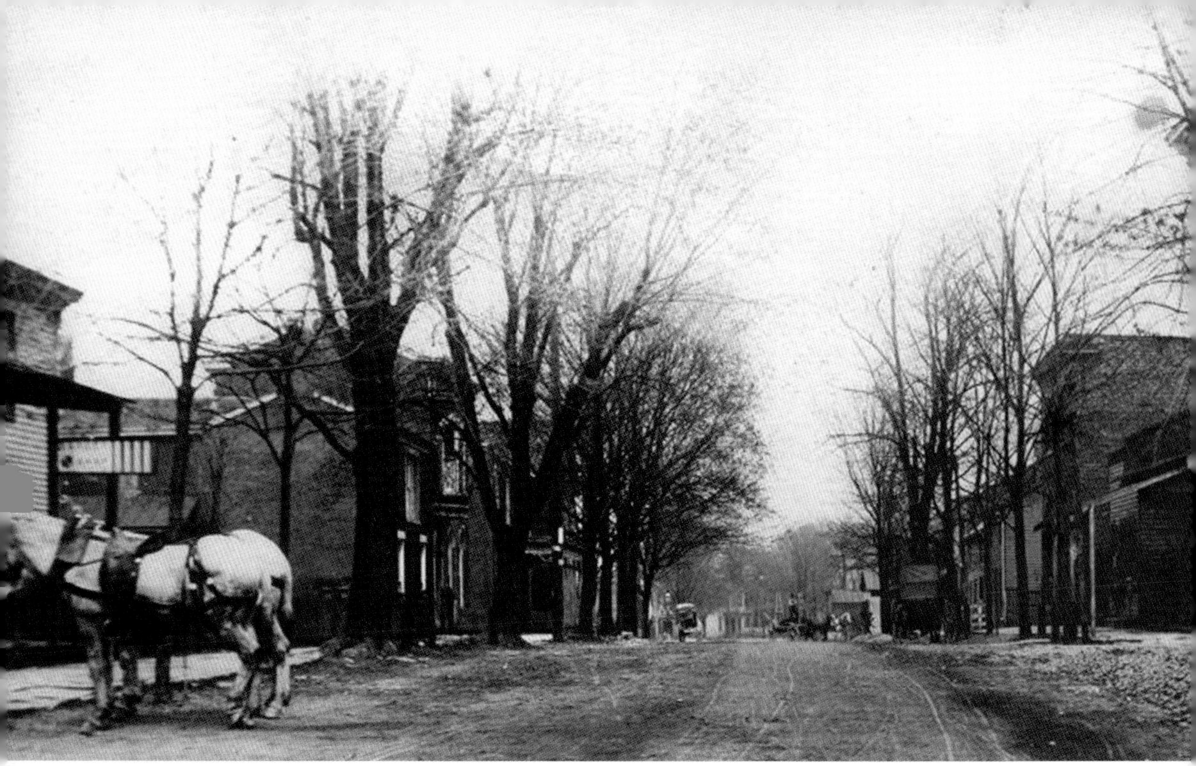

STRINGTOWN ON THE PIKE. In this *c.* 1905 photograph, the Stringtown/Main Street area of Florence consists of a dirt road as well as some of the historic buildings that still stand. The road was most commonly known as Lexington Pike at the time. The Stringtown Restaurant building can be seen in both pictures as well as several other structures. The horses, in the vintage image, are tied up in front of the building on the left in the modern photograph.

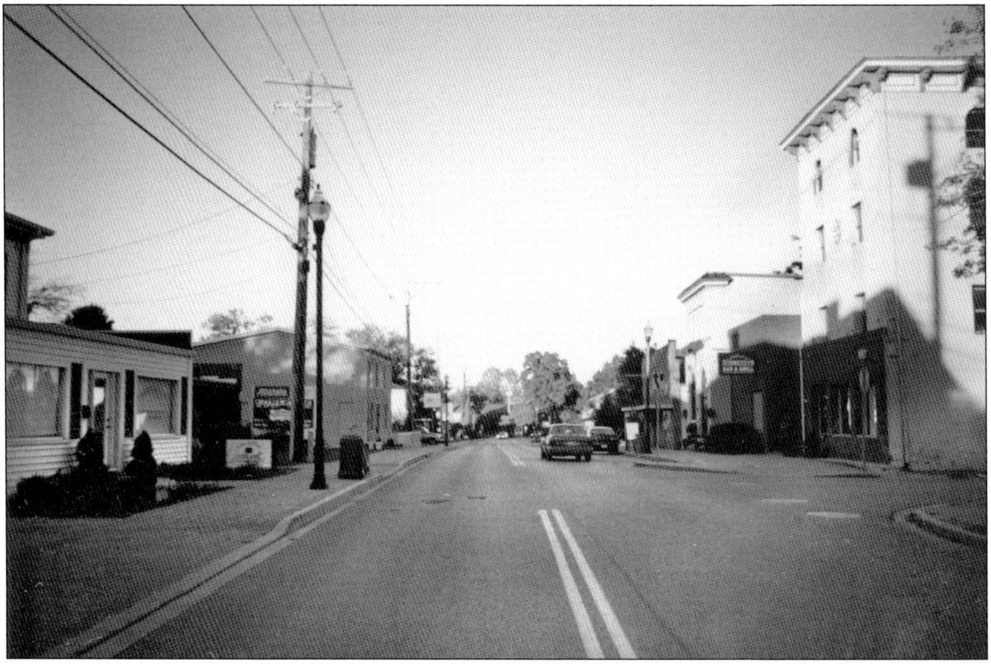

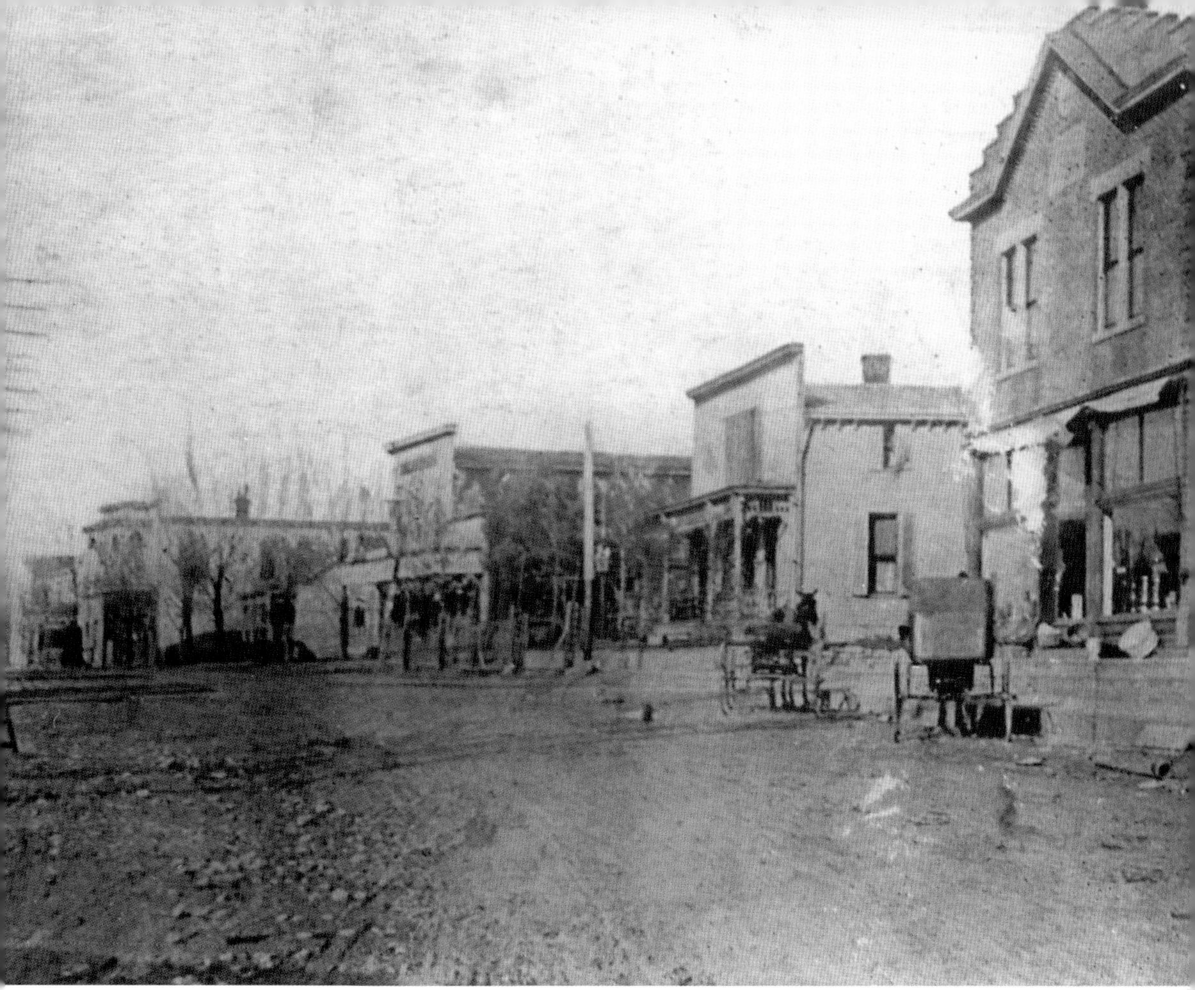

WALTON'S MAIN STREET. This *c.* 1908 photograph is of Main Street in Walton looking north. The Odd Fellows Hall is the first building on the right in the vintage photograph. The recent picture shows a wider range of the street, and the Odd Fellows Hall can be seen farther up. Later the Odd Fellows Hall housed the Masons, a drug store, and now a law office.

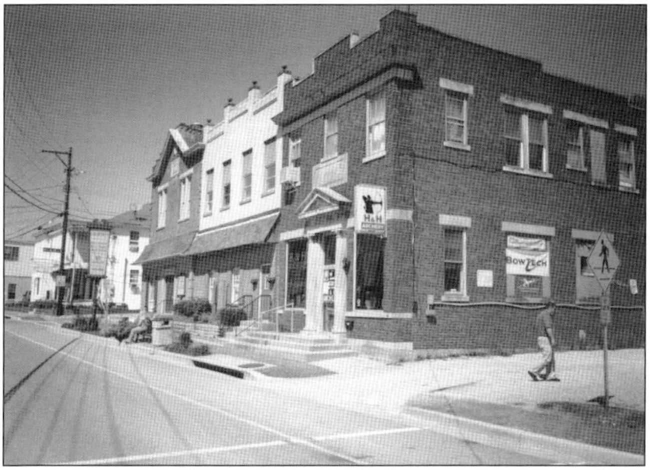

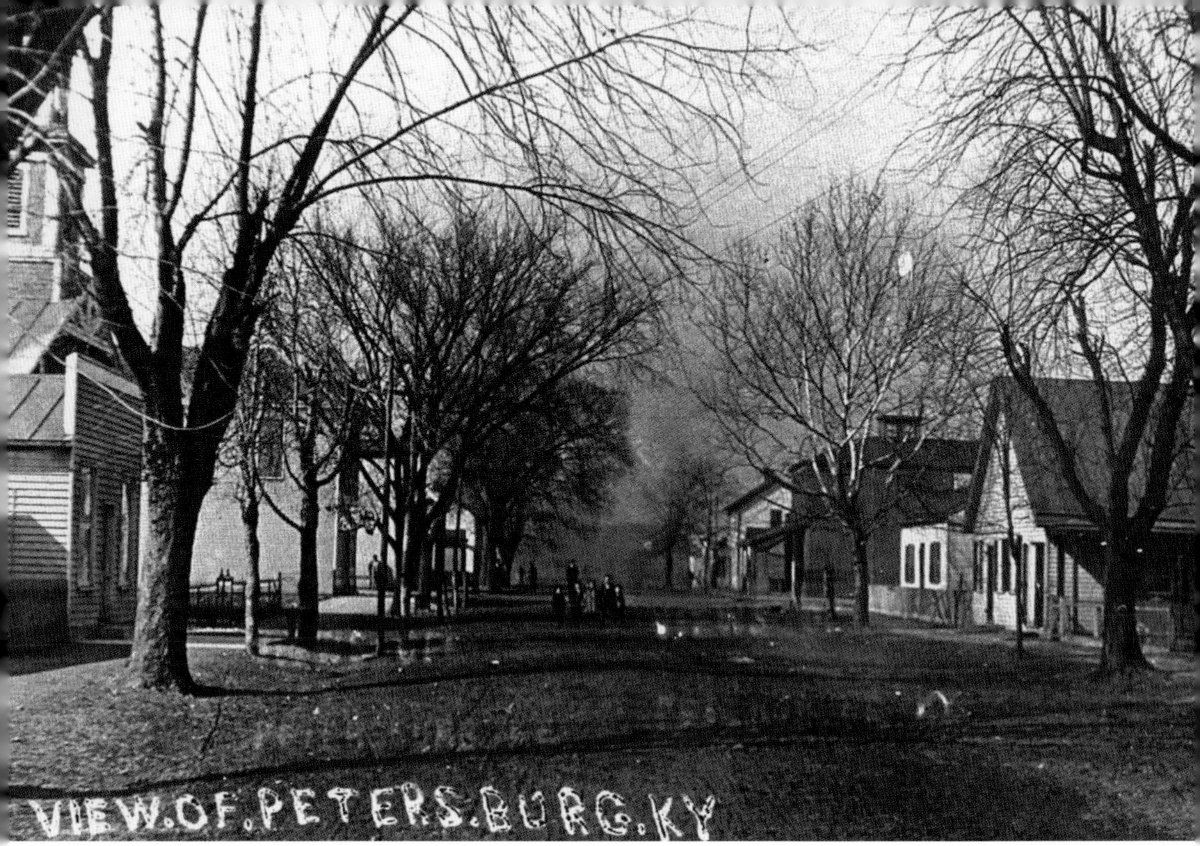

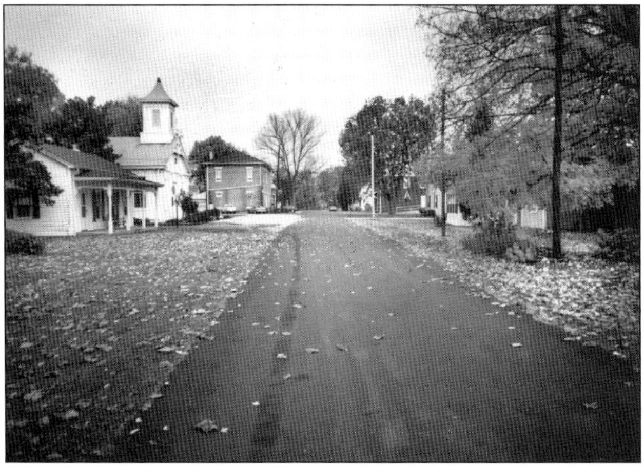

VIEW OF PETERSBURG. Petersburg is the oldest town in Boone County and is situated on ancient American Indian lands. Settled by North Carolina Baptist preacher John Tanner in 1789, it became known as Petersburg in 1818. This undated image shows Tanner Street looking toward the river. The Petersburg Christian Church, built in 1840, appears on the left in both pictures.

Chapter 2
SCHOOLS

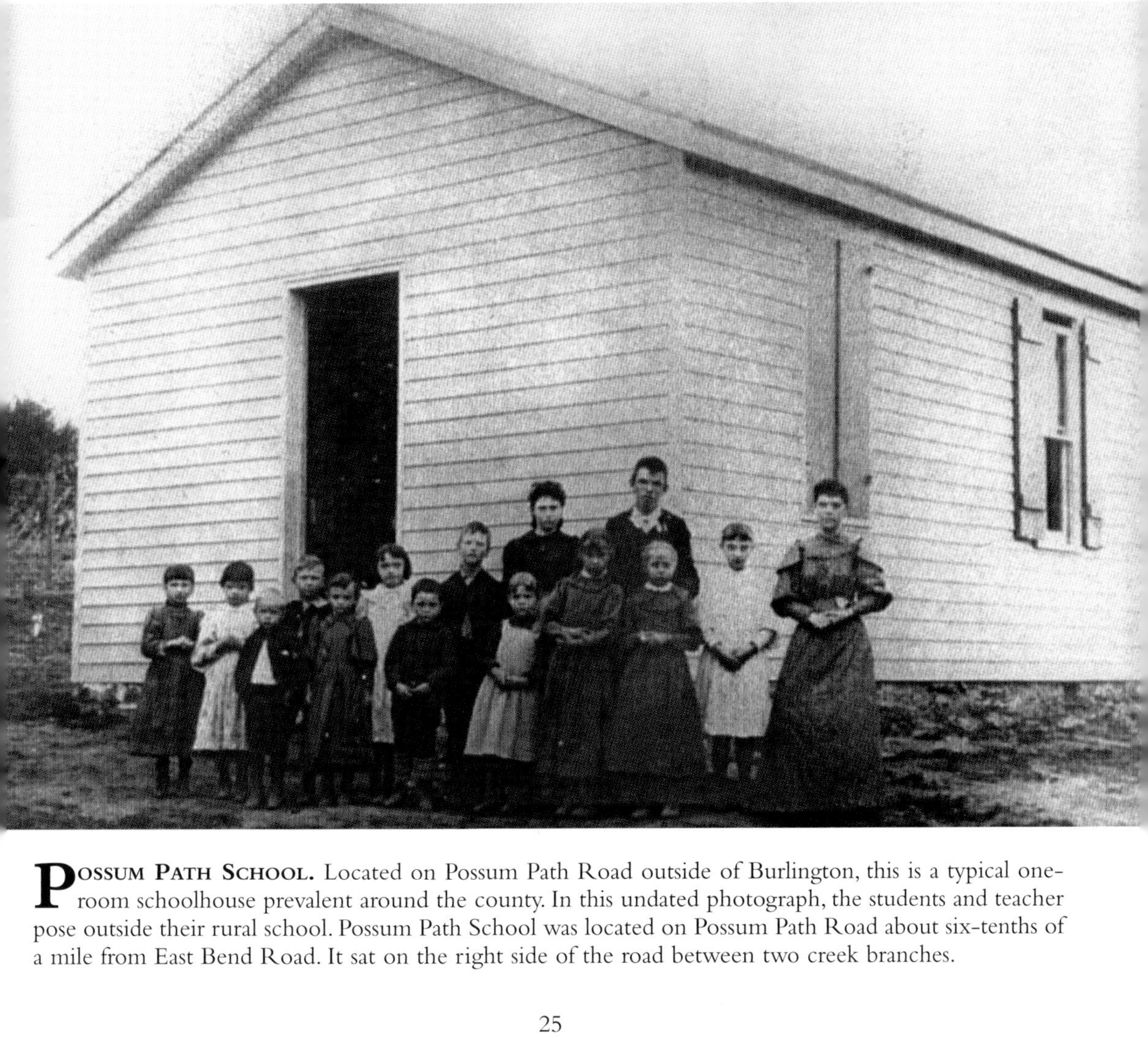

POSSUM PATH SCHOOL. Located on Possum Path Road outside of Burlington, this is a typical one-room schoolhouse prevalent around the county. In this undated photograph, the students and teacher pose outside their rural school. Possum Path School was located on Possum Path Road about six-tenths of a mile from East Bend Road. It sat on the right side of the road between two creek branches.

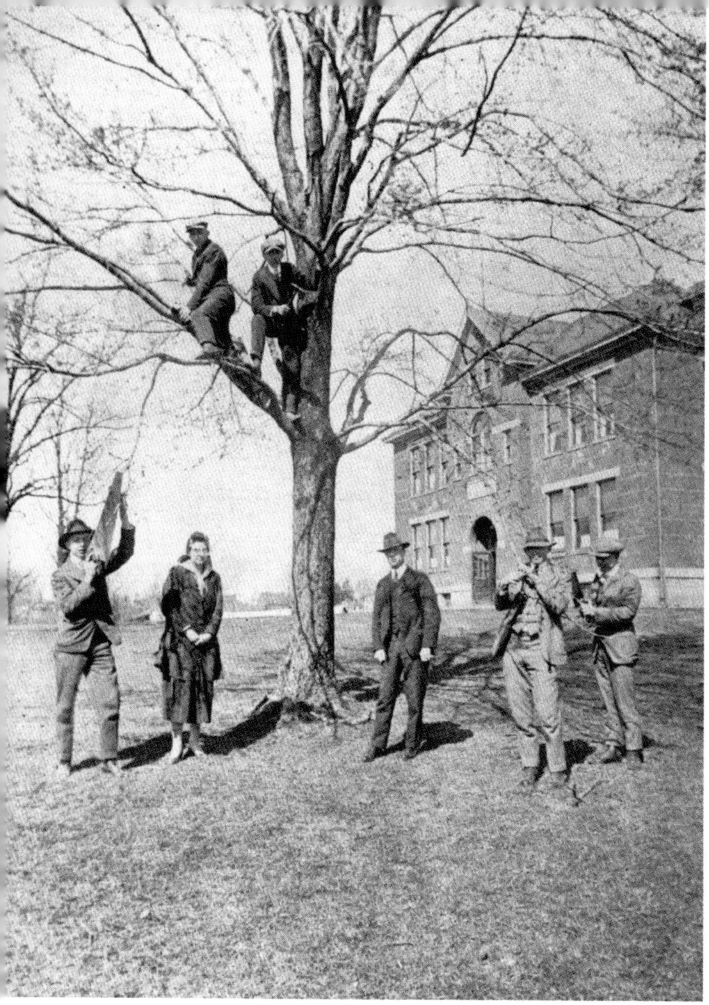

BOONE COUNTY HIGH SCHOOL. Boone County High School was located on the site that today houses the Burlington Elementary School. In this undated photograph, the agricultural club poses outside the old building. The new building opened on September 25, 1939, and served as the high school. Now an elementary school, it has been expanded to accommodate the tremendous growth of the school system. When the new building opened in 1939, it housed 228 students.

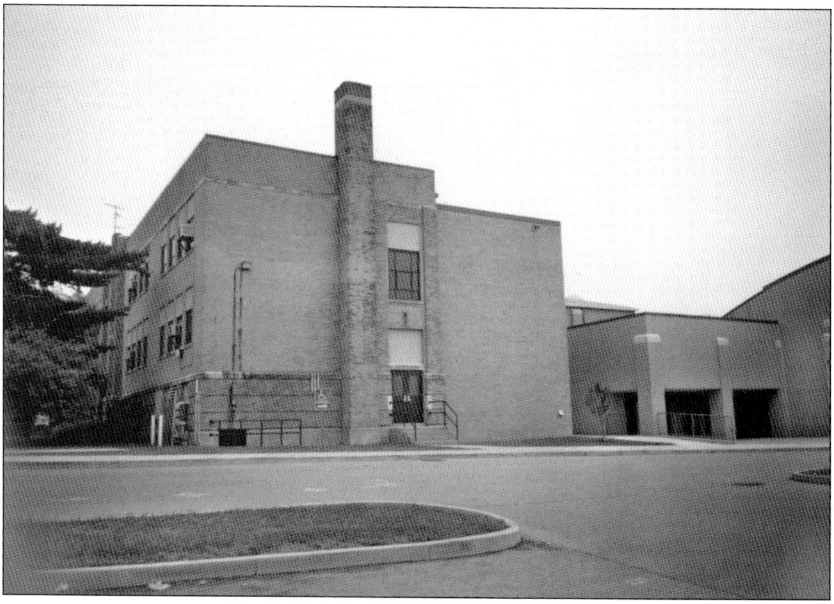

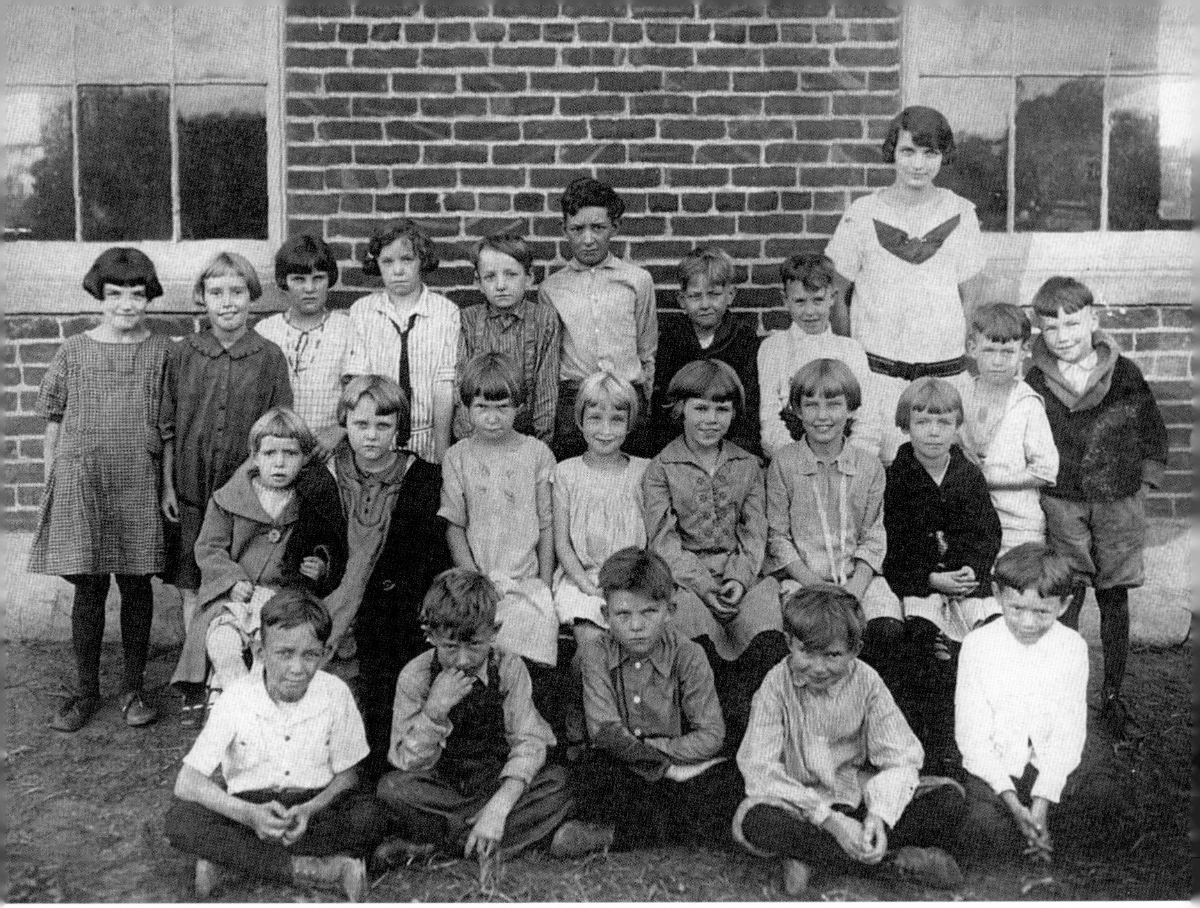

BELLEVIEW SCHOOL. Students, some happy and some sad, pose outside the old school located in Belleview. The community was settled in the early 1800s, and the school opened approximately 100 years later. It is located on Kentucky Route 18 and sits almost directly across from the newer school, Kelly Elementary. The school still retains some of its charm, as do many of the buildings in Belleview. The old school today is a private business.

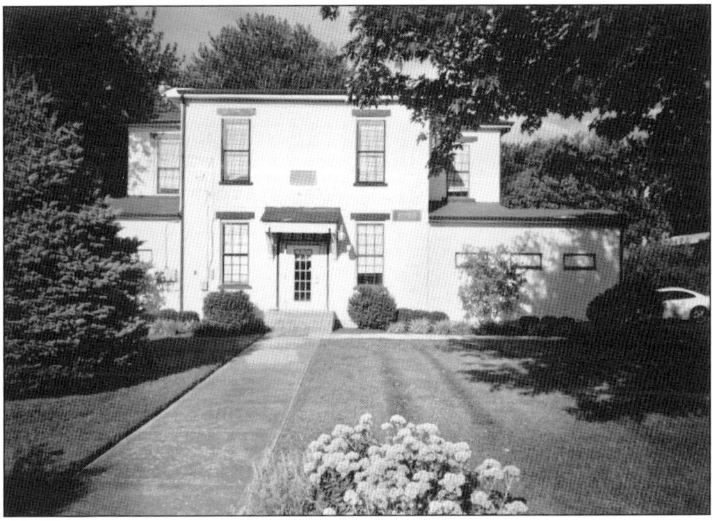

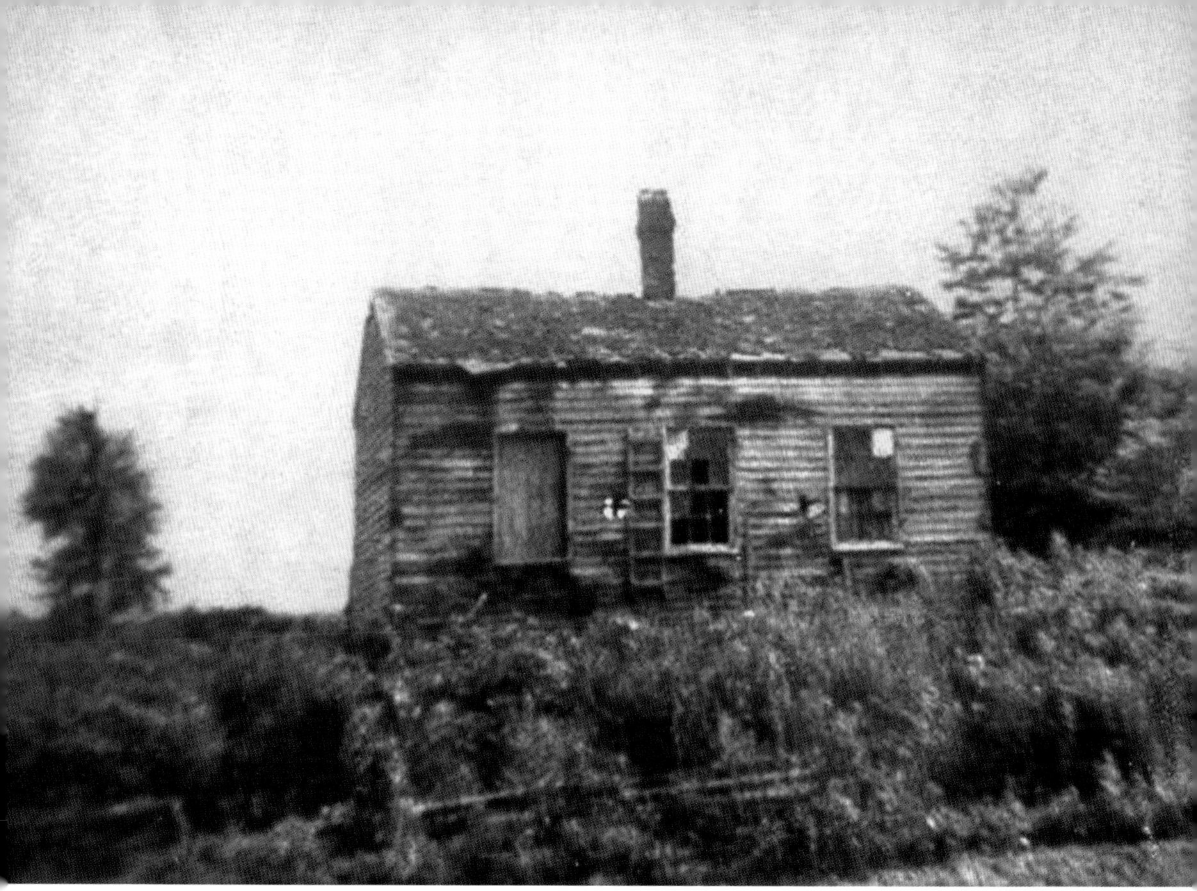

BURLINGTON'S FIRST SCHOOL. The first school in Burlington was this wooden structure located on Orient Street, between Burlington Pike and Gallatin Street. At the time, an alley sat to the north of the school. The school is long gone, and the lot sits empty behind the county parking lot. Taken from Orient Street, the recent picture shows the Boone County Administration Building in the far distance.

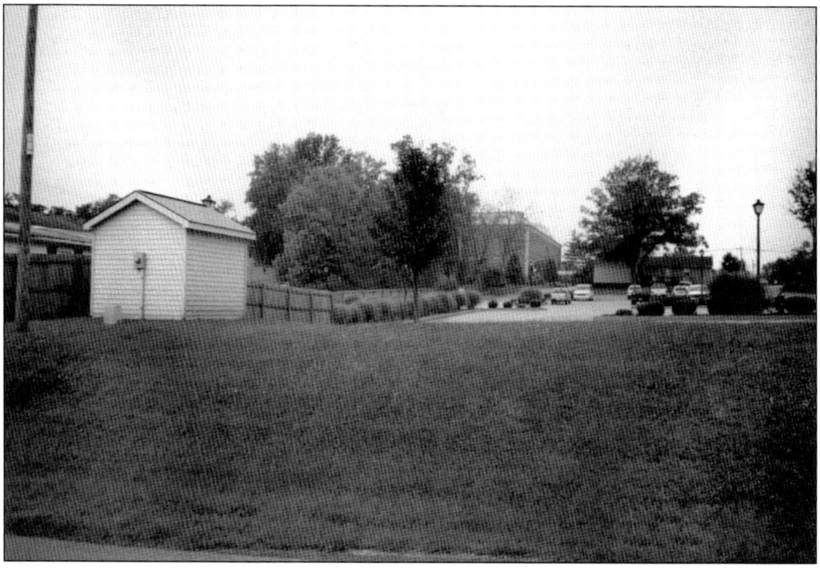

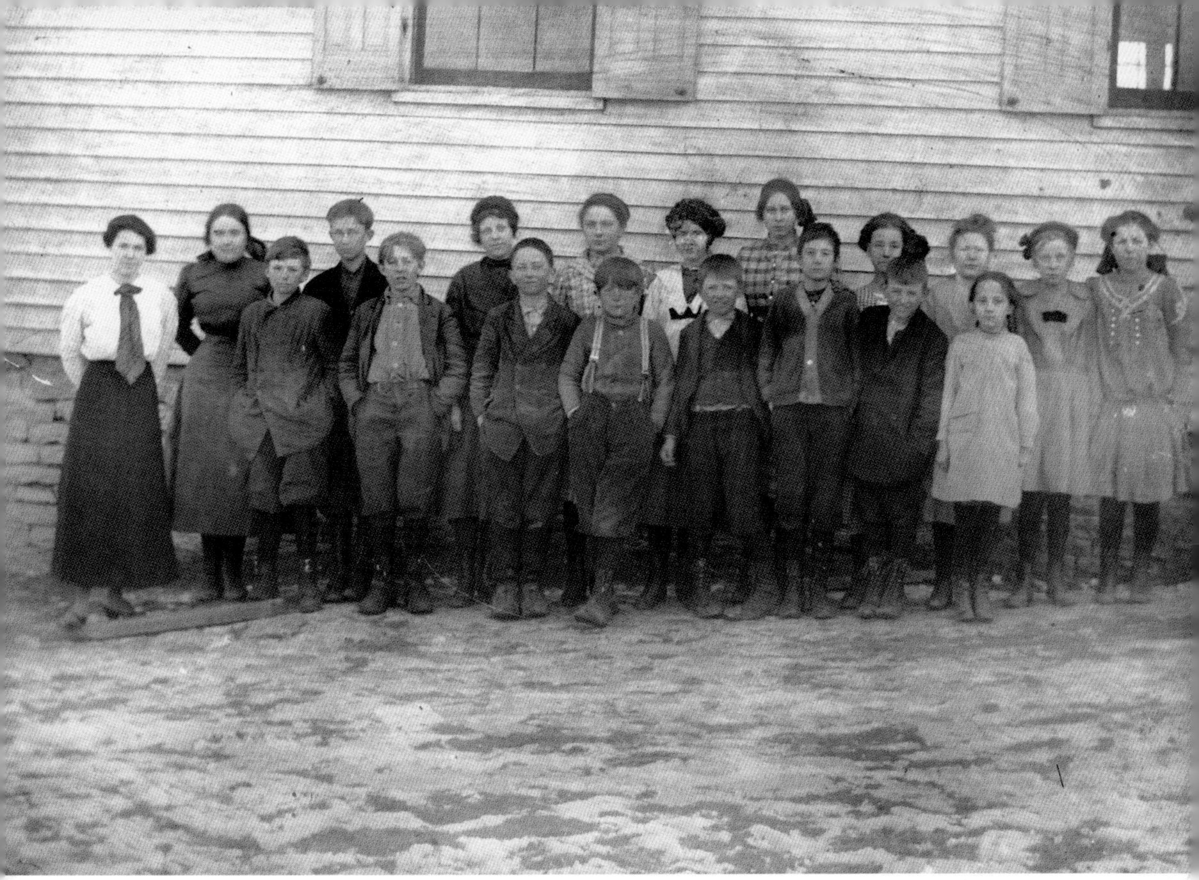

KENSINGTON SCHOOL. The Kensington School was located at Kensington Crossing near Walton. The crossing was a railroad stop on the Southern Line. This picture was taken in 1913, and the person in the second row, fourth from the right, is ? Readnour. Today the school is a single-family home. Both photographs are taken from the same side of the building.

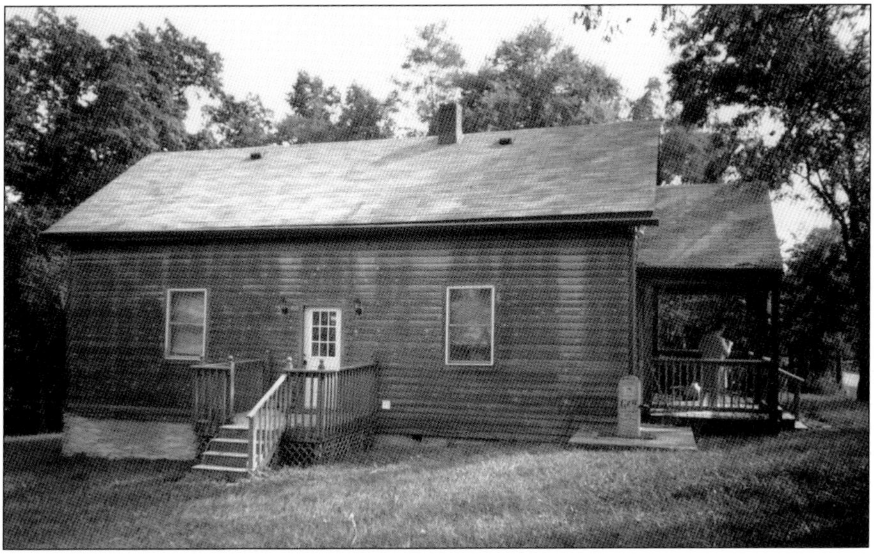

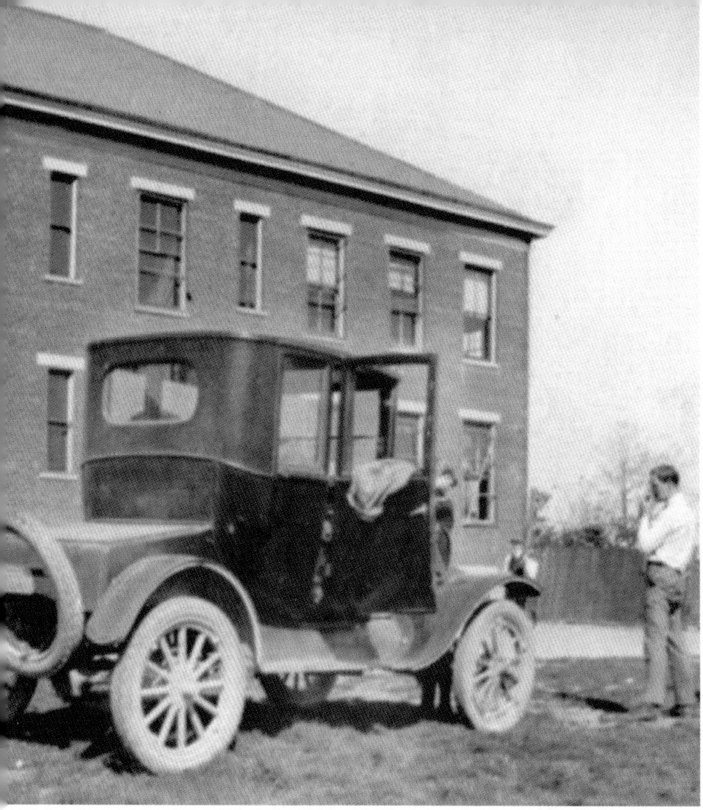

WALTON SCHOOL. The Walton School, a two-story structure built in 1902, was the first public high school in the county. It housed 12 grades, with the high school located on the second floor. In this 1923 photograph, a car sits on the front lawn. Today the school building is used for apartments.

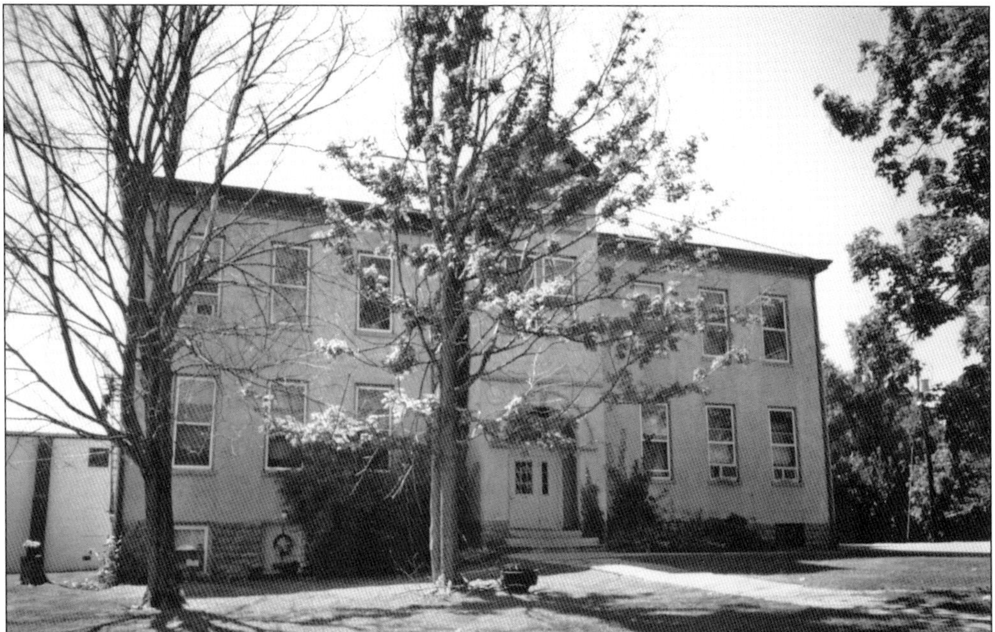

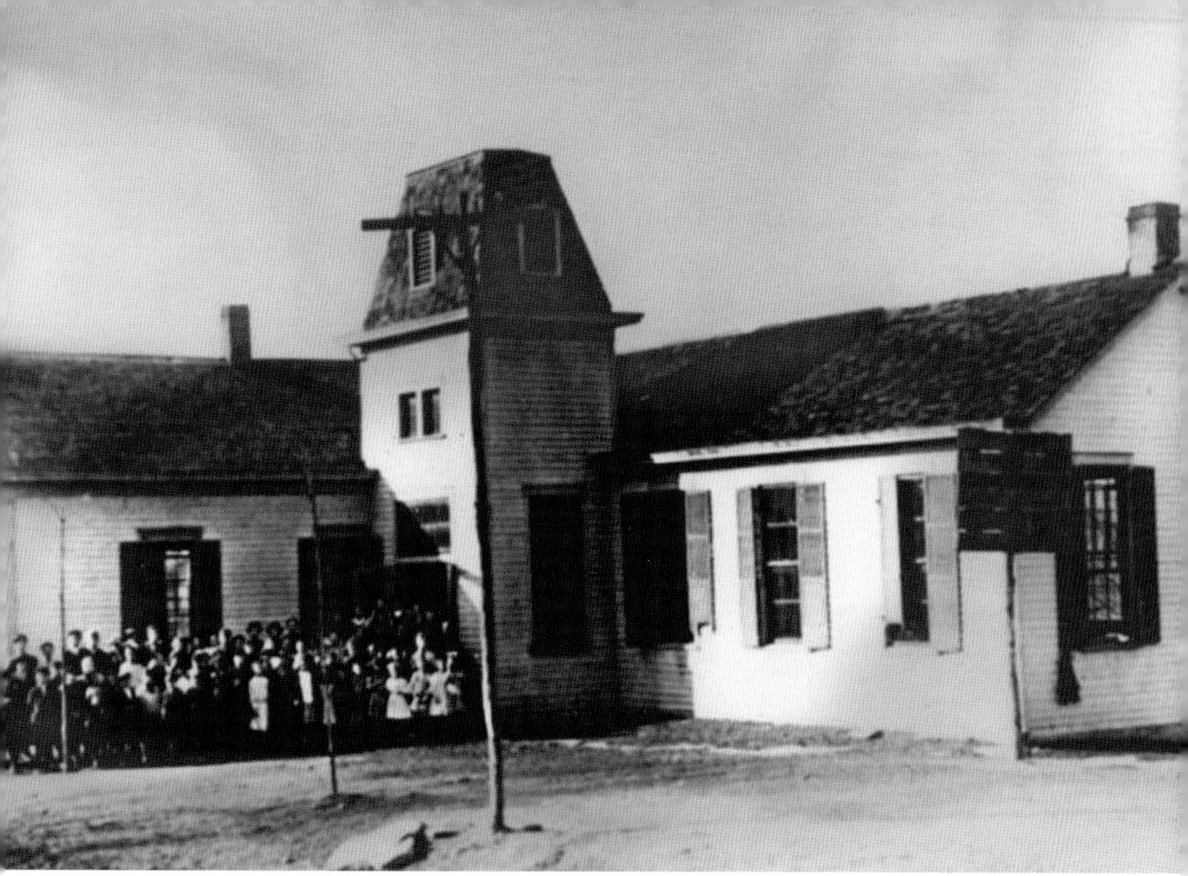

OLD UNION SCHOOL. The old Union School was an L-shaped building that today is a private residence. The central tower is gone. A small school of only a few rooms, it housed all grades. Eventually the building became a high school. The building is located on Mt. Zion Road near the new Union Municipal Building.

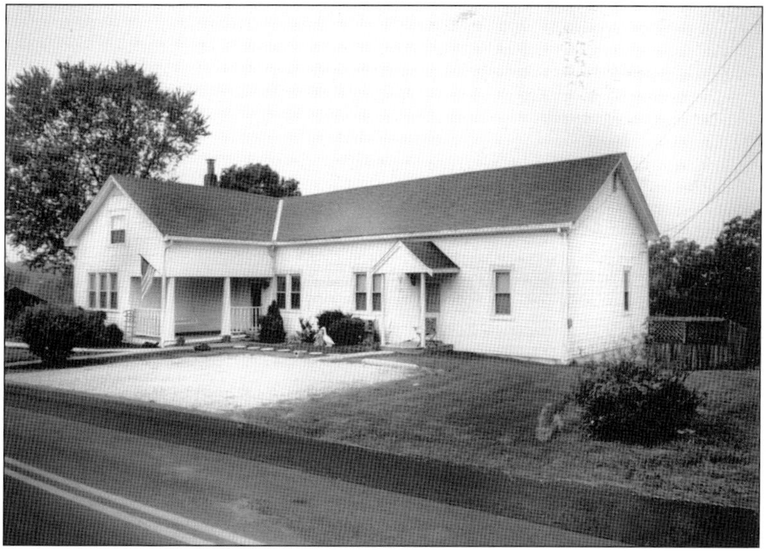

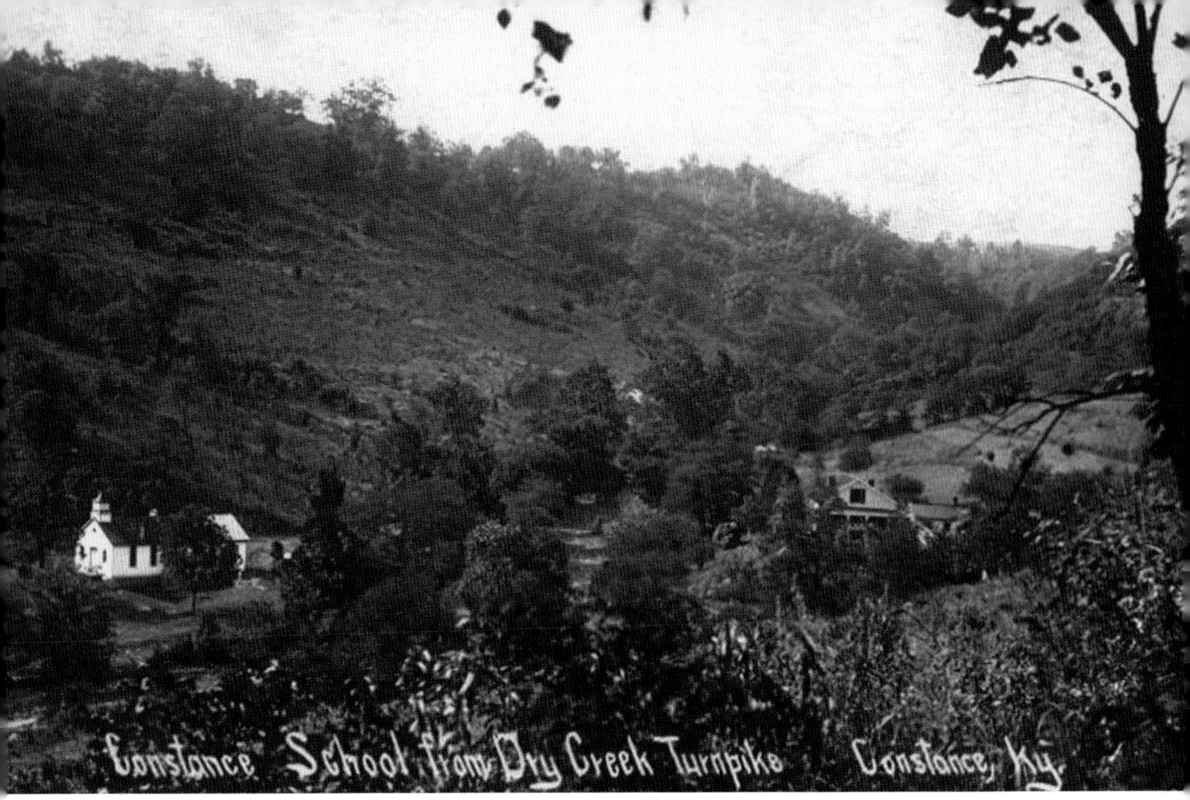

CONSTANCE SCHOOL. The Constance School can be seen from this early picture lying in the Dry Creek Valley. Through the years, Constance had several school buildings, the first built in 1868 near Anderson Ferry. The valley today serves as home to the main Sanitation District Number 1 of Northern Kentucky sewage treatment plant. However, the building shown in the recent picture is a small water facility just below Point Pleasant Road.

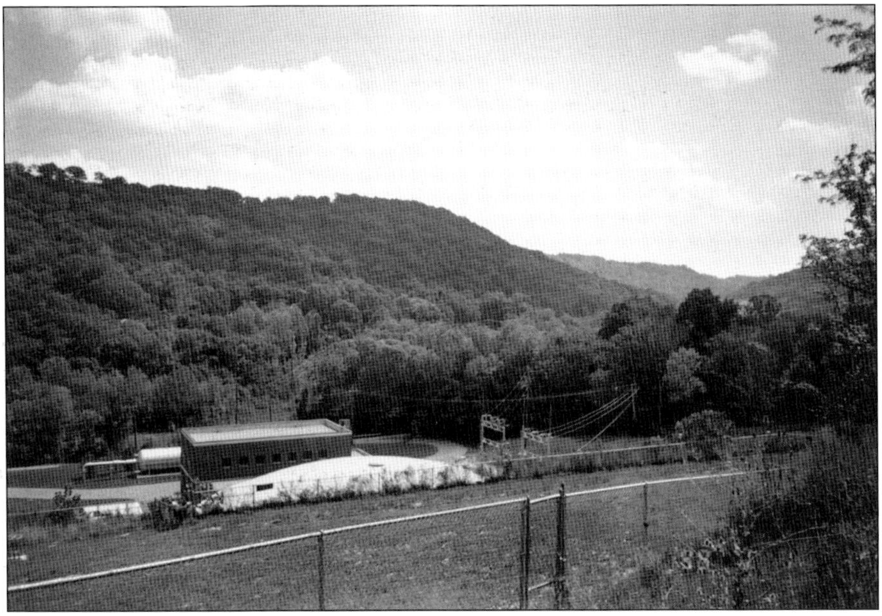

Chapter 3
CHURCHES

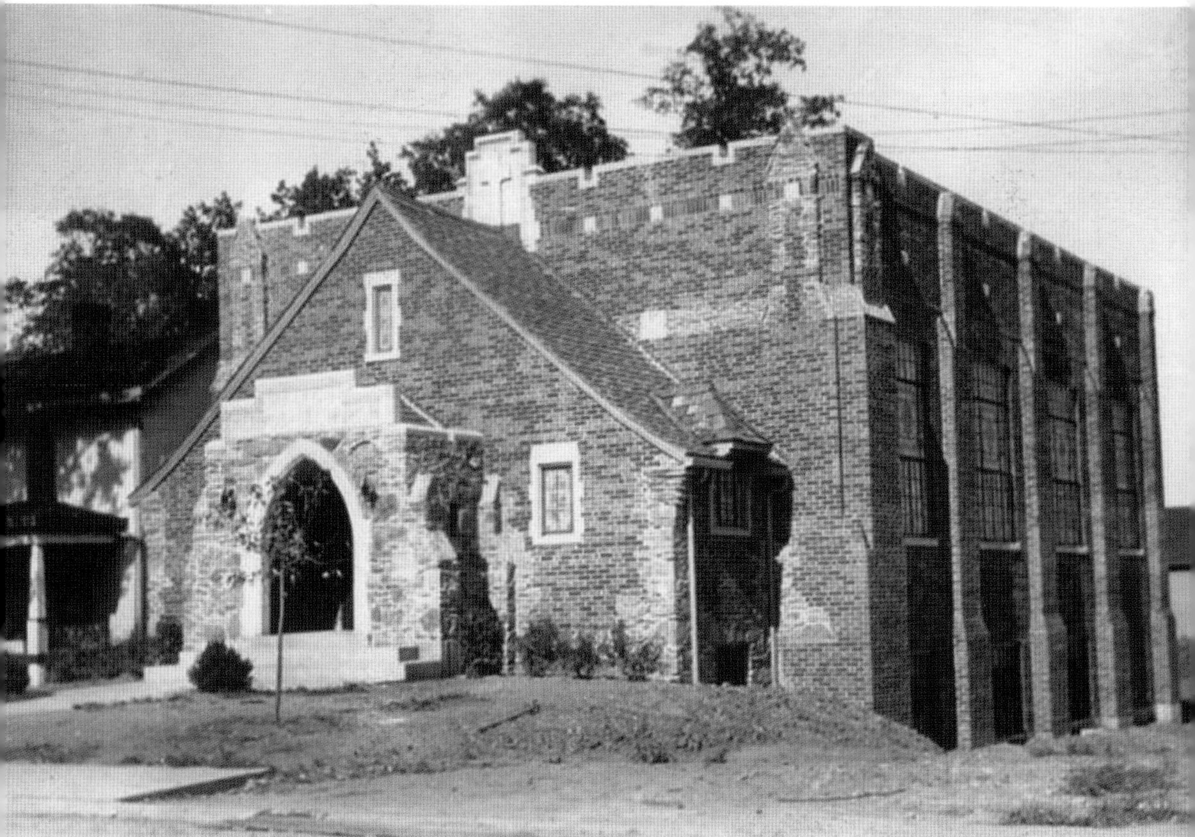

WALTON UNITED METHODIST CHURCH. The United Methodist Church in Walton is often thought of as the area's most beautifully designed church of the 20th century. Many note its unique blend of Tudor Revival and Craftsman elements. Its arched doorway, roofs, and gabled portal add to the beauty. Founded in 1879, Walton United Methodist began with eight members. The first minister was W. W. Spates. The current building was built in the 1920s during the ministry of John H. Lewis.

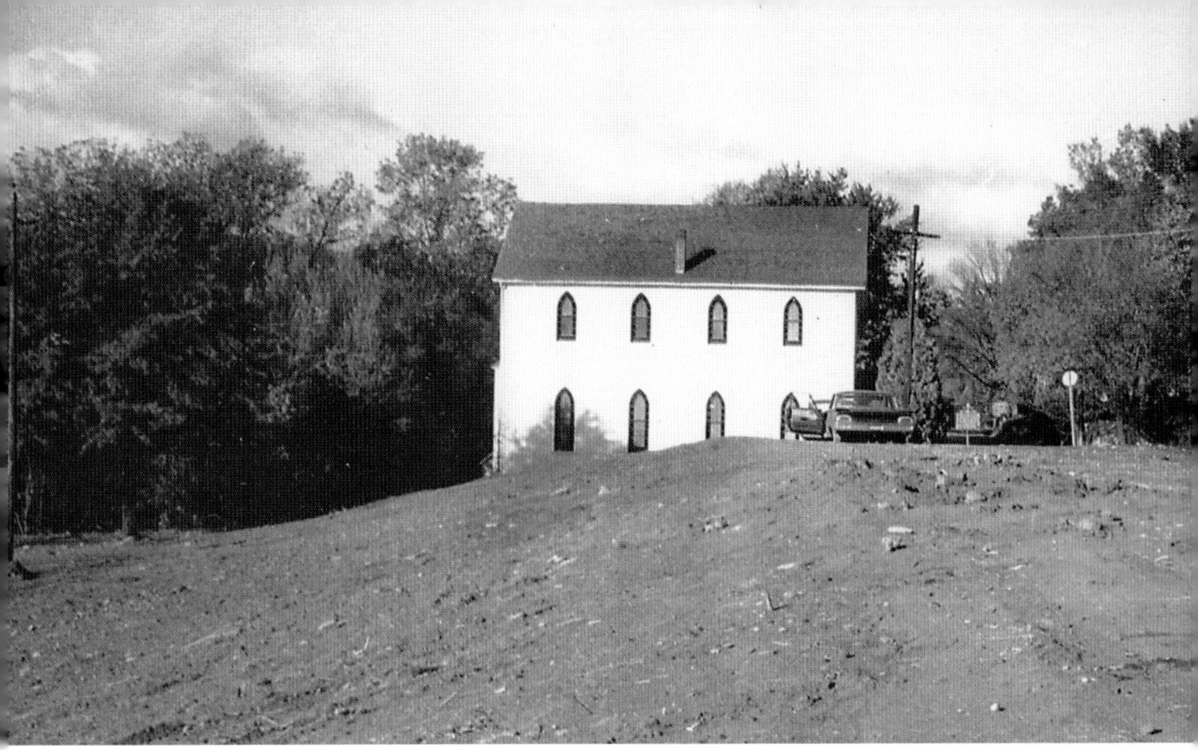

BIG BONE METHODIST CHURCH. Built in 1888, the Big Bone Methodist Church sits near the entrance to the nearby Big Bone Lick State Park. It is a very nice example of Gothic Revival architecture with Queen Anne elements. The congregation of this church was organized in 1887. A few years ago, the State of Kentucky bought the church and today it is being preserved.

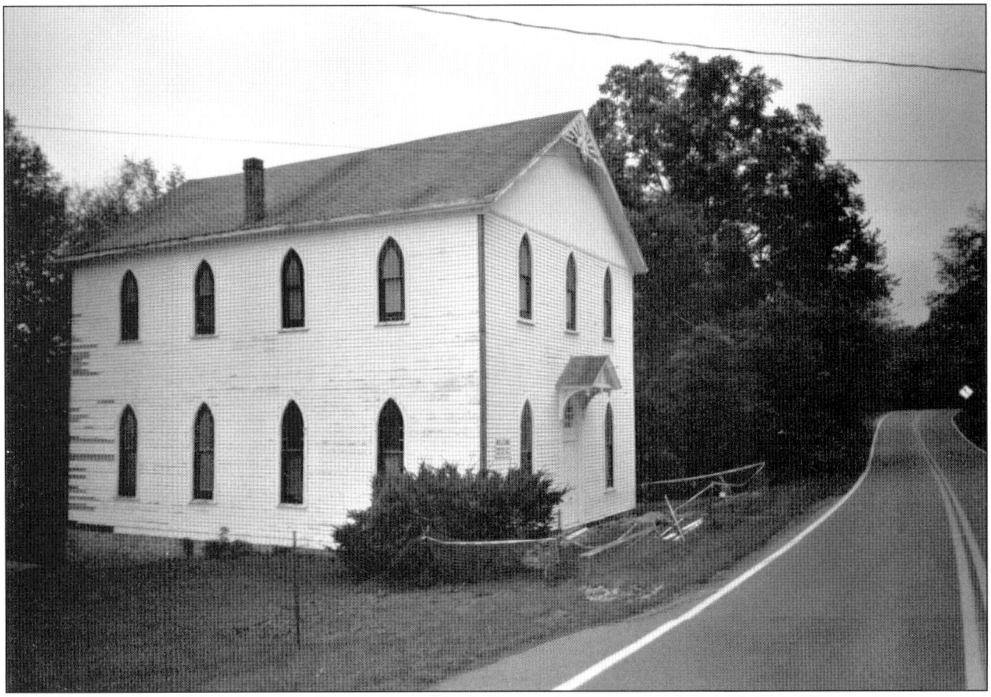

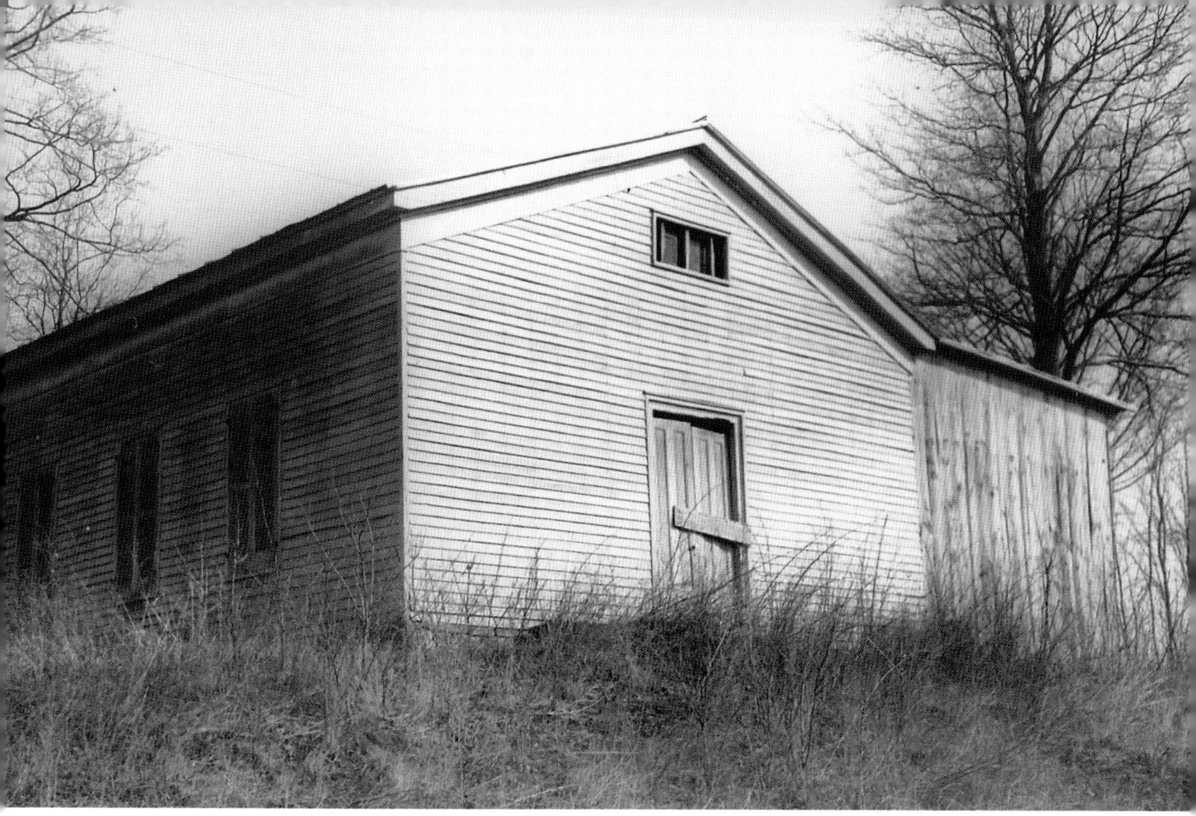

EBENEZER LUTHERAN CHURCH. The Ebenezer Lutheran Church was organized on January 22, 1856, and disbanded in the early 1930s. It then merged with Hopeful Lutheran Church. The picture is of the original church built in 1856. It was taken after the church was no longer in use, and thus it appears somewhat run down. In fact, it was most likely used as a tobacco barn. It was located in the middle of what is now the southbound exit of Mt. Zion Road.

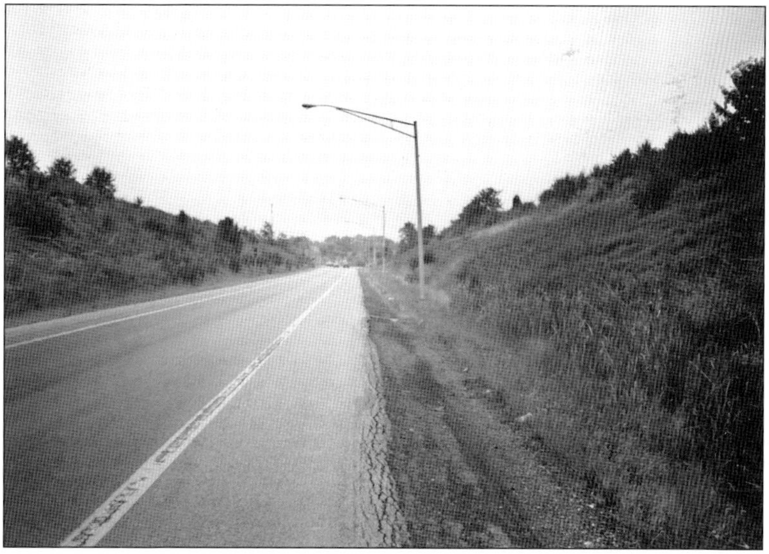

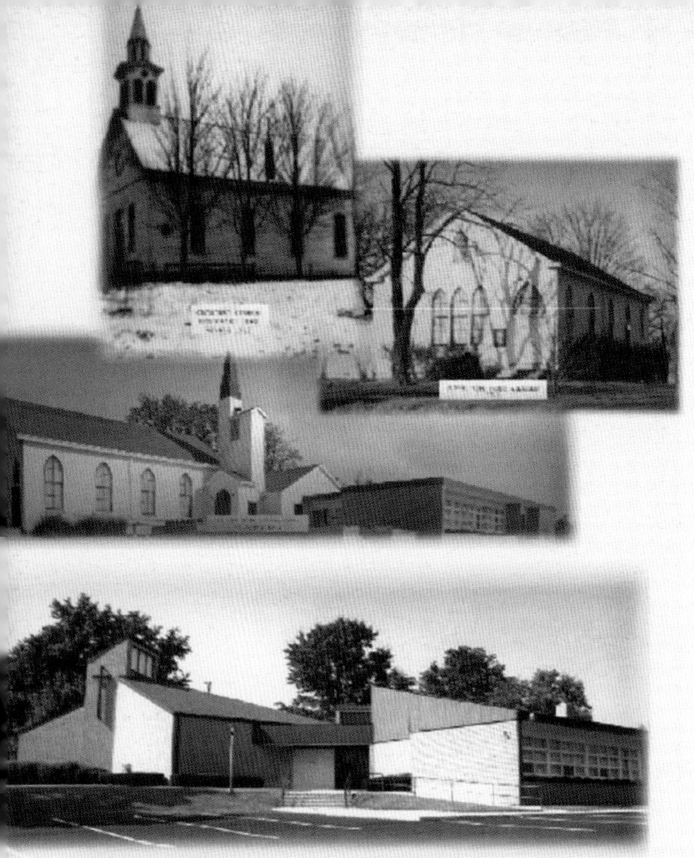

BULLITTSVILLE CHRISTIAN CHURCH. The Bullittsville Christian Church is a Protestant denomination of the Christian Church (Disciples of Christ). In 1879, the Bullittsville Christian Church was organized with 19 members. The collage of pictures shows each church building through the years. In March 2003, the church called its first female minister, Trish Standifur, seen standing outside the church located on Kentucky Route 20.

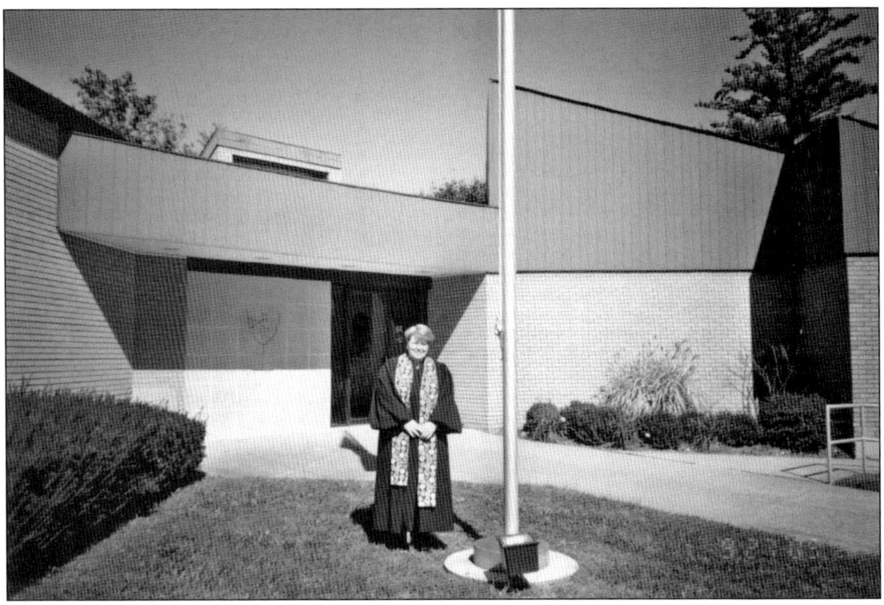

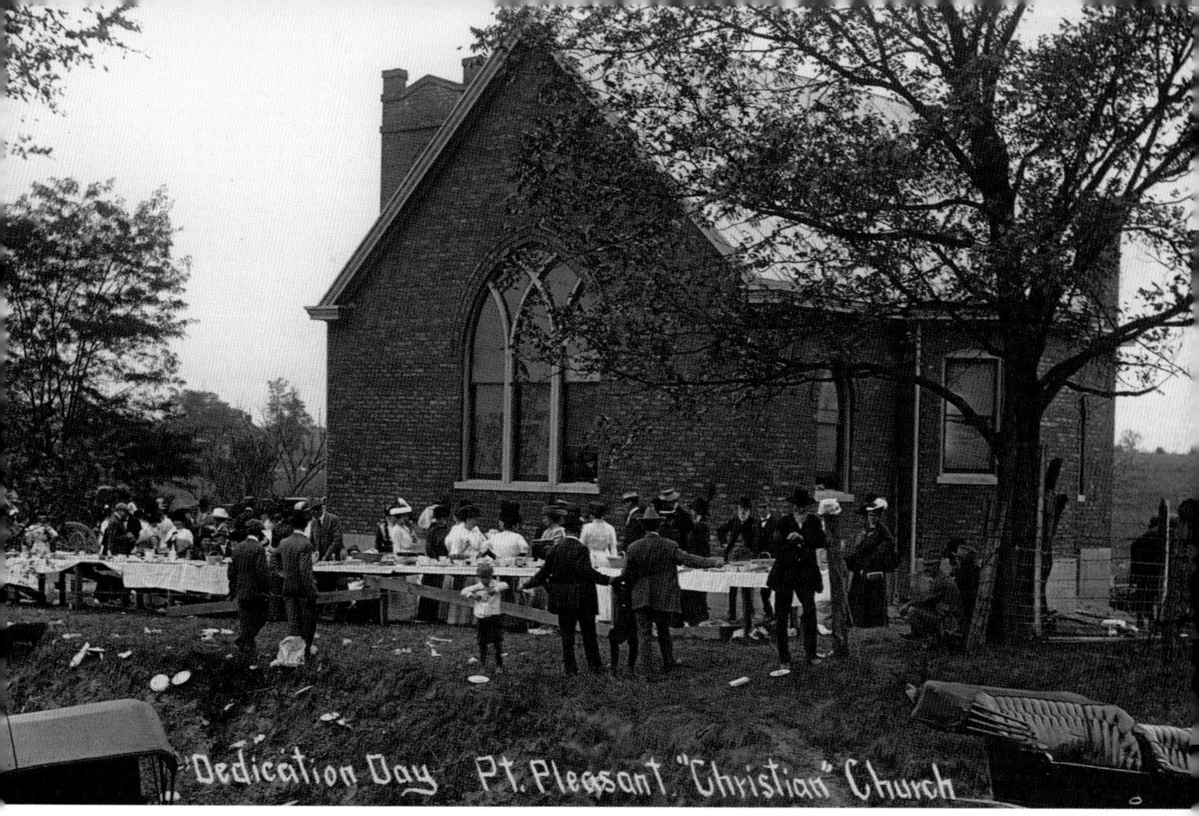

POINT PLEASANT CHURCH OF CHRIST. Point Pleasant Christian Church was dedicated in 1914. The congregation dispersed and left the building around 1938. The Church of Christ took it over and held its first service in May 1956. In 1970, the church was demolished because of I-275 construction. It sat in the westbound lane just before the Point Pleasant Road Bridge. Minister Ralph Denham served the church for 50 years and stands in front of the new church, built down the road from the old. Mr. Denham passed away a few weeks after this photograph was taken.

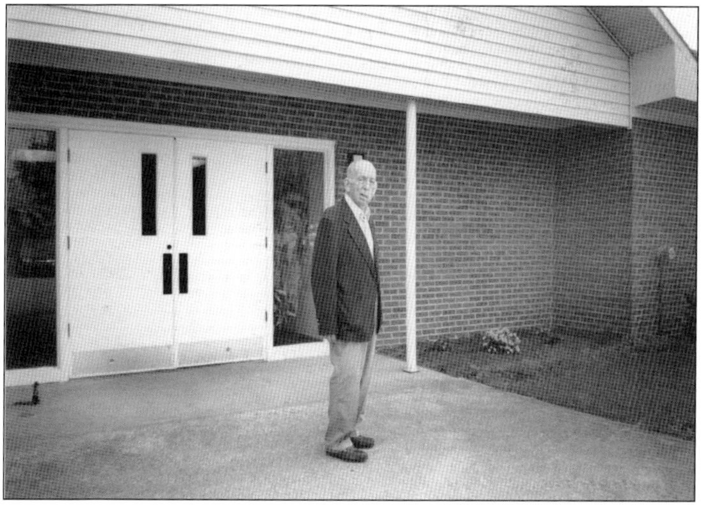

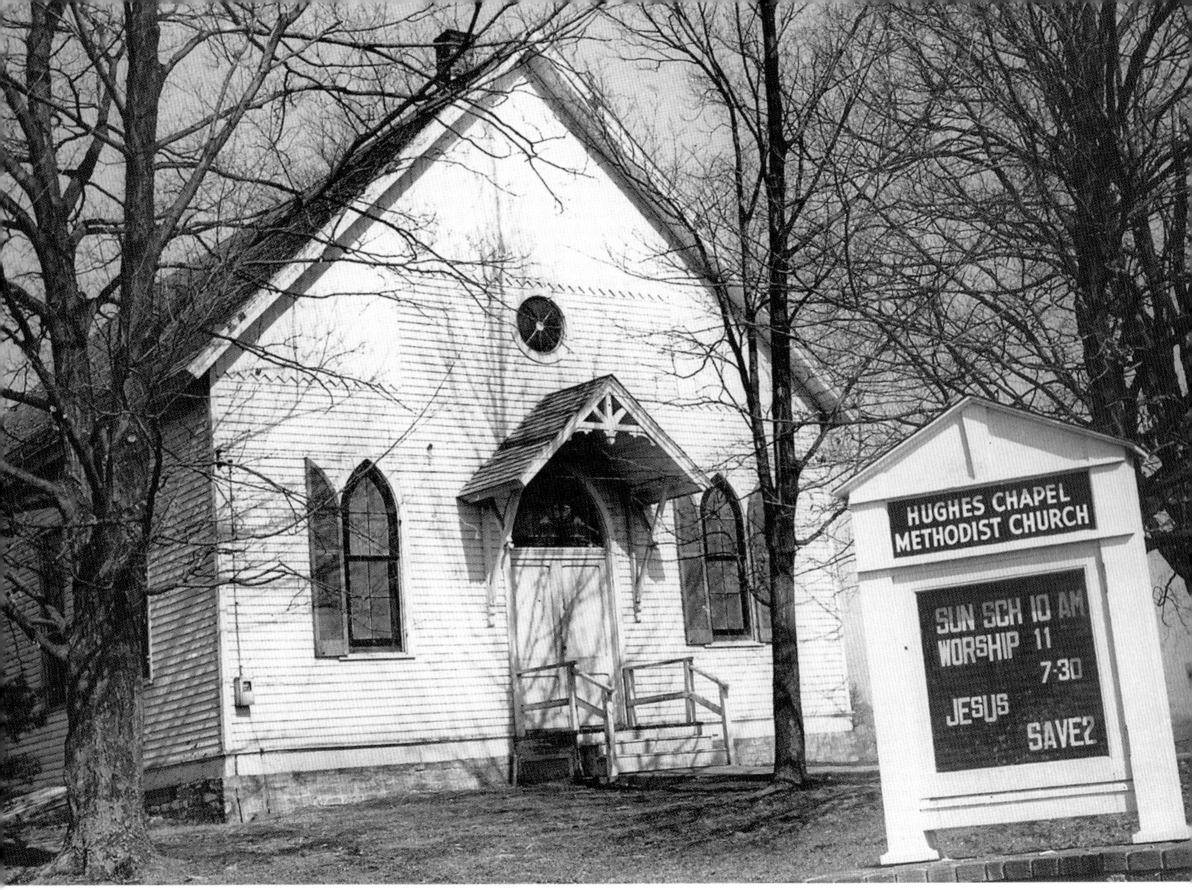

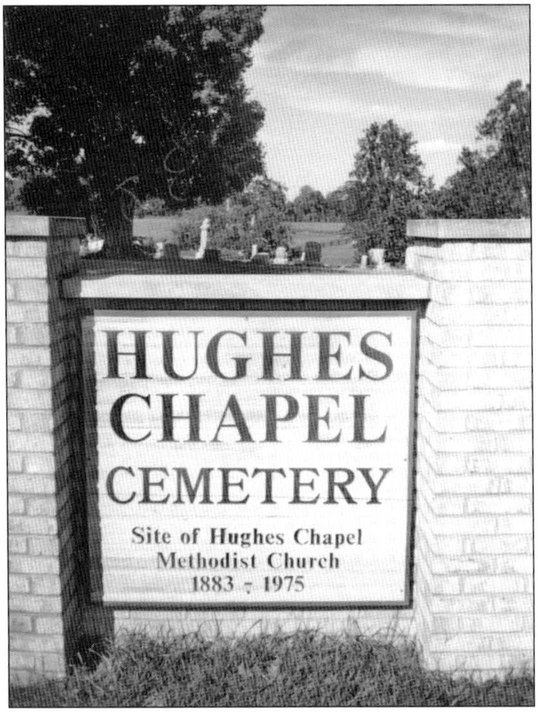

HUGHES CHAPEL CHURCH. Hughes Chapel Methodist Church was located at the corner of U.S. 42 and Richwood Road (Route 338) from 1883 to 1975. The church can be seen in its beautiful and historic form in this undated photograph. The church lot is now home exclusively to the Hughes Chapel Cemetery. The cemetery offers the opportunity for a peaceful roadside stroll through some historic grave sites.

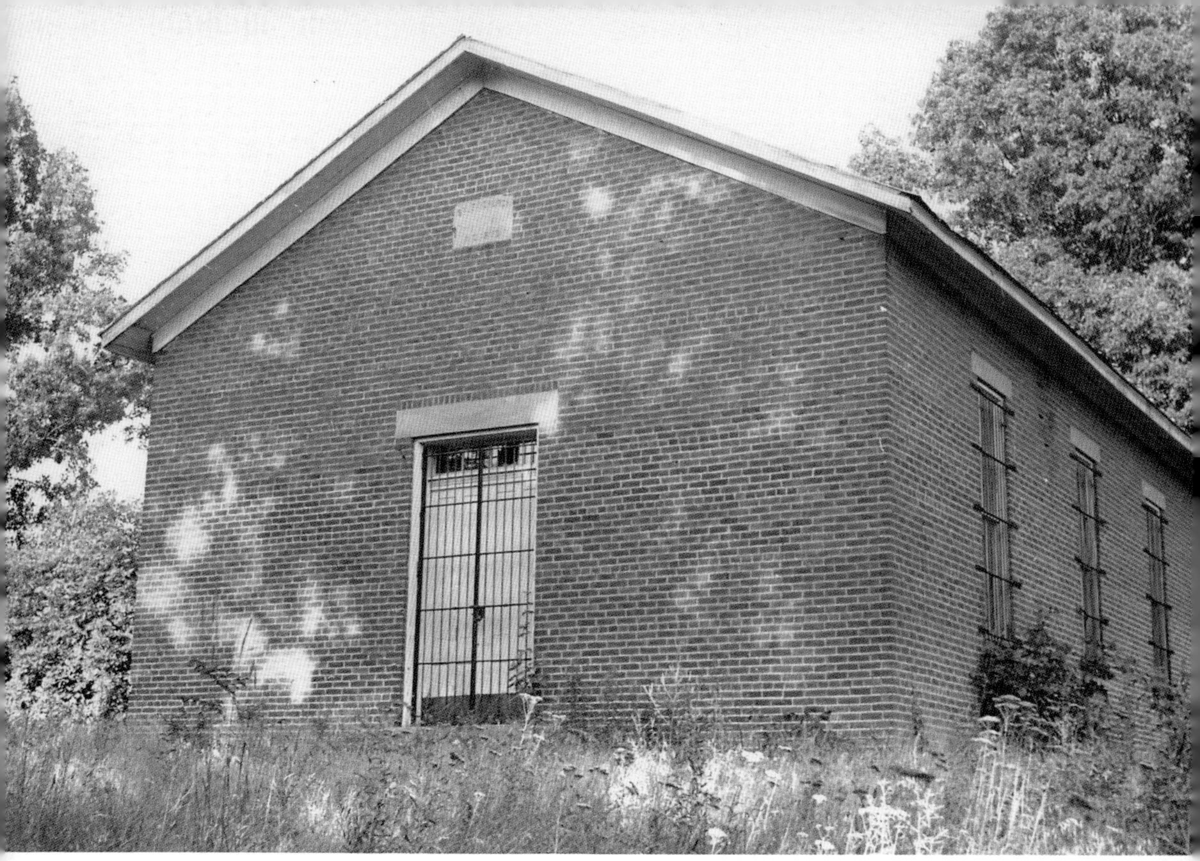

SALEM BAPTIST CHURCH. This beautiful church lies hidden on Oak Creek Road, off Walton Verona Road near a campground. The church has a long history, and the building appears to have not changed much through the years. The members have done an excellent job preserving the church and the historic atmosphere of the surroundings. A cemetery adjoins the church in a magnificent and beautiful setting.

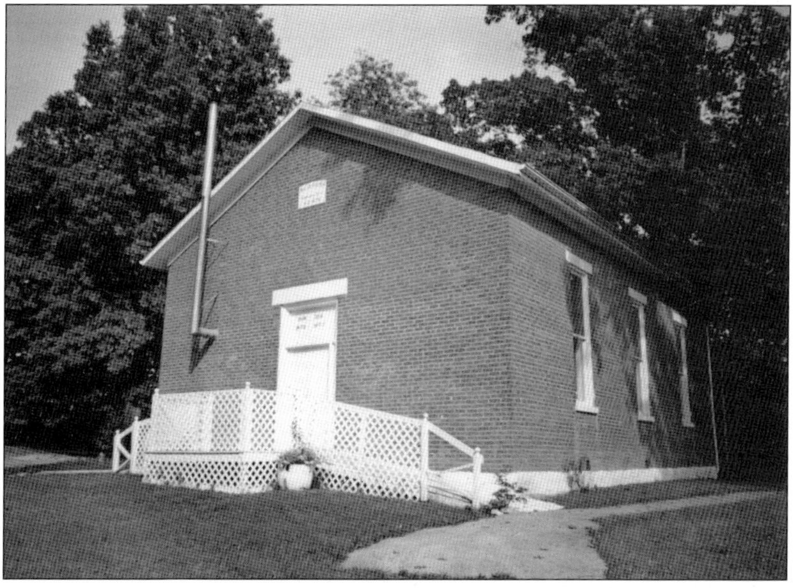

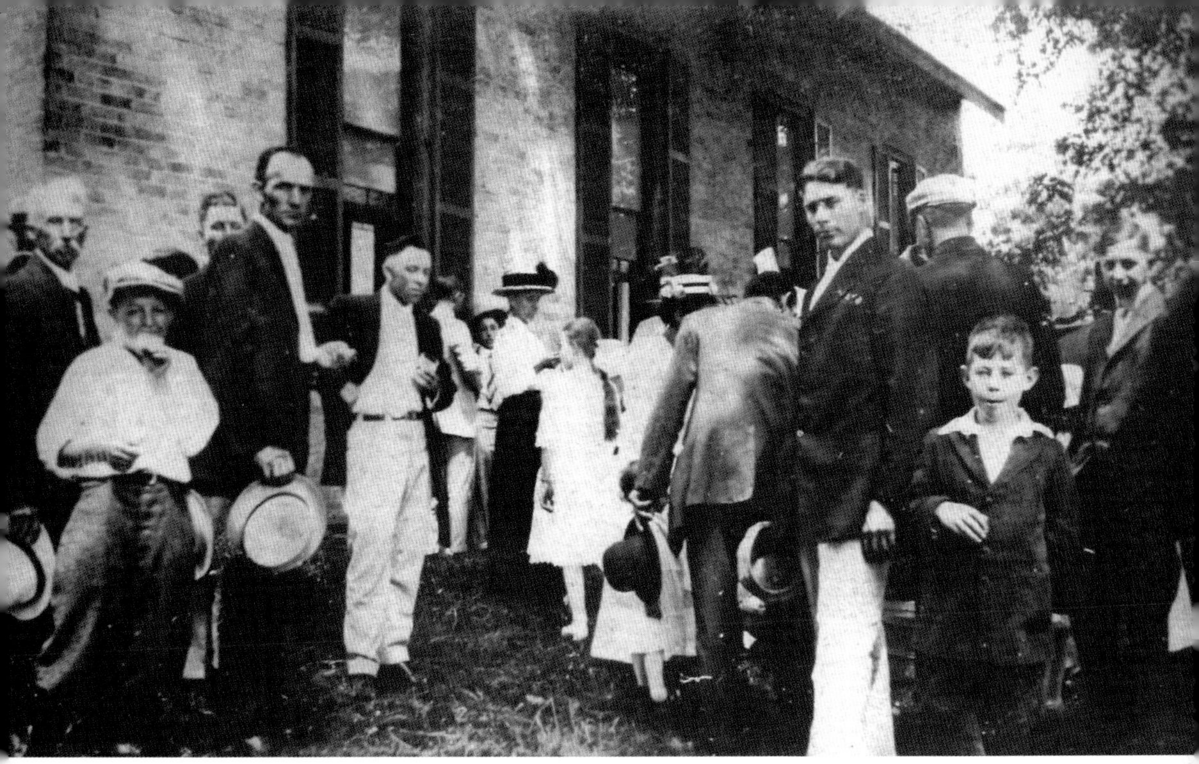

EAST BEND METHODIST CHURCH. East Bend Methodist Church is a simple Greek Revival church located near Piatt's Landing. Most likely built shortly after the Civil War, the church has a historic cemetery that is still in use. Modern graves are located in the front of the church, and those behind it date back centuries. The church sits empty but is being preserved for future use as a community room for the Rabbit Hash/East Bend area.

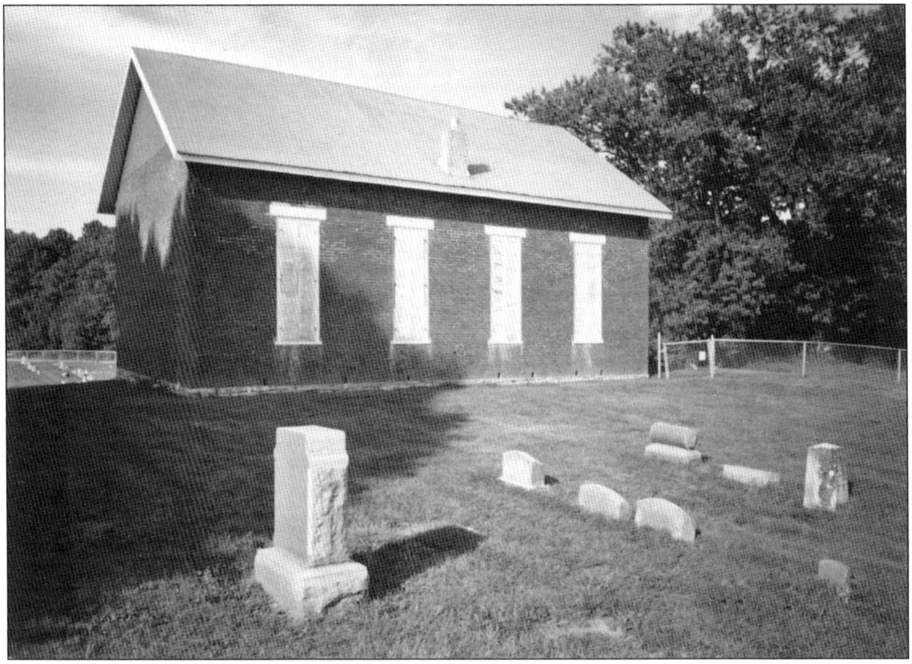

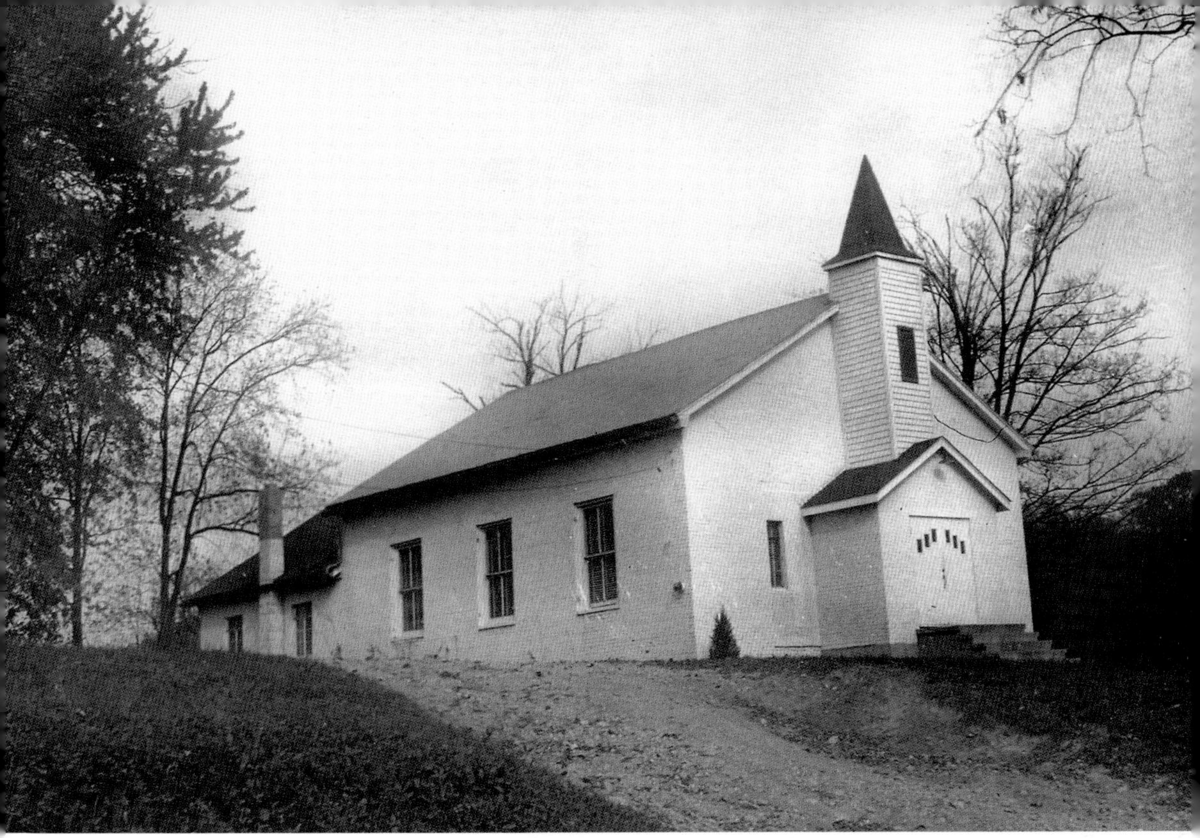

EAST BEND BAPTIST CHURCH. Established in 1819, the East Bend Baptist Church (built in 1826) is located at the corner of Route 338 and Lower River Road near Rabbit Hash. It rests on the top of a small hill, giving it a special and historic look. The church has served the community for many years and is located near the middle of the most historic corridor in the county, running from Big Bone to Petersburg.

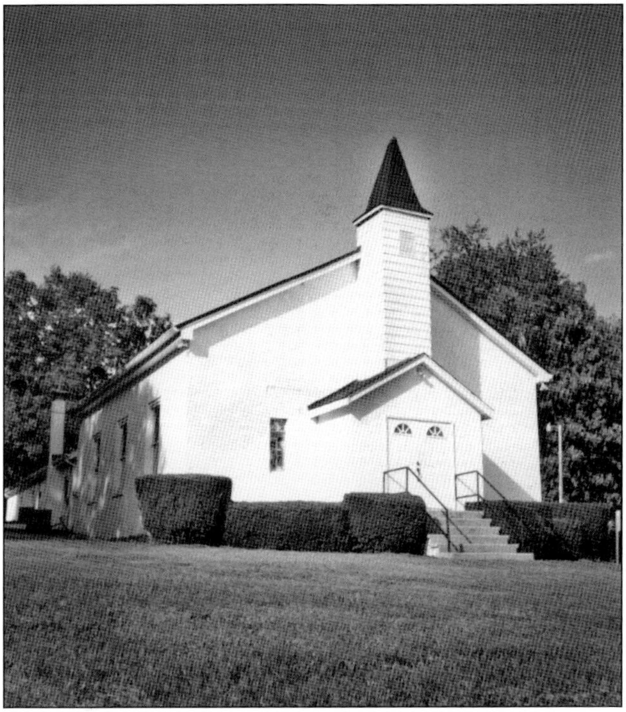

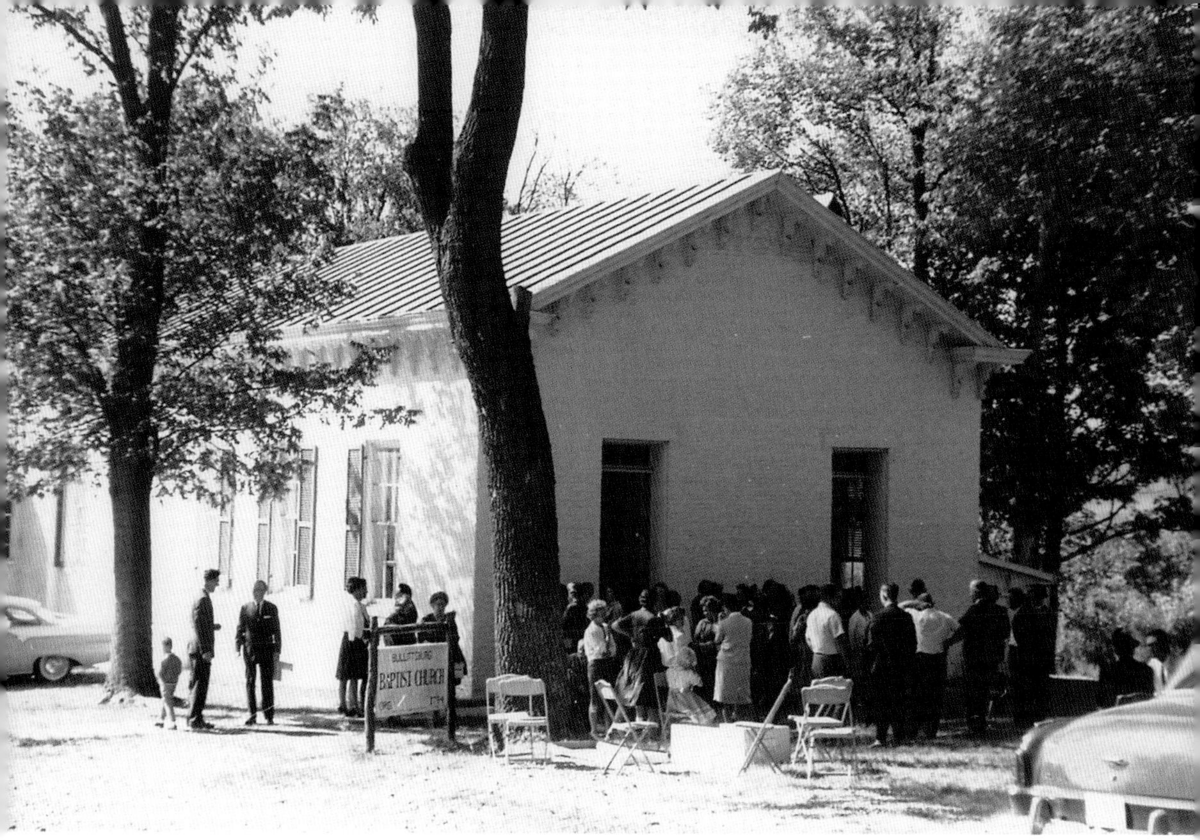

BULLITTSBURG BAPTIST. Bullittsburg Baptist is the oldest active church in Boone County, organized in 1794. It is known for many things, including assisting in the formation of many other county churches. Visiting the church is a step into Boone County history. The grounds contain a beautiful 1819 church, a cemetery started around the time of the Civil War, a burial vault constructed in 1878, and a baptismal pool built by a local stonemason in 1878 that is still sometimes used today.

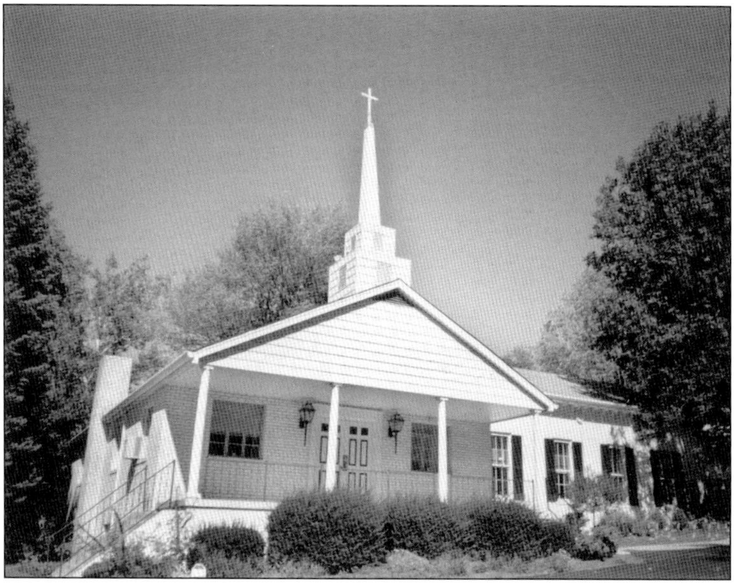

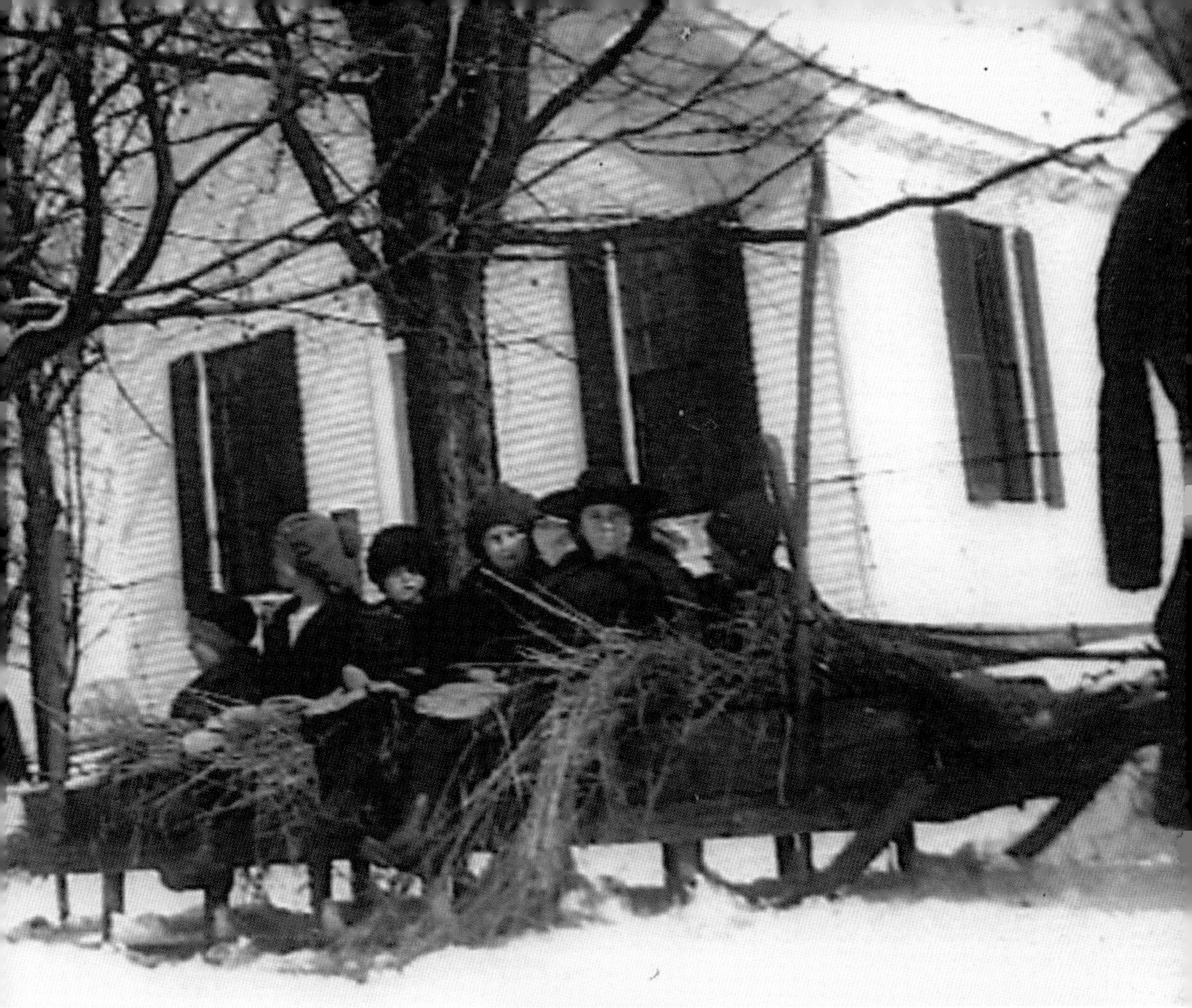

RICHWOOD PRESBYTERIAN CHURCH. The Presbyterian church was established in 1834, and the current sanctuary was constructed in 1870. Richwood was actually named after the church that has long been the central part of the community. The church was founded by Joseph Harrison, the first cousin of Pres. William Henry Harrison. In this undated photograph of a snow-covered churchyard, children on a sled are being pulled by a horse. The church remains one of the most beautiful in the county and is surrounded by a historic cemetery.

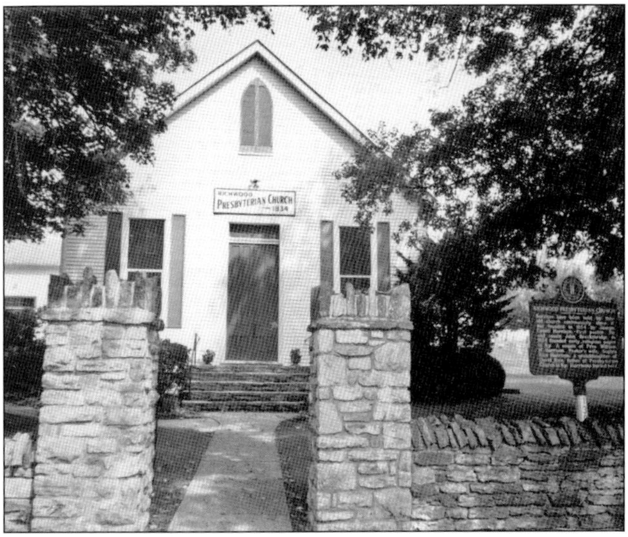

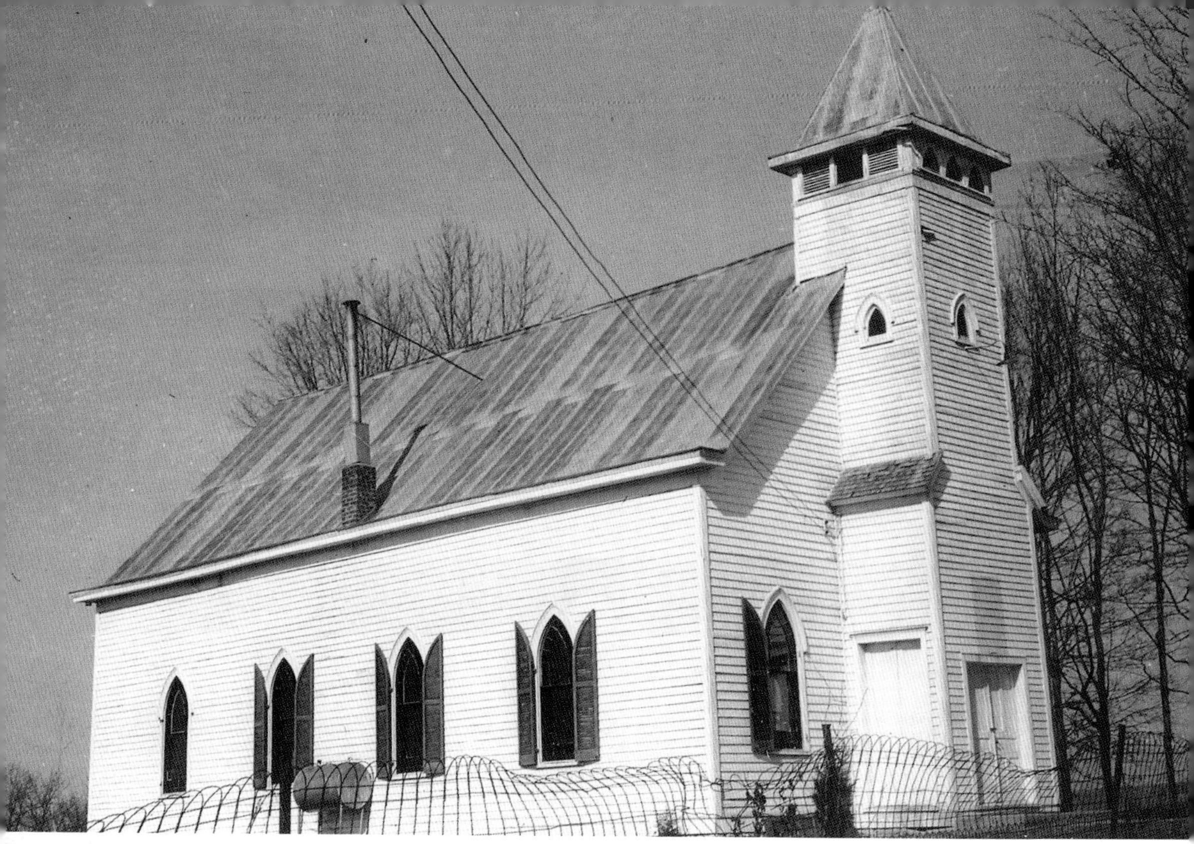

BEAVERLICK CHRISTIAN CHURCH. Beaverlick is a small village lying on the Louisville Turnpike (U.S. 42) not far from Big Bone State Park. The Beaverlick Christian Church is a fine example of the history of this crossroads community. A cemetery sits alongside the church, and combined they provide one of the most attractive spots along the route.

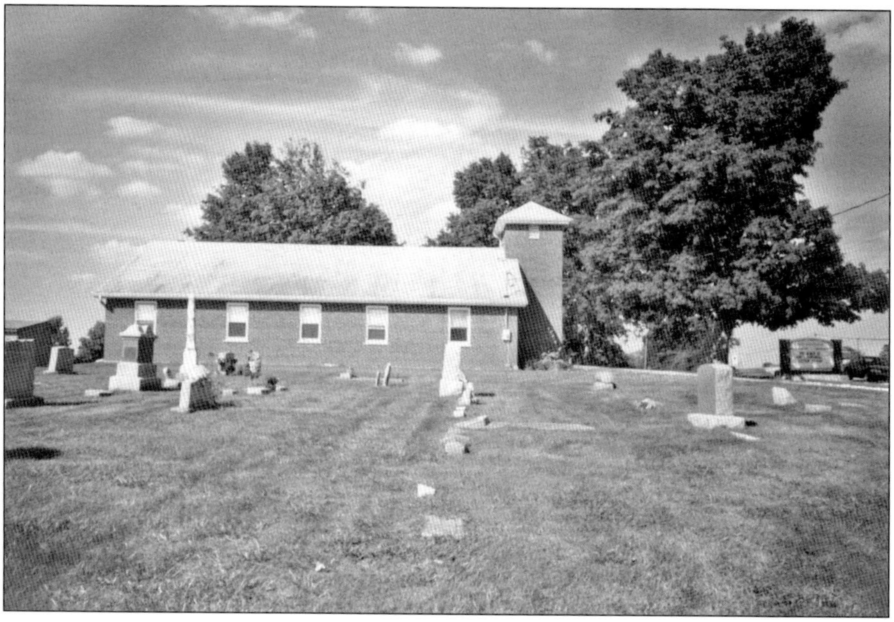

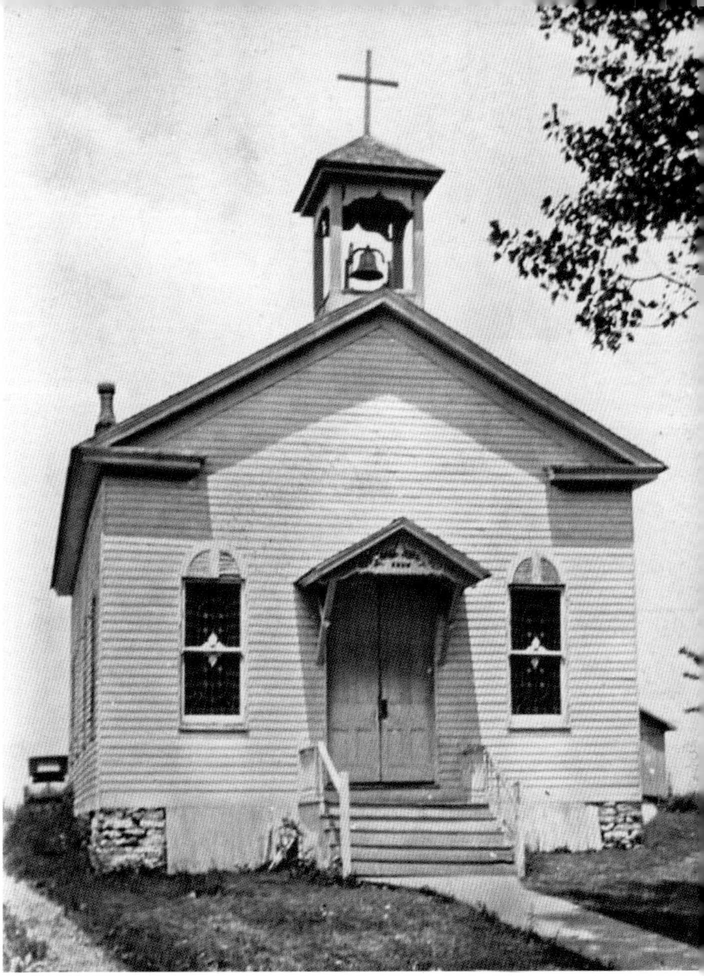

VERONA'S ST. PATRICK'S CHURCH. St. Patrick's Catholic Church was founded around 1850 and was extremely important to the community of Verona, especially the Irish citizens. St. Patrick's and All Saints Church in Walton have merged. The former spot of St. Patrick's is a vacant lot across from the former Verona Deposit Bank.

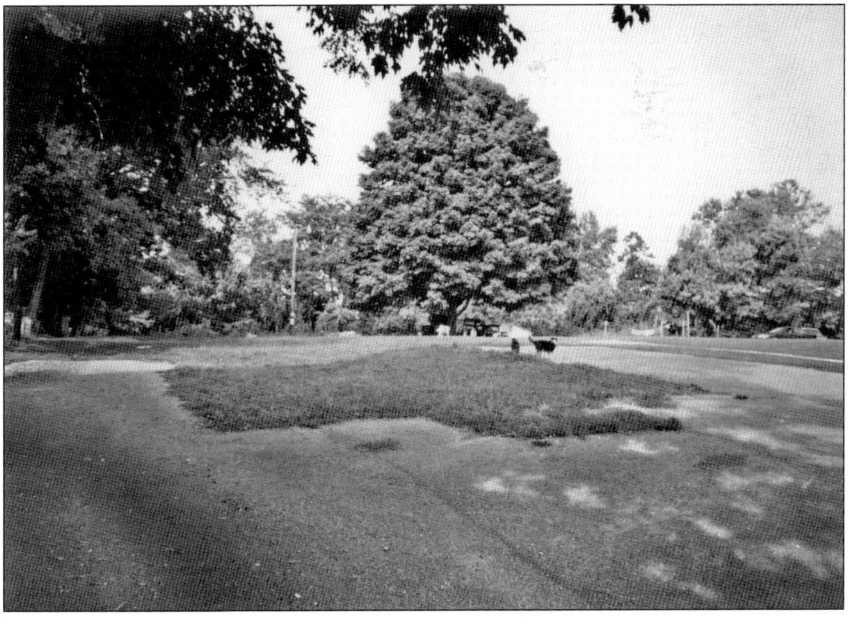

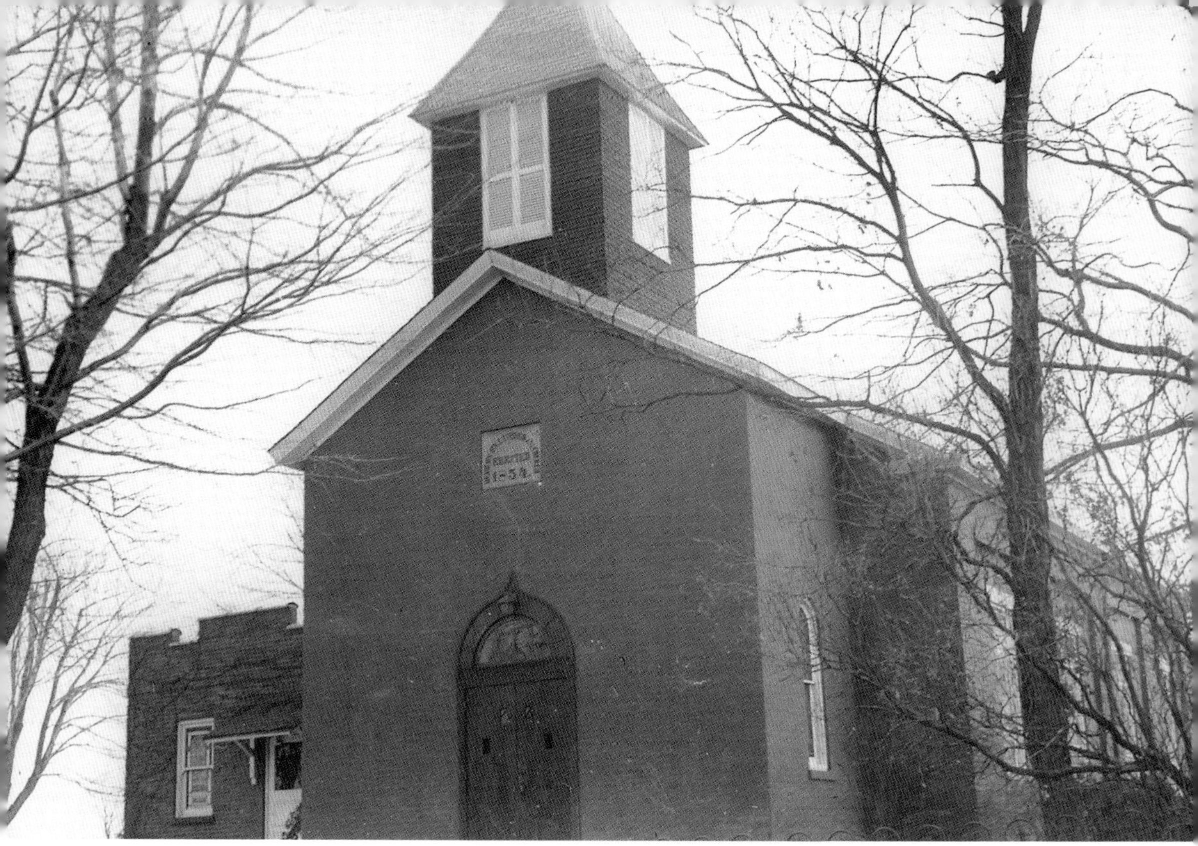

HEBRON LUTHERAN CHURCH. The Hebron community took its name from the Lutheran church that was formed in the mid-1800s. Located on Limaburg Road, the church was founded by members of the strong Lutheran church on Hopeful Road in Florence. As the church grew, so did the Hebron farming community. Today a new structure sits on the same land as the old church, surrounded by a large historic cemetery.

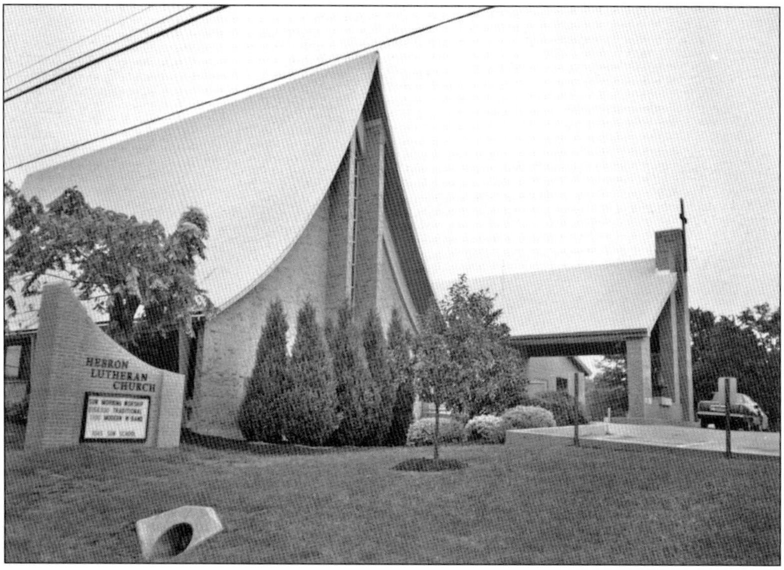

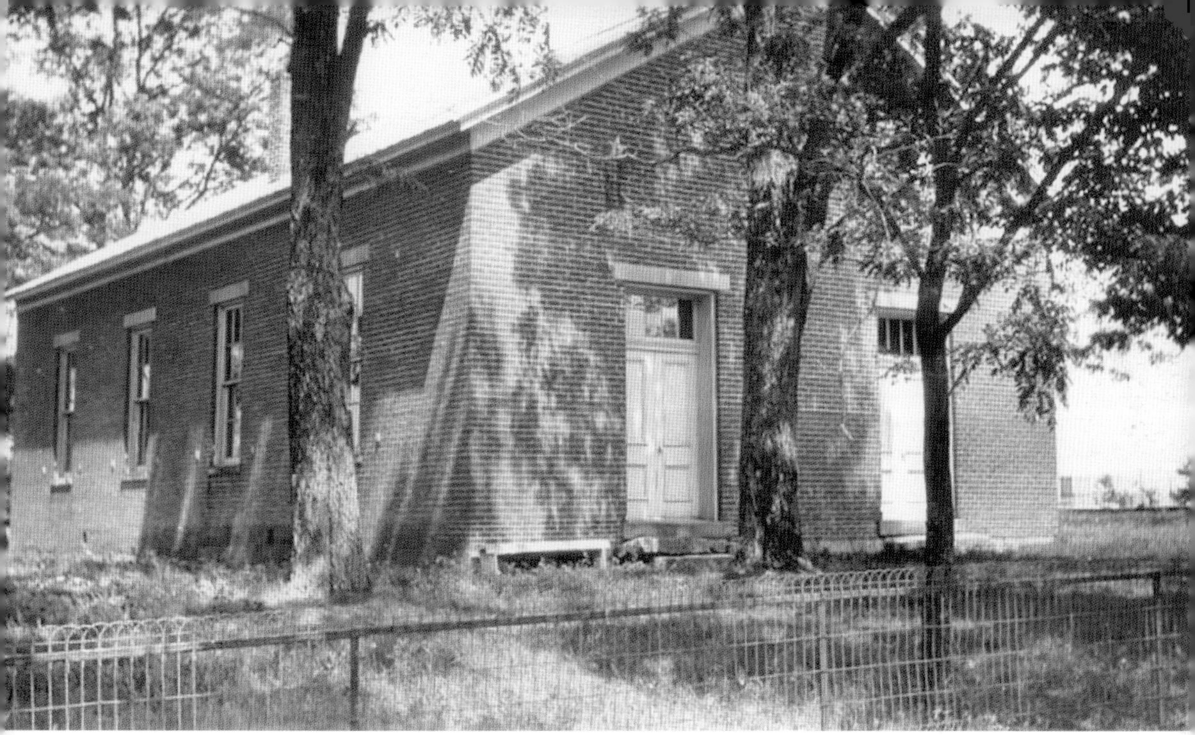

NEW BETHEL BAPTIST CHURCH. The New Bethel Baptist Church was established in 1831 by local farmers. The history of the church and the community seem to have grown together, and today the church remains a vibrant institution. The church has had several buildings such as the one pictured here, located at the New Bethel Cemetery. Today the church is located in the center of town.

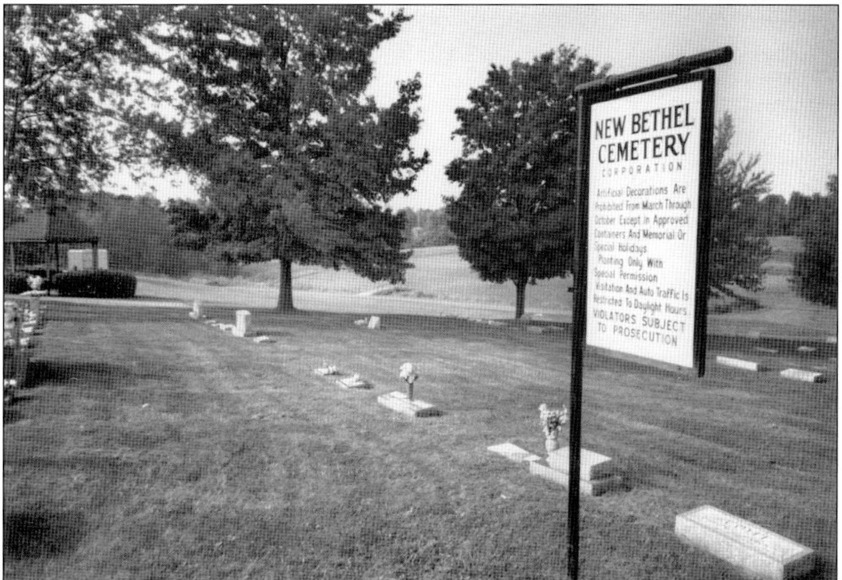

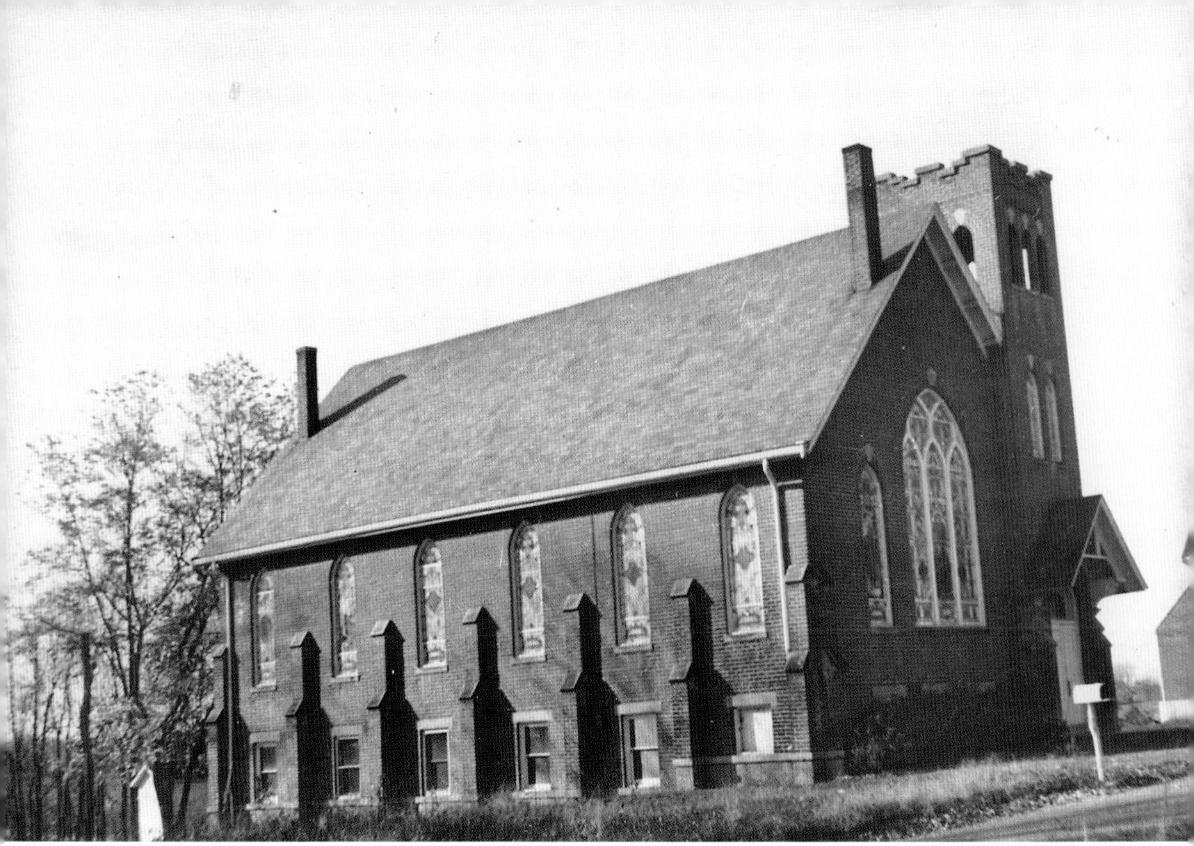

HOPEFUL LUTHERAN. The Hopeful Lutheran Church was founded in 1806, and the first church on its present site was built in 1837. The current church was built in 1917. The church is thriving, and a new sanctuary is under construction at the time of this 2005 photograph. The church is to be applauded for preserving the old church, which it will use for weddings and funerals. The new building will match the old. This represents historic preservation at its best.

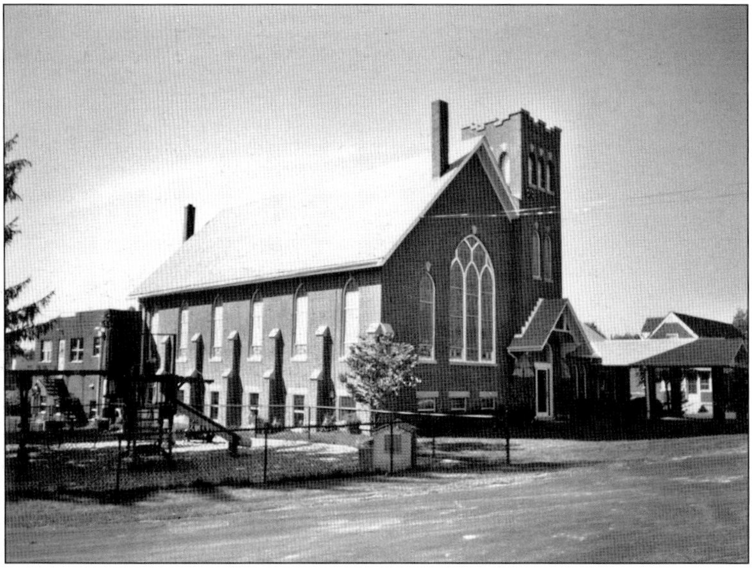

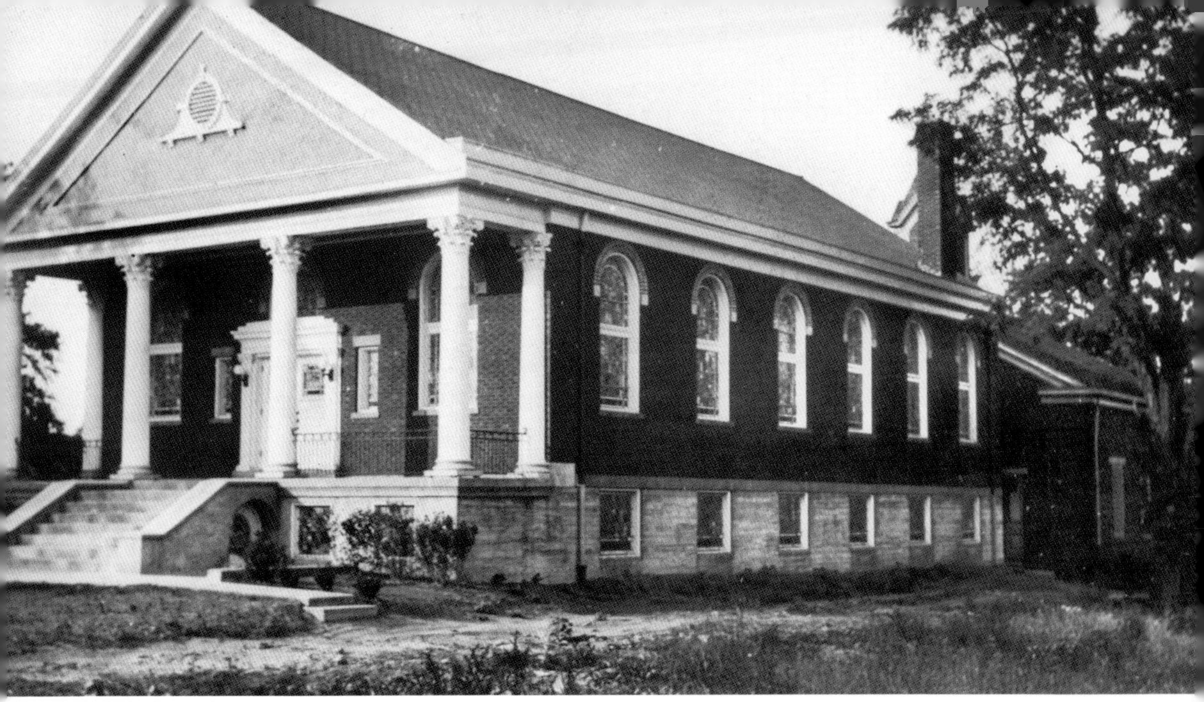

FLORENCE BAPTIST CHURCH. This 1930 photograph shows the Florence Baptist Church on Main Street in Florence. The church has been greatly expanded, but an excellent job was done to preserve the historic structure. As can be seen, the expansion project incorporated the old church into its design. The modern photograph was taken in 2005, the 150th anniversary of the church.

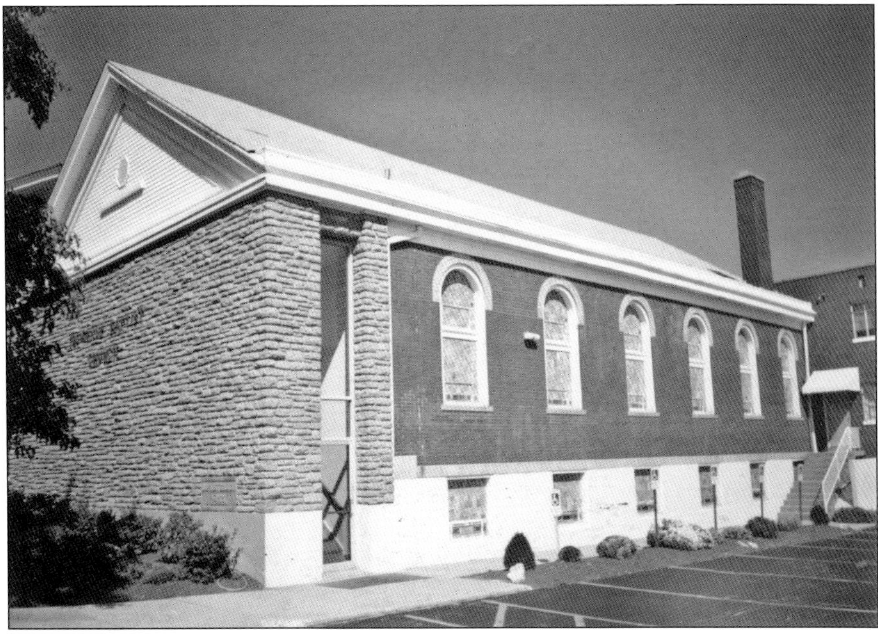

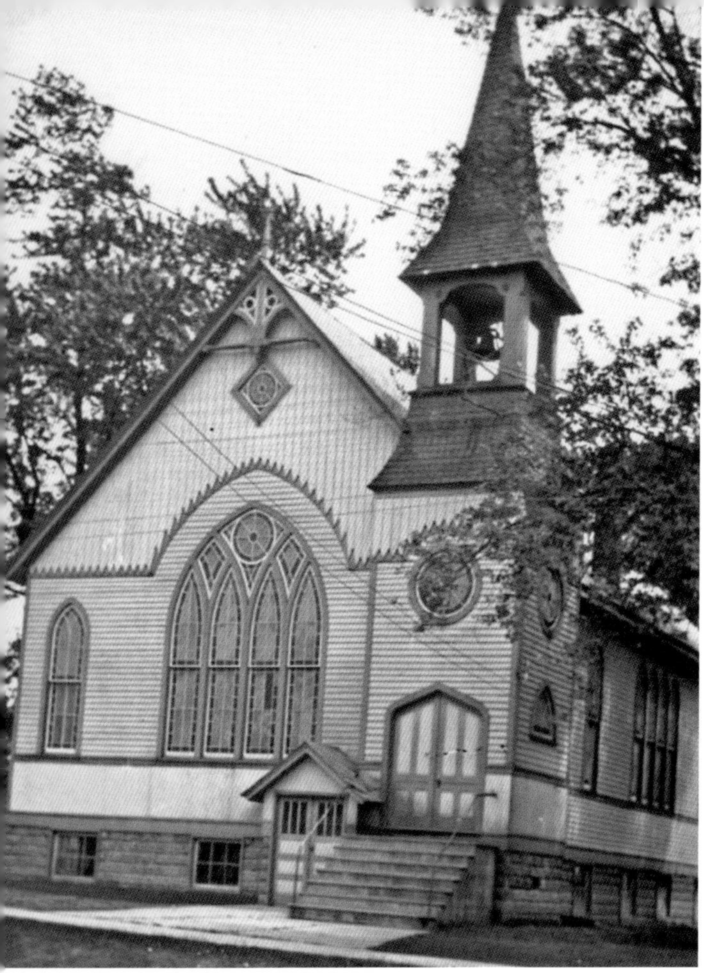

BURLINGTON **B**APTIST **C**HURCH. One of the most active churches in the county is the Burlington Baptist Church. It was founded in 1842 and in the mid-1800s was one of four churches serving Burlington. The church has always played a prominent role in Burlington, both physically and spiritually. The current church was built in 1979 and sits in the heart of town. Today the church offers many programs for the community. The two pictures compare the old church and the new.

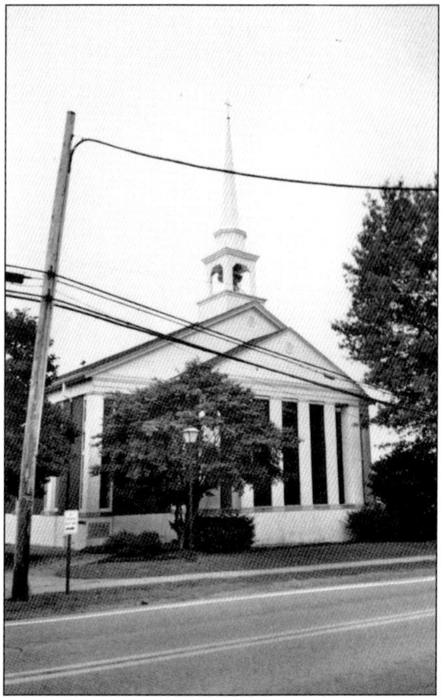

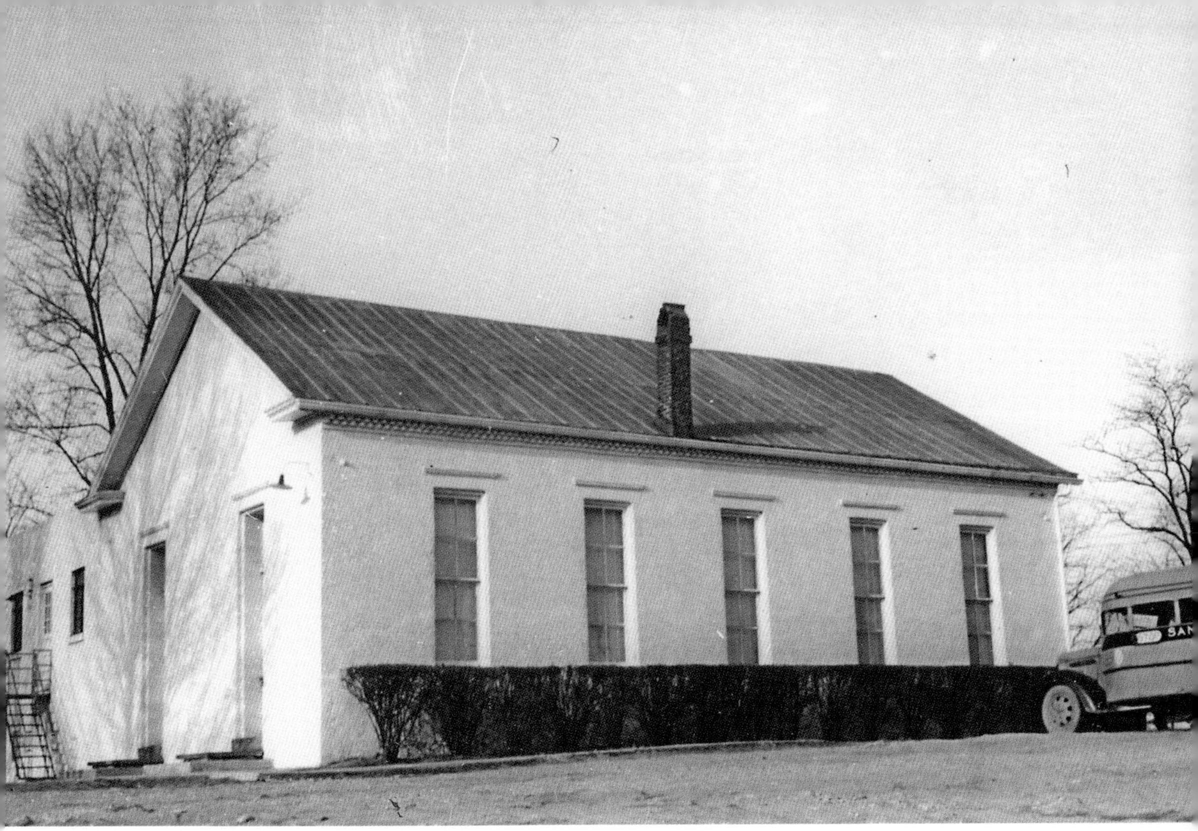

SAND RUN BAPTIST CHURCH. The original structure of the Sand Run Baptist Church was built in 1819, and the congregation consisted of 77 original members. The current building was opened in 1976, the year of the United States Bicentennial. Sand Run is located on North Bend Road in Francisville, and behind the church is a historic cemetery that contains the remains of many church leaders. The current building, although fairly new, has a nice historic feel to it, accentuated by the stained-glass windows.

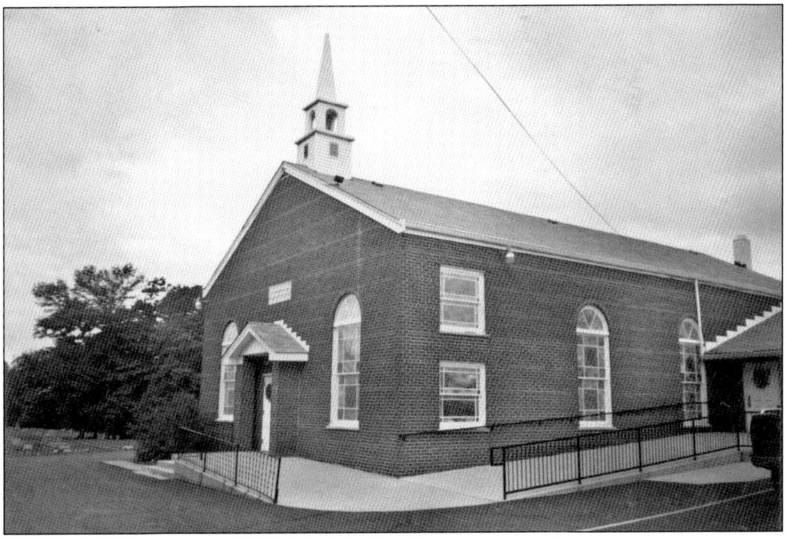

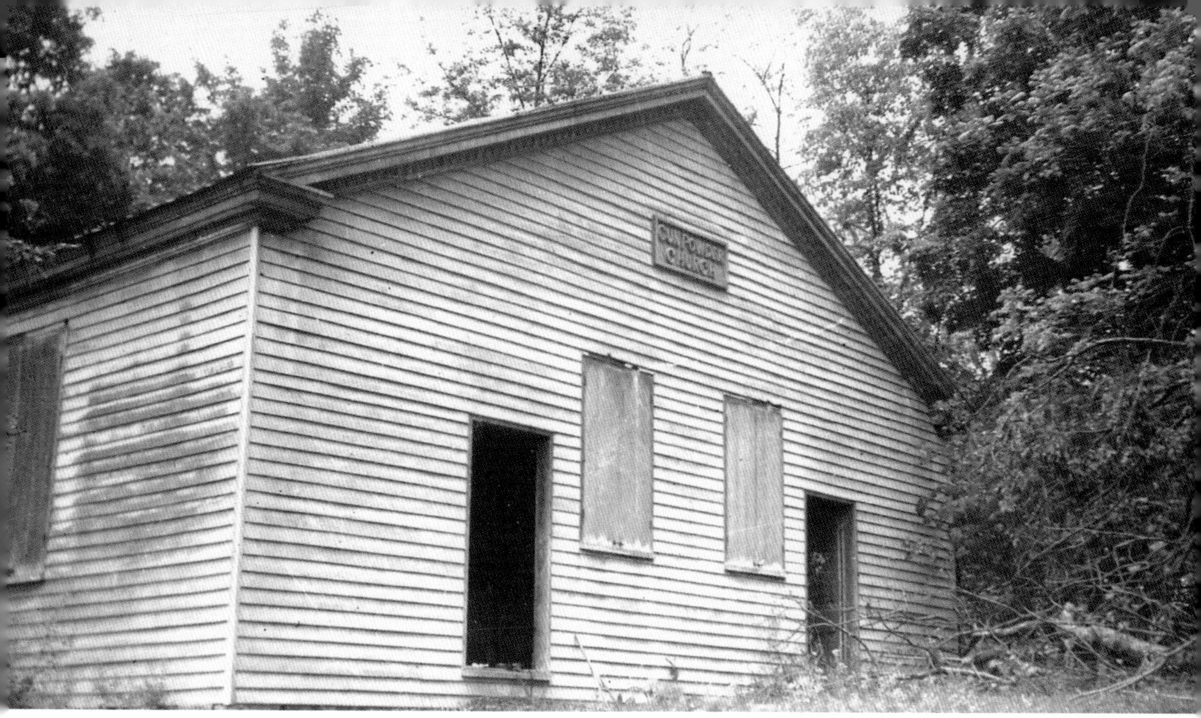

GUNPOWDER BAPTIST CHURCH. Gunpowder Baptist Church organized in 1812, and the sanctuary pictured here was built in the 1850s. It sat almost literally on the Gunpowder Creek, supposedly on an island that is now filled around. It is located off Pleasant Valley Road at the bridge going over Gunpowder Creek. The church sat approximately 100 yards upstream from the bridge. The structure stood for about 150 years. In 2002, it was moved and rebuilt as a home on a farm on Richwood Road.

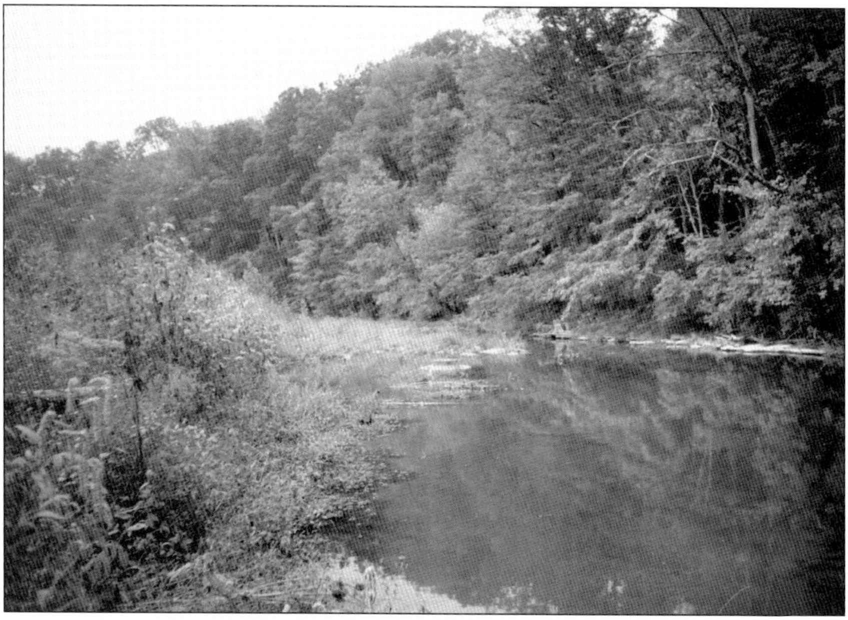

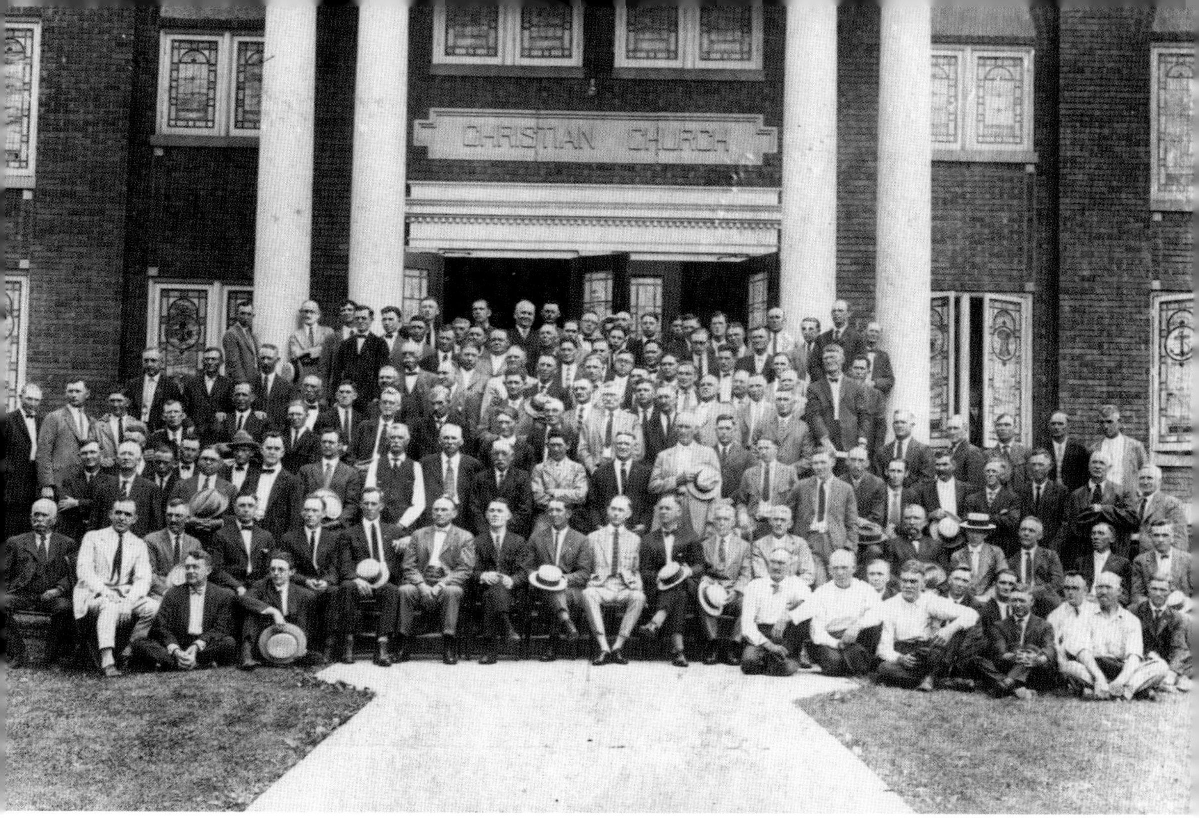

WALTON CHRISTIAN CHURCH. The Walton Christian Church (Disciples of Christ) was founded in 1876. The first church building was on High Street. On May 5, 1918, a new building, shown here, was dedicated on Main Street. On Thanksgiving Day 1947, it was destroyed by fire. The present building was dedicated on August 14, 1949. Pictured in front of the new building is Pastor Kevin Russell.

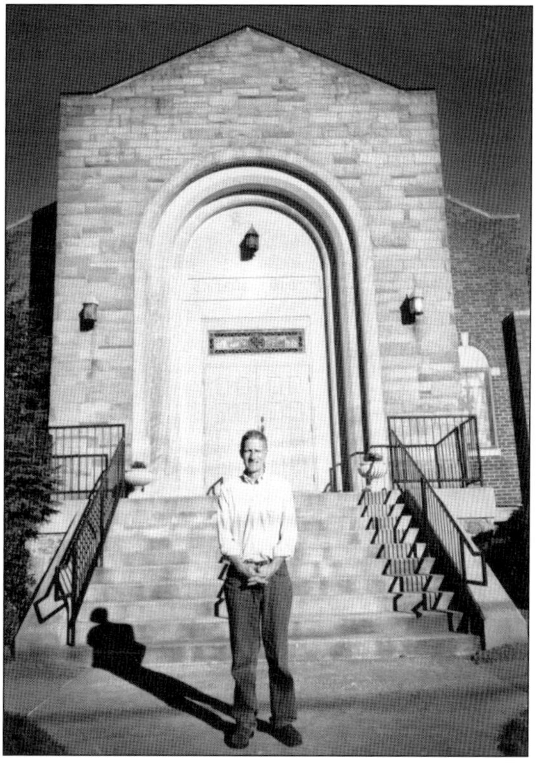

Bellevue, Ky., Sep the 28 1916

This is to Certify, *that* Pope Bros

has purchased and paid for Lot No. 15 *in the* north side of

Bellevue Baptist Church Cemetery,

AT BELLEVUE, BOONE COUNTY, KENTUCKY,

and that he is entitled to full control of same, so far as does not conflict with the rules of the Cemetery as adopted; and we, the Trustees of the Bellevue Baptist Church Cemetery Company, hereby convey to him Lot No. 15 *in said Cemetery, subject to the conditions of the Charter and By-Laws under which said Cemetery is controlled.*

Witness *our hands, this the* 28 *day of* Sep 1916

.... *Pres't.*

G. J. Roberts *Sec'y.*

W. L. RIDDELL, BURLINGTON, KY.

BELLEVIEW CEMETERY. This Baptist cemetery is located in the heart of the community in western Boone County. It is associated with the Belleview Baptist Church, one of the most important and historically significant churches in the county. This historic cemetery houses many important people from Boone County's past. Most prominent is the Brady Mausoleum, the final resting place of the Brady family, including Robert, who rode with Gen. John Hunt Morgan during the Civil War. The mausoleum was constructed around the same time as this lot document.

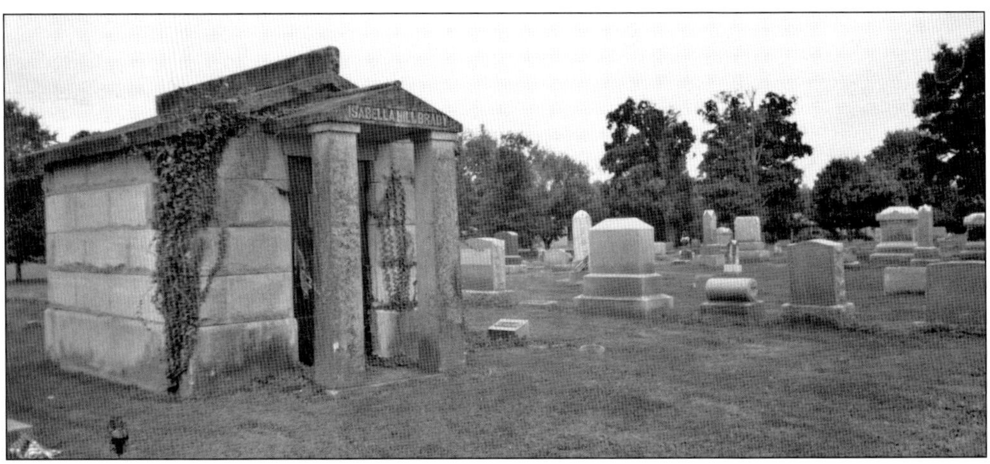

Chapter 4
COMMUNITIES

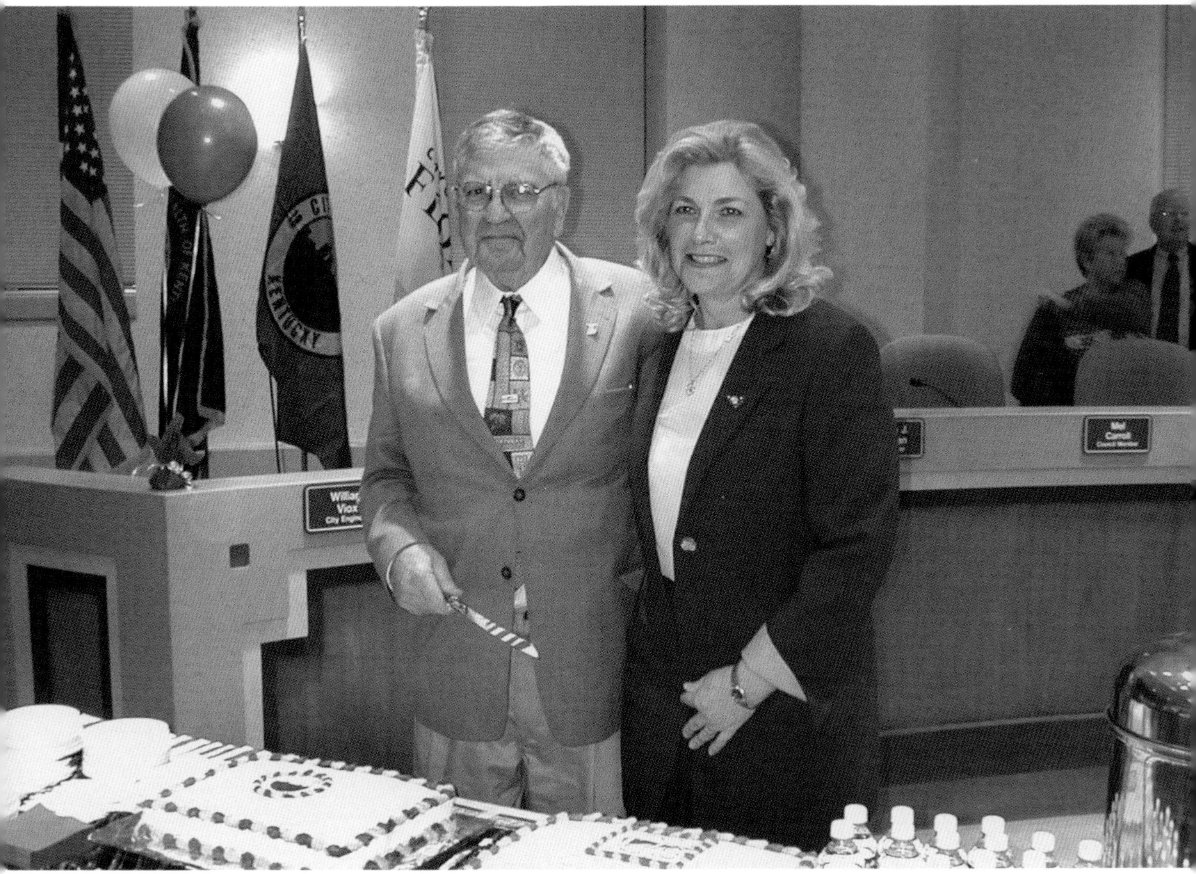

MAYORS OF FLORENCE. Pictured on the left is former mayor of Florence Carol M. "Hop" Ewing. Mayor Ewing was most instrumental in the 1970s in the development of Mall Road and the Florence Mall, which led to the modern commercial growth of the city. He is pictured with his daughter, Diane Ewing-Whalen, the current mayor of the city. In this 2005 picture, they help celebrate the 175th anniversary of Florence. Ewing Boulevard is named after the former mayor.

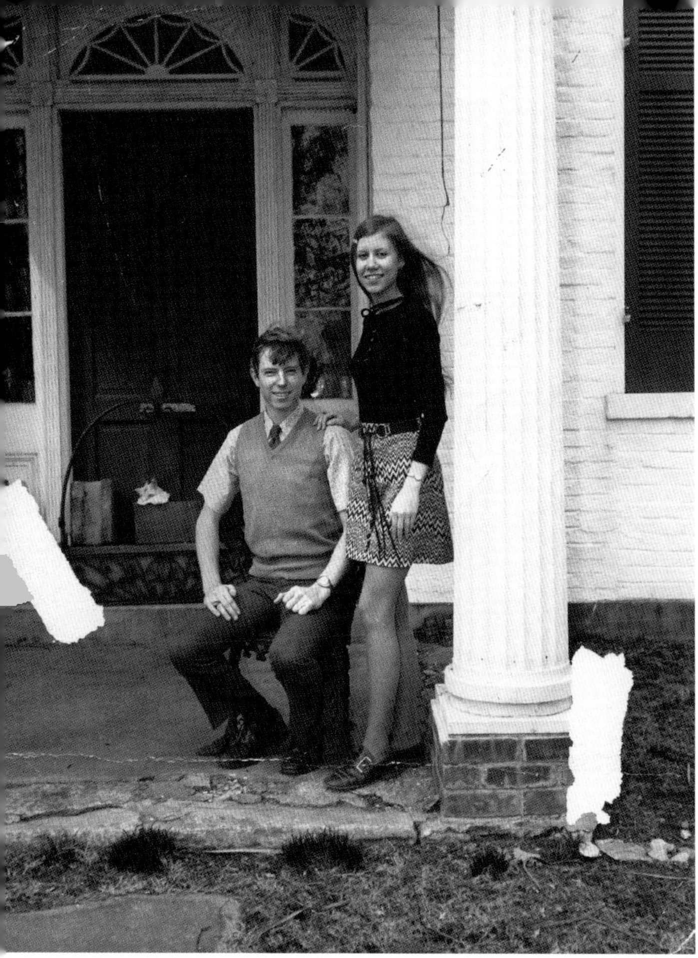

COL. ABNER GAINES HOUSE. This fine house was built by Abner Gaines around 1814 and was unique by having a second floor. It served many purposes for Gaines, including inn, tavern, and stagecoach stop. Gaines served as a county justice and sheriff. His son, John, was a congressman and governor of the Oregon Territory. Pictured in 1972 in the Federal-style doorway are Mr. and Miss Walton-Verona High School, Dean Ward and Donna Coyle, now married for 28 years.

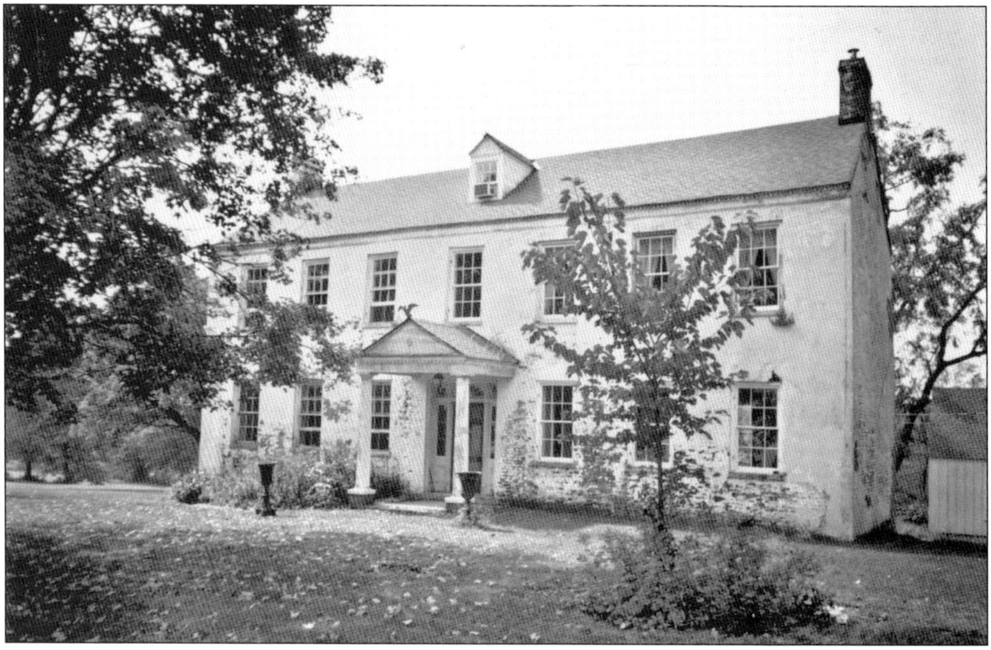

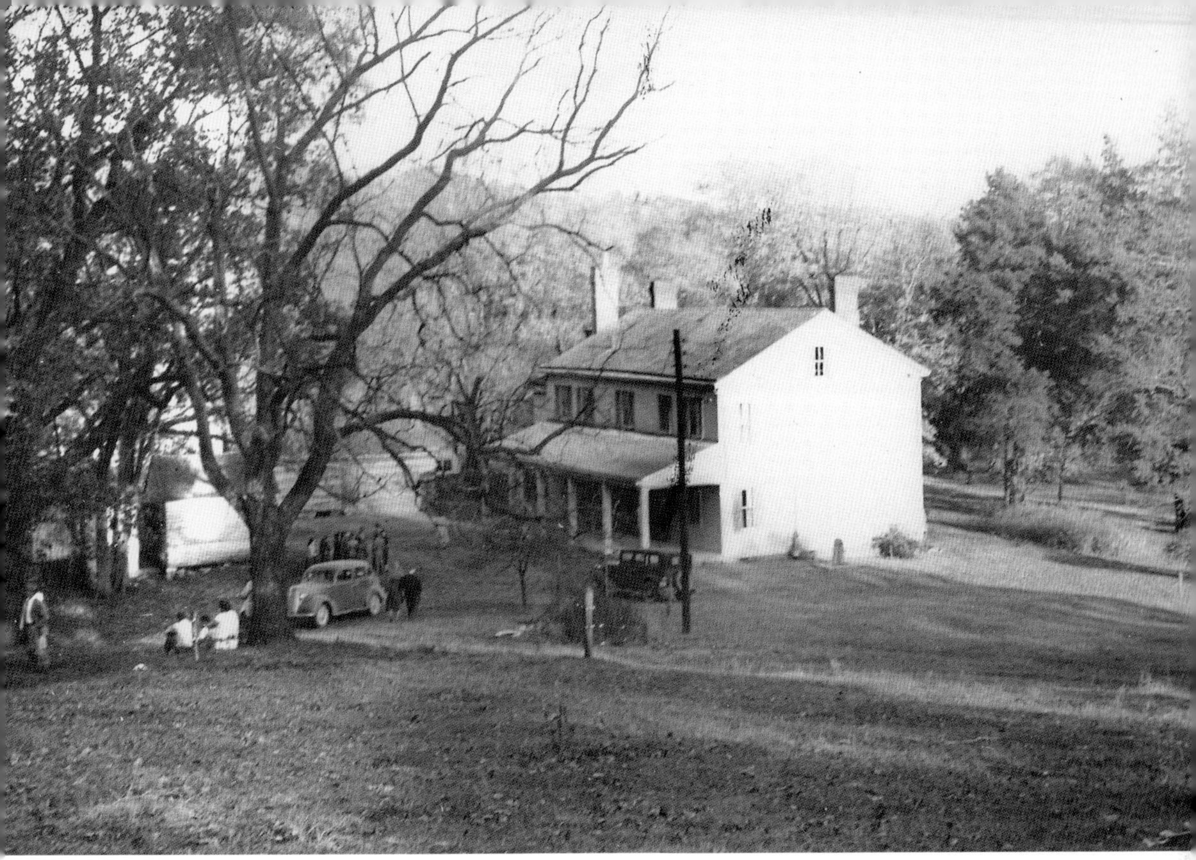

DINSMORE HOMESTEAD. Perhaps the most historically significant residence in the county, the Dinsmore Homestead was built in 1842. Generations of Dinsmores lived in the home for 150 years. This vintage view shows the back of the home from the hill leading to the family cemetery. The current image features Rembrandt, the dog, visiting the homestead, which serves as a museum and an excellent area for hiking.

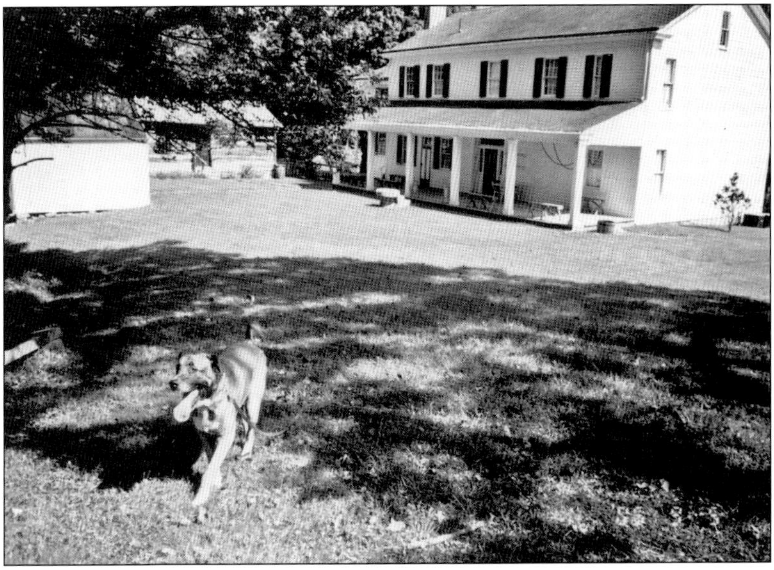

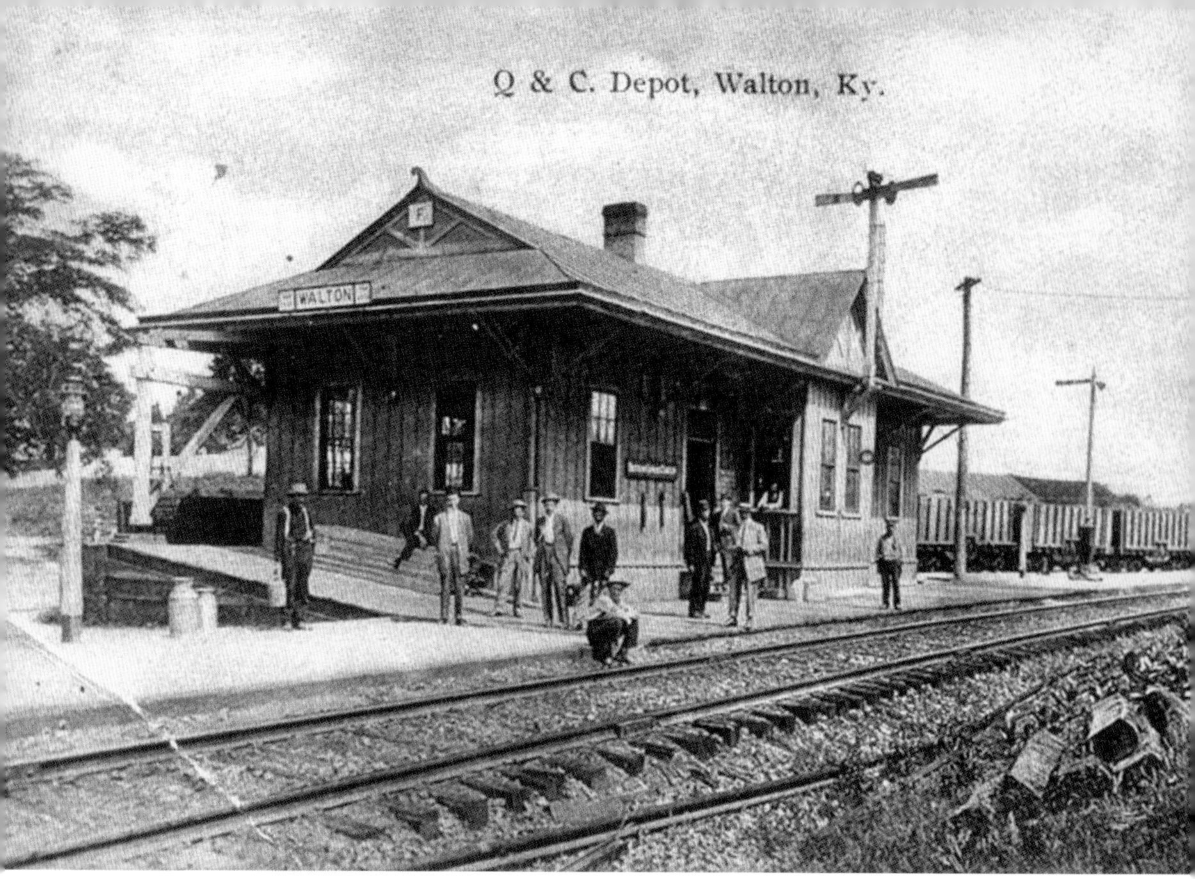

THE TRAIN DEPOT OF WALTON. The city of Walton developed as a railroad town, with tracks running along both sides of Main Street. The image shows the Louisville & Nashville Railroad Depot, and it sat behind the old Dixie State Bank, as seen in the background of the current view. The current view is from the opposite end of the depot from the historic image. It shows the remains of the concrete support for the pole used by passing trains to grab mail.

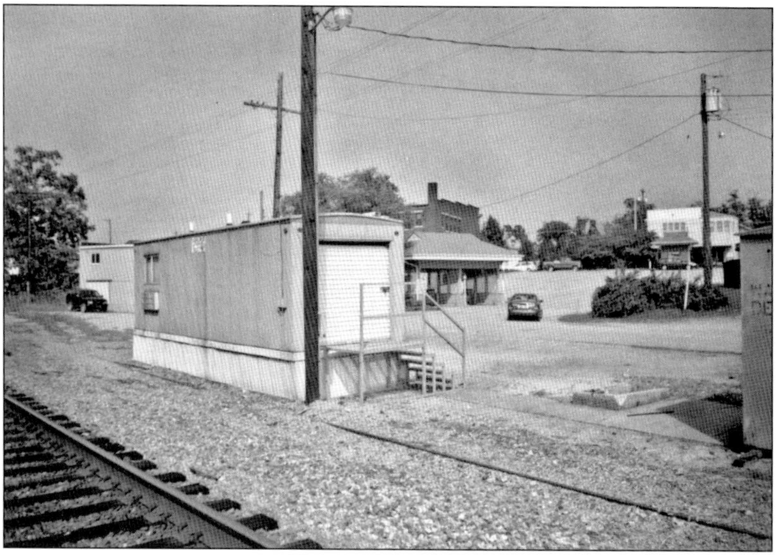

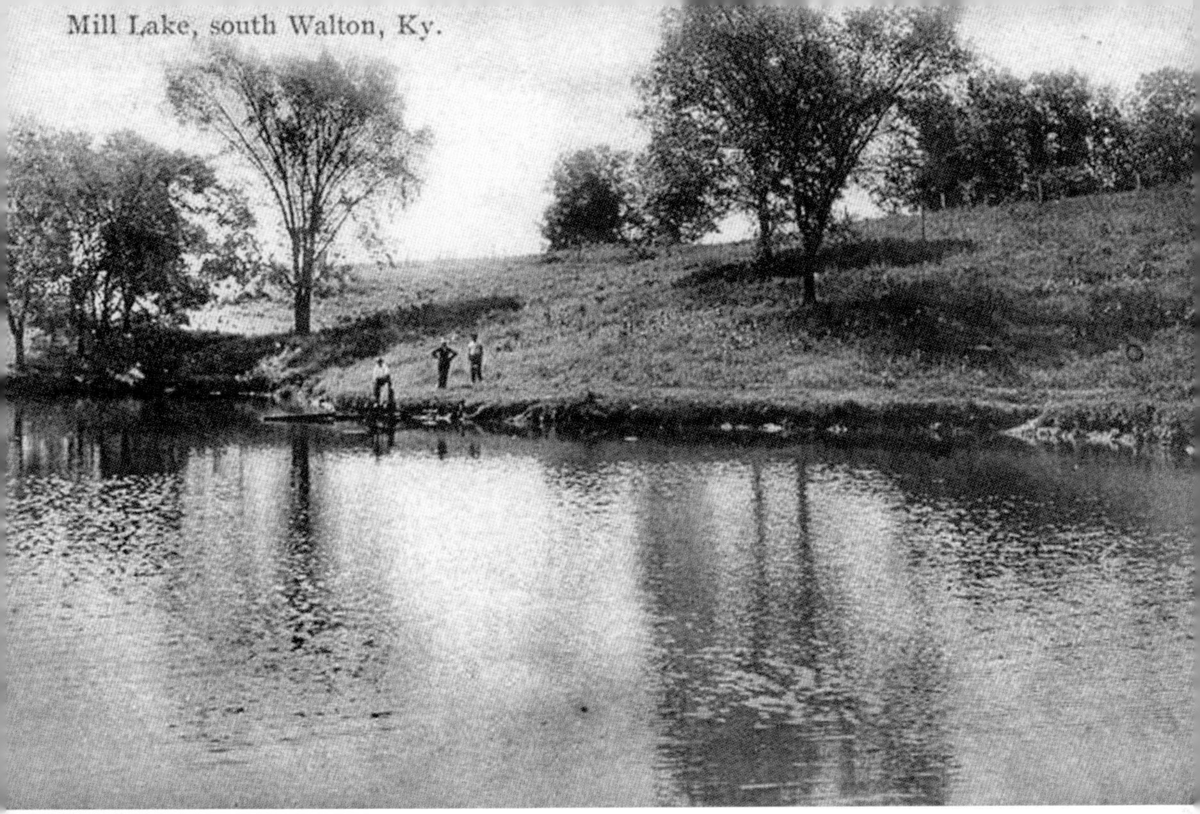

WALTON MILL POND. This pond was created when the Cincinnati Southern Railroad built a dam while constructing the tracks in the mid-1870s. Jack Rouse remembers the pond and the steam gristmill and stands above the sloped yard that made up part of the pond. It was located along the southern side of Loreco Street and ran down from near Rouse's position almost to the railroad tracks. The railroad later destroyed the dam, and the pond drained.

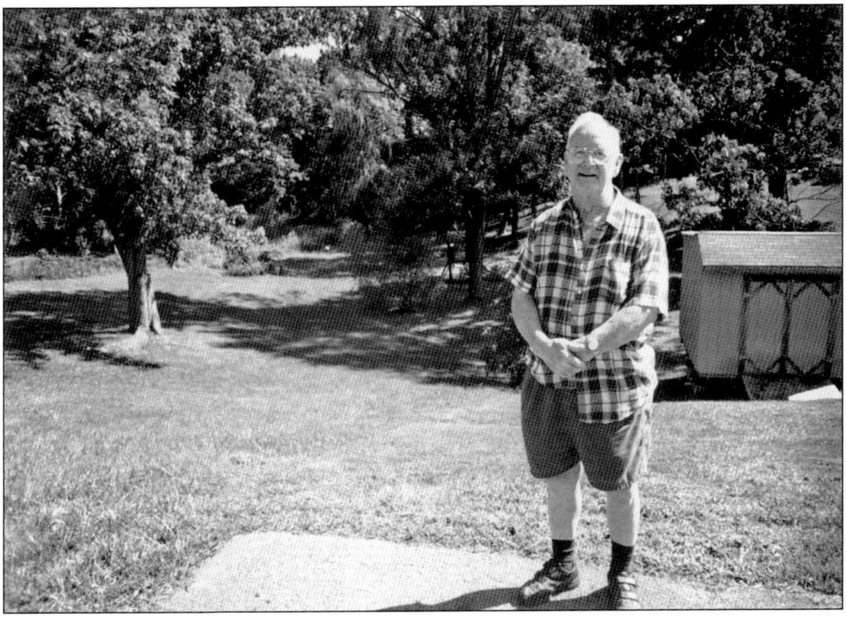

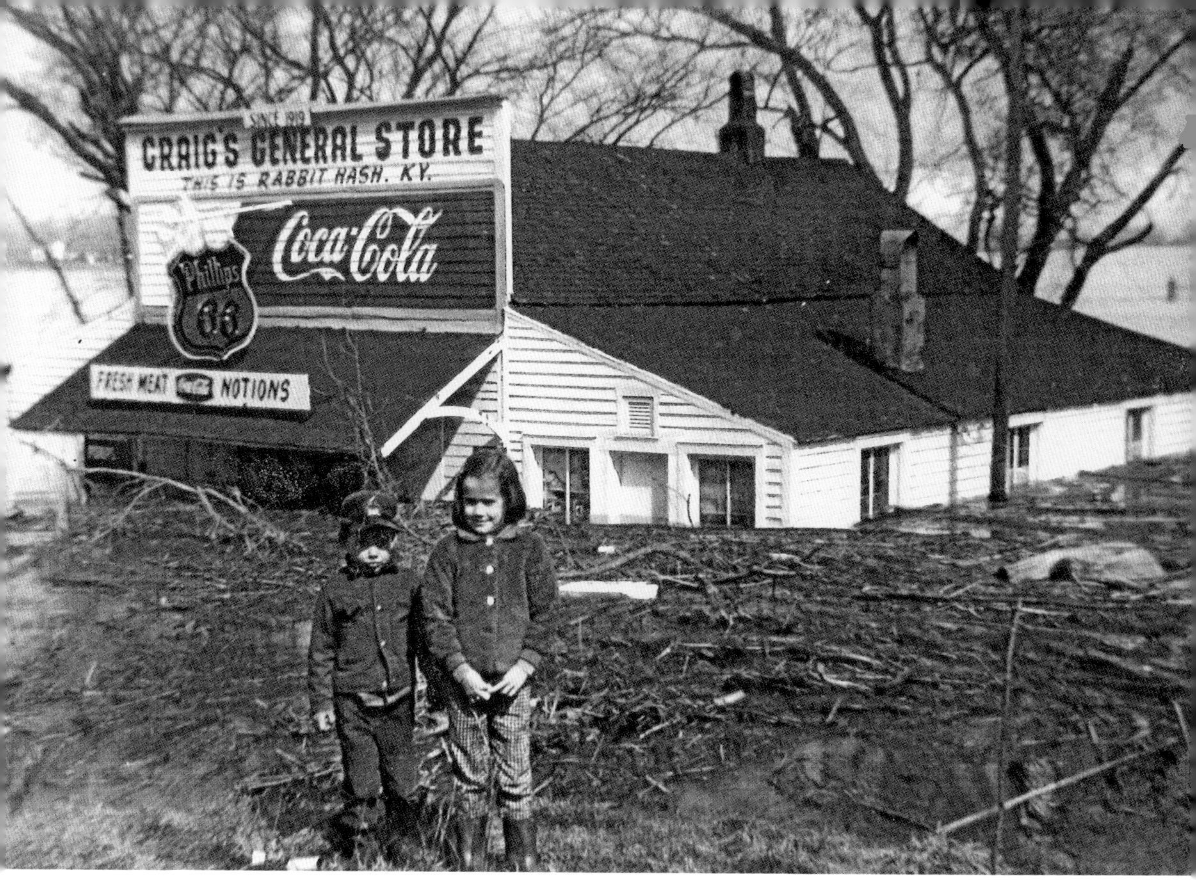

OH, THOSE FLOODS! One constant about living on the Ohio River is floods. In recent memories, the floods of 1937 and 1997 stand out. This picture shows the 1937 flood almost to the roof of Craig's General Store in Rabbit Hash. The flood reached 80 feet and caused $20 million damage in affected areas. In 1997, waters again filled the store, reaching 65 feet. Ethan Schrage (front) and Andrew Schrage (back) stand in the same area as the children from the 1937 flood.

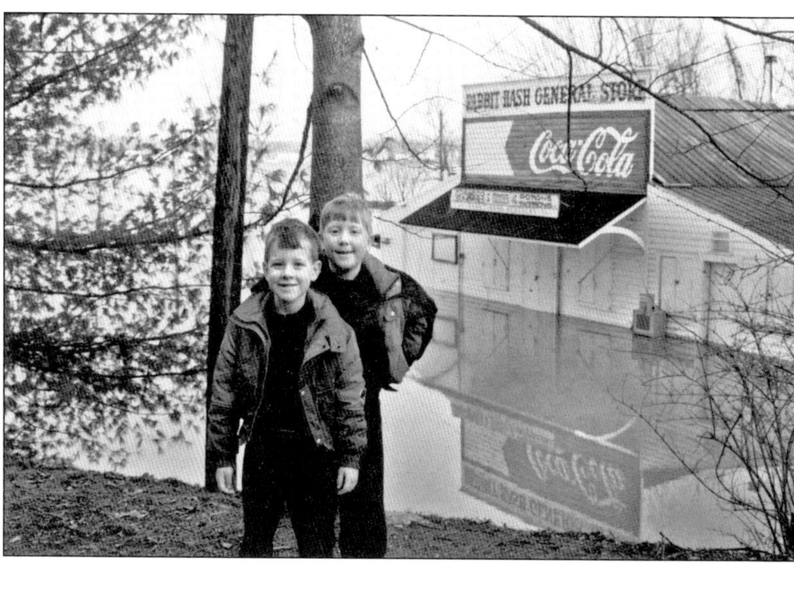

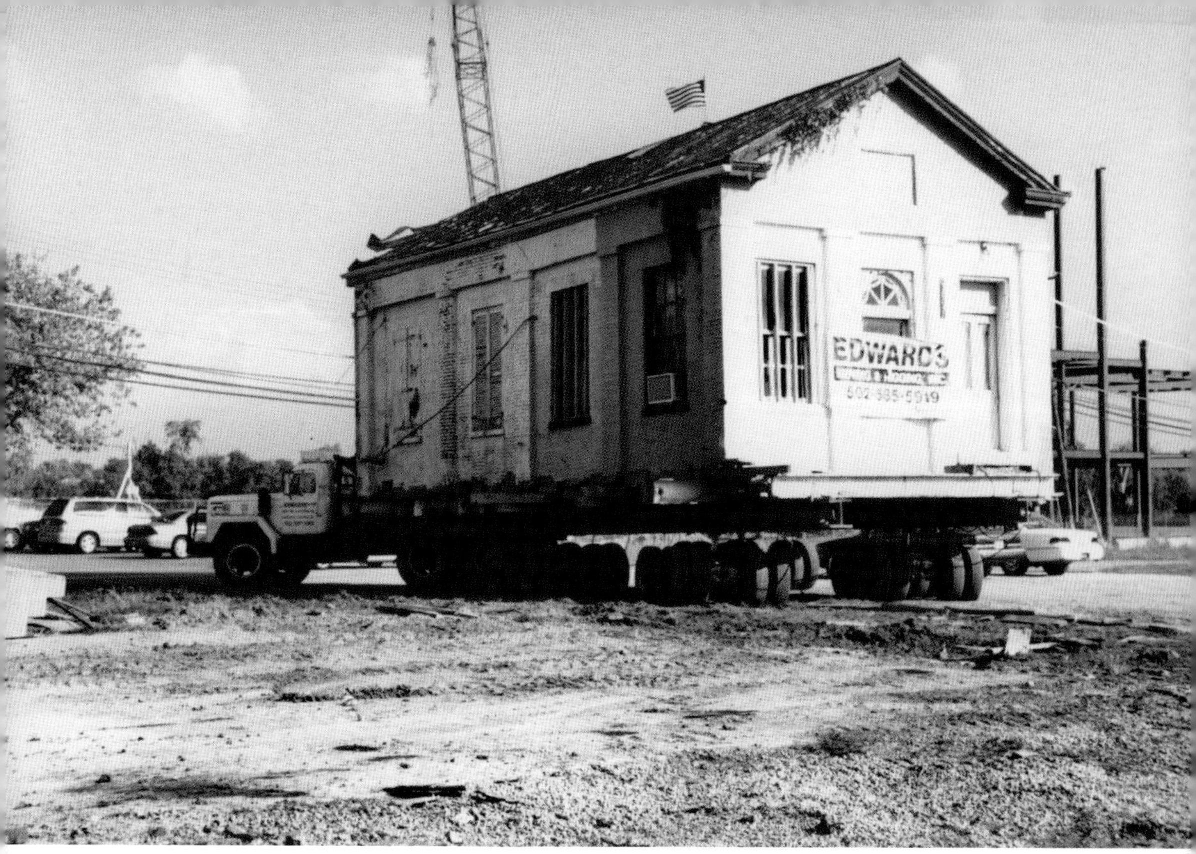

ON THE MOVE—AGAIN. A Greek Revival building built in 1889, the old clerk's building is shown on its second move. It originally served as the Boone County Deposit Bank from 1889 to 1924 and was located across from the old Boone County Courthouse. When a new bank was constructed in 1924, the old bank building was moved to a spot on the southwest corner of Burlington Pike and Jefferson Street. In the picture, it is being moved to its third location behind the County Administration Building.

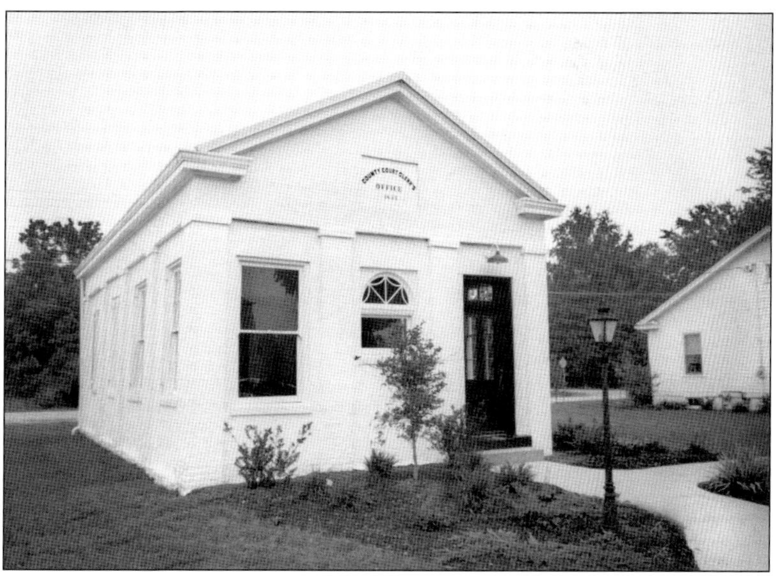

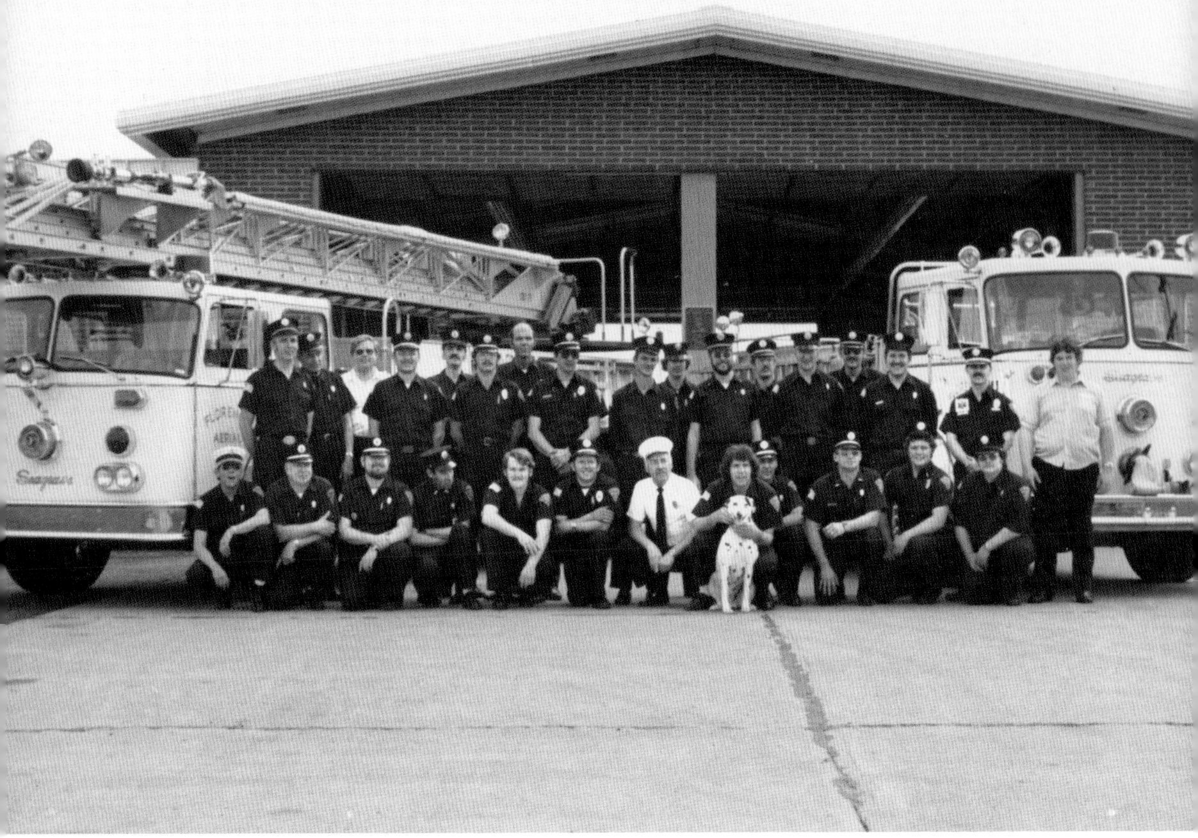

FLORENCE FIRE DEPARTMENT. This early-1980s picture shows the entire Florence Fire Department outside Hue Station on Industrial Road. Pictured in the white cap is Chief Don Roberts, who died in 2005. To his immediate right is future chief Tom Olier. The fire dog is Smokey. In the second row, second from left, is Junior Hue, a volunteer for 50 years. The station is named after his father. Future-mayor Roger Rolfes is in the second row, 11th from the left.

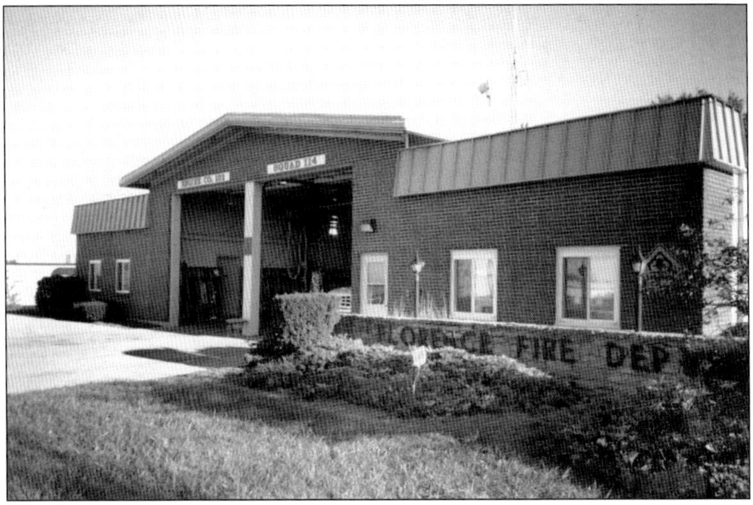

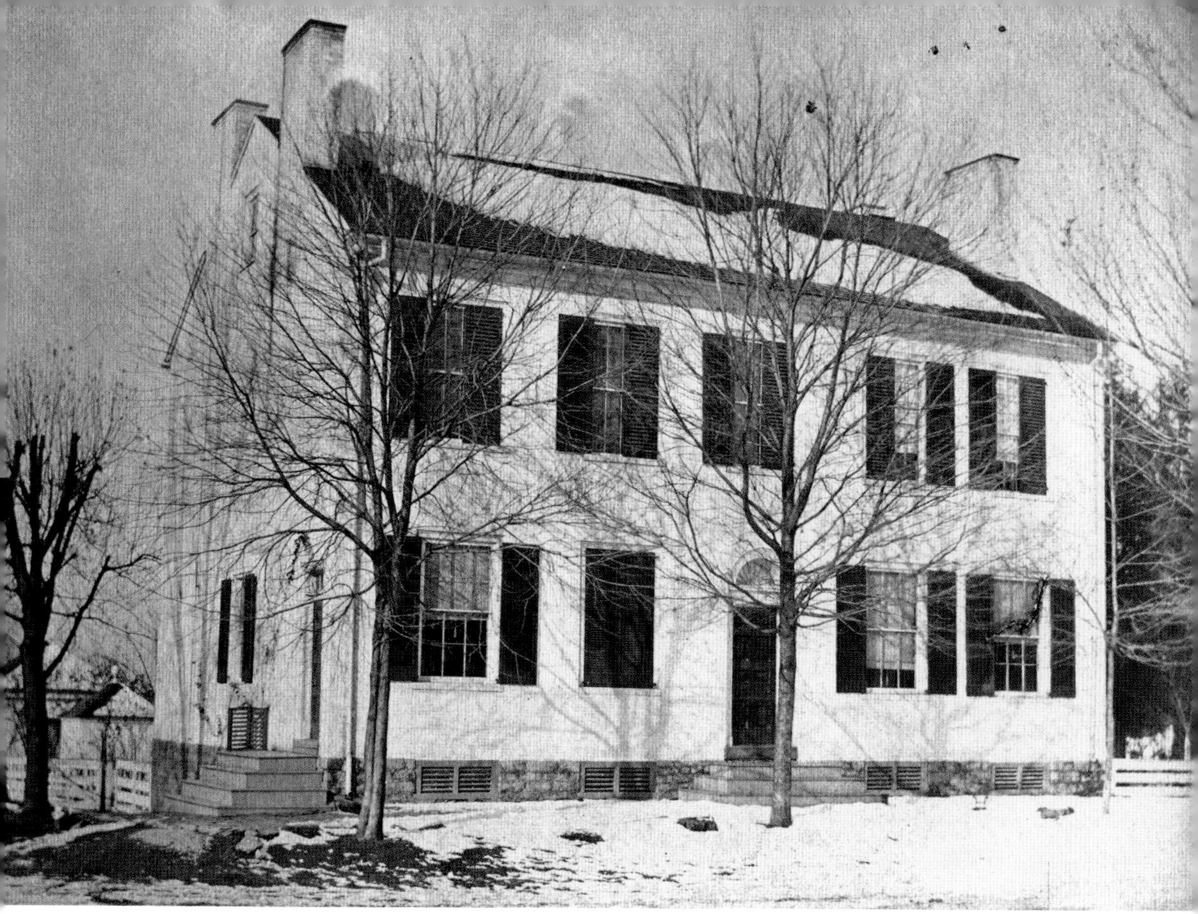

TOUSEY HOUSE. Built around 1822, the Erastus Tousey House has served as a store, hotel, residence, and now as a restaurant. It is a wonderfully preserved building located in the heart of Burlington. Rehabilitated in 2001, it opened as a restaurant and is an excellent example of a Federal brick home. The Tousey House Restaurant is also an example of how a historic structure can be preserved and used as an economic resource.

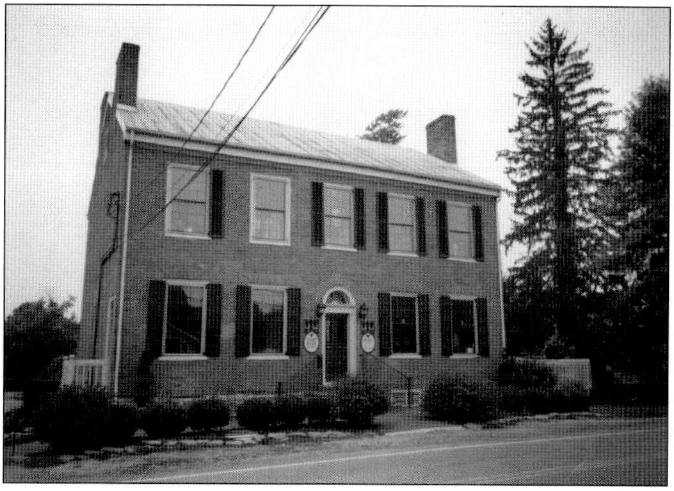

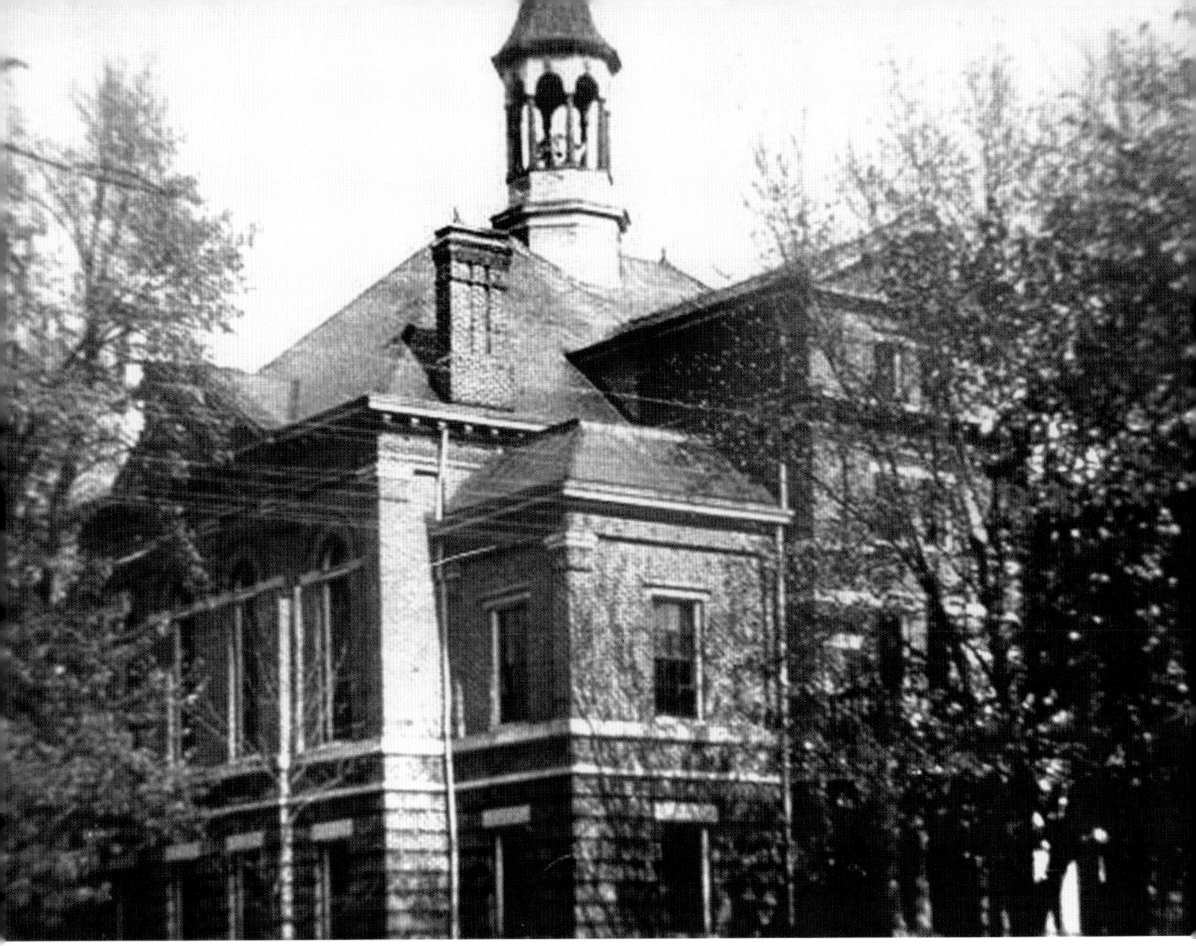

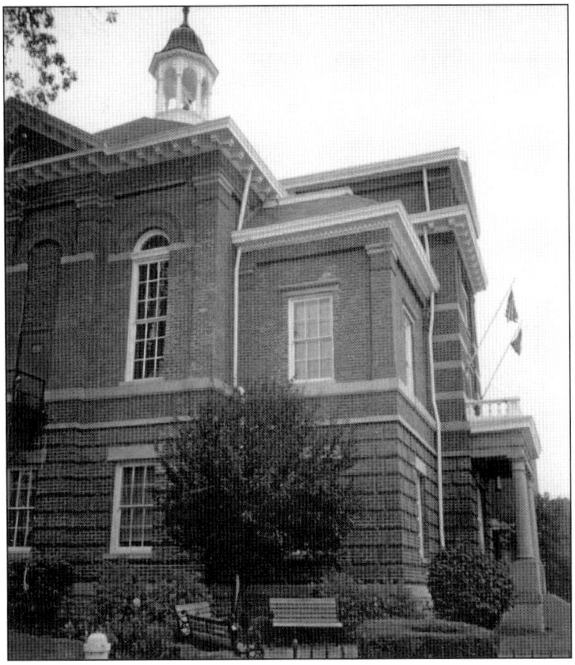

Old Boone County Courthouse. Built in 1889 and shown here in 1915, this courthouse is the third one to sit on the corner of Burlington Pike and Jefferson Street. In 1960, a brick addition was added. A few years ago, the county fiscal court remodeled the outside of the building, enhancing its preservation and historical integrity. From the side view, a time capsule can be seen on the right that was placed during the county's bicentennial celebration.

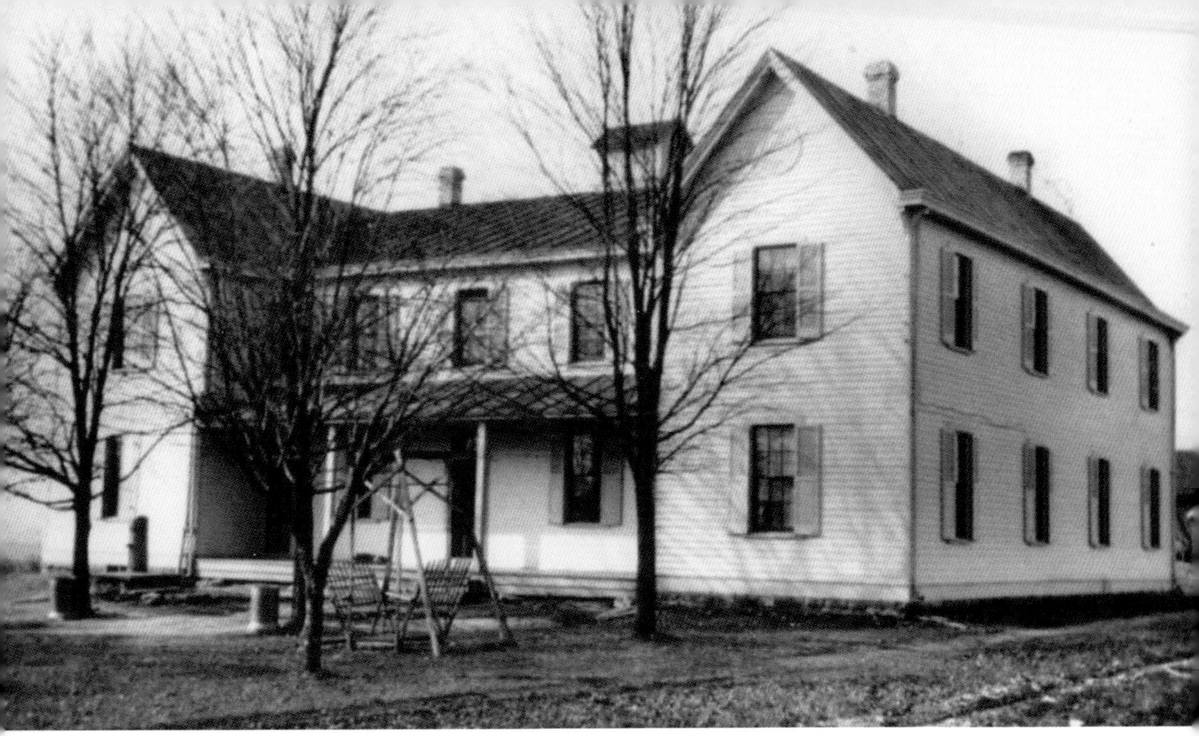

THE INFIRMARY. Built sometime in the 1870s, the Infirmary was home to the indigent of the county. It remained in operation until almost 1970. The picture was taken in 1918, and the building had no modern conveniences. It is on the site of what today is known as the Maplewood Children's Home located near the Boone County Fairgrounds and the public works department.

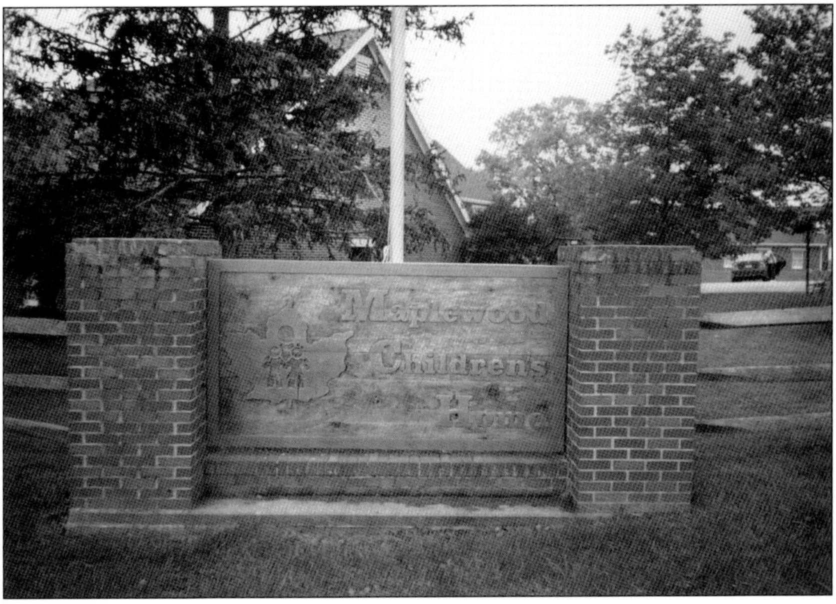

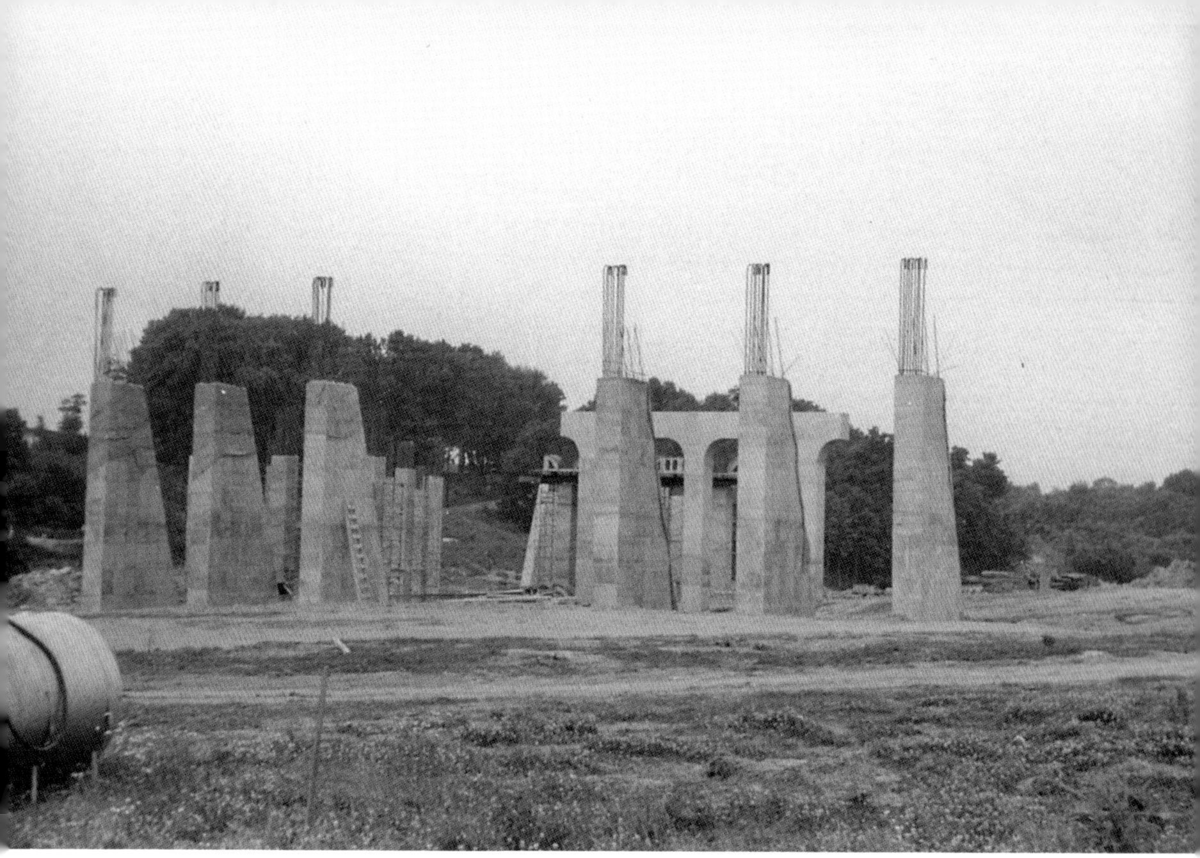

CONSTRUCTION OF INTERSTATE 75. The Northern Kentucky section of Interstate 75 was built in the early 1960s. Construction of the overpass on U.S. 42 in Florence involved concrete, and it was arched, unlike the ones north of the river. In Ohio, they were straight arches and involved steel beams. The same overpass location today is a major road within Florence, and the entire expressway area has been reconstructed.

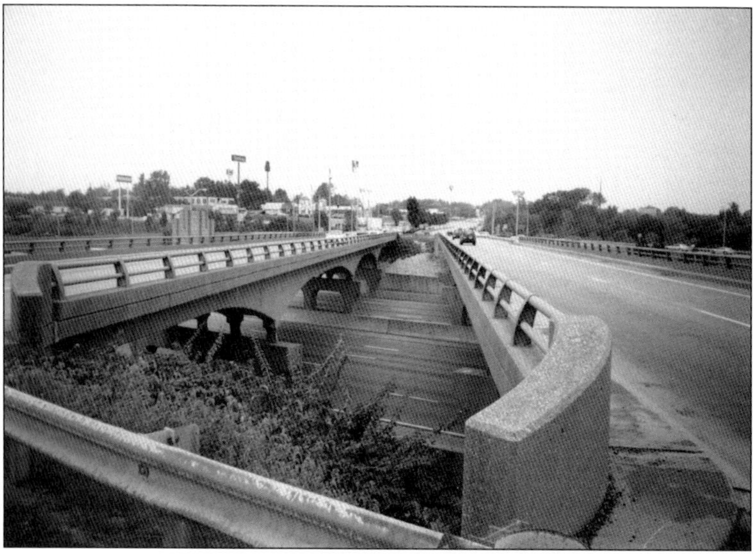

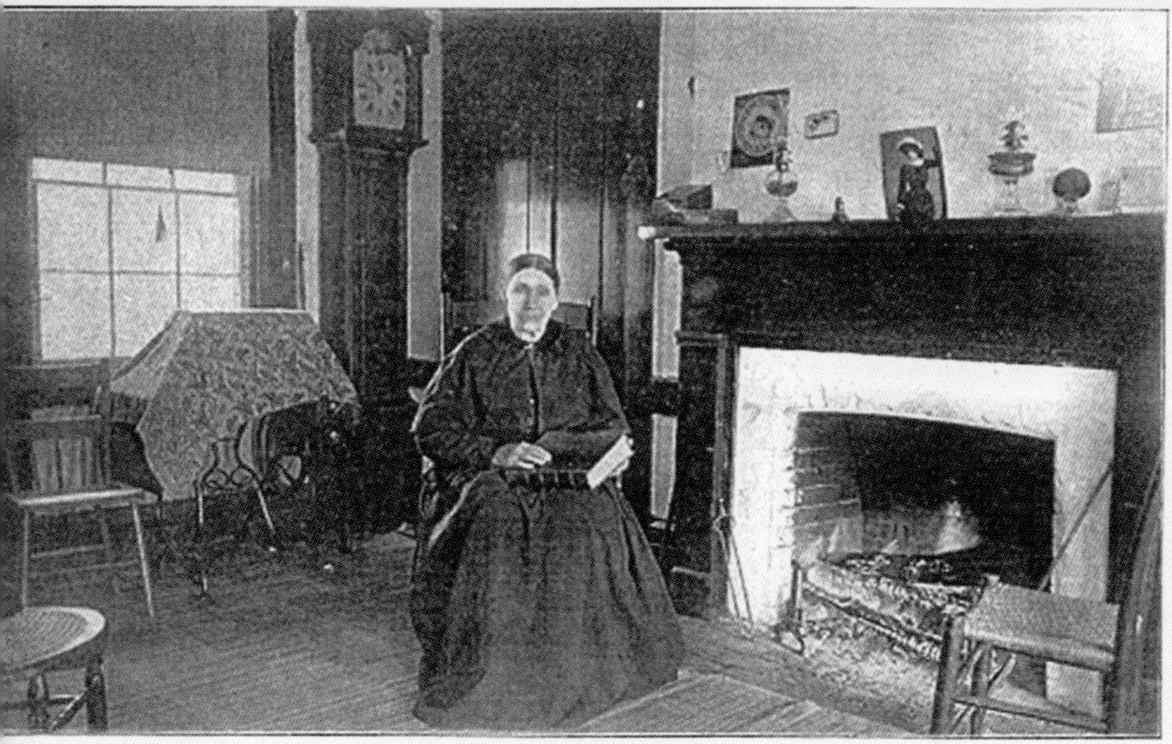

"OLD KENTUCKY HOME."

"OLD KENTUCKY HOME." This photograph shows an aspect of Kentucky life within the confines of a home. The cozy fireplace of this house is long gone. This "old Kentucky home" sat on the location of the old Flicks Grocery on Burlington Pike. Flicks Grocery relocated to Hebron in 2005. The site will become the new home of the main branch of the Boone County Public Library.

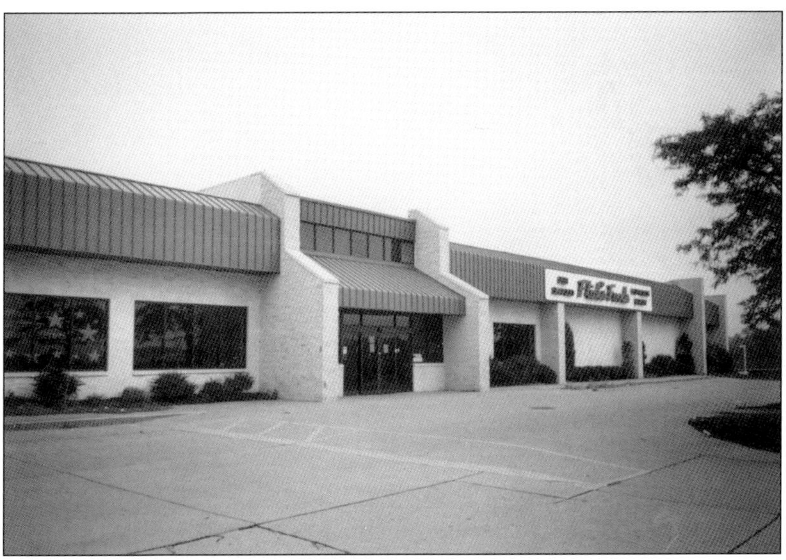

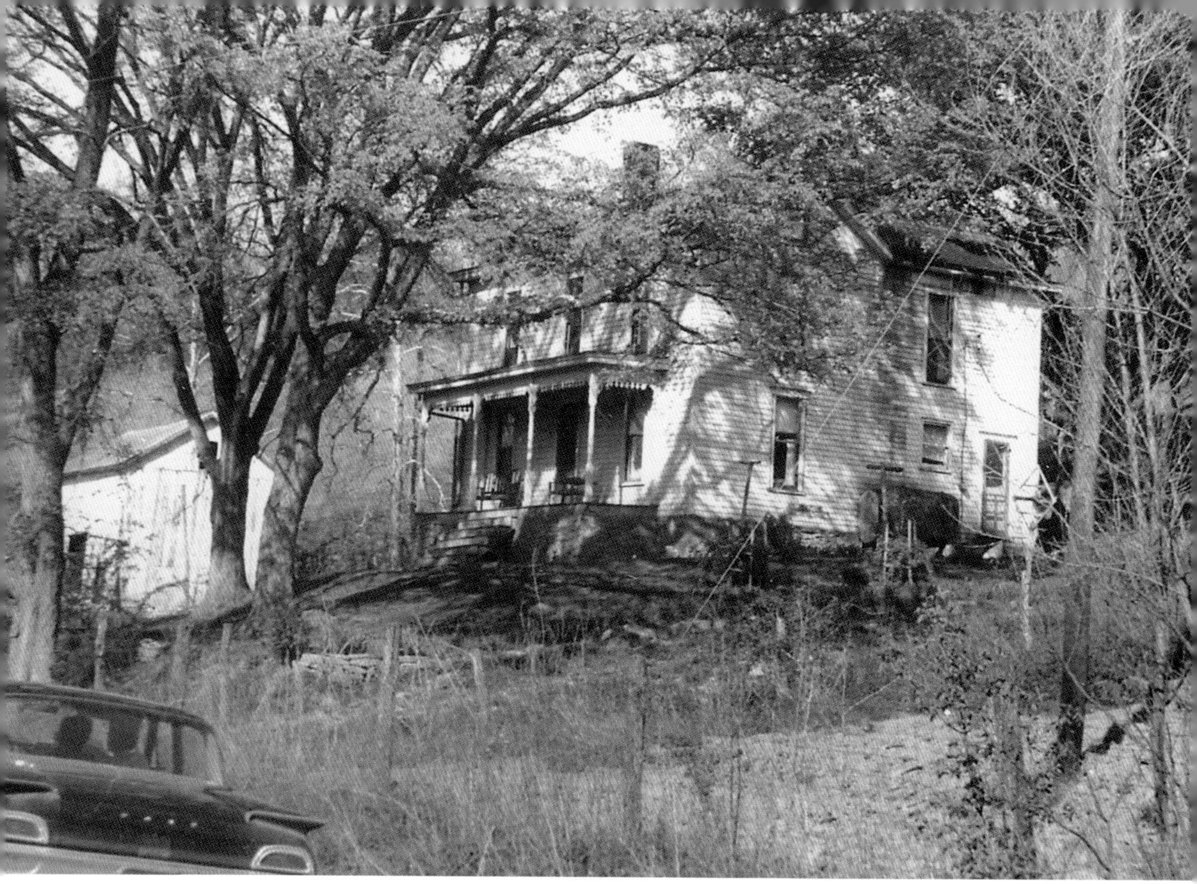

DR. STEVENSON HOUSE. The Dr. John Stevenson House is located on Beaver Road just across from Big Bone Lick State Park. It is the only remaining structure from the resort days of Big Bone Lick. The house was built around 1870 and today is well preserved and beautifully landscaped. Dr. Stevenson believed that the resort had medical benefits.

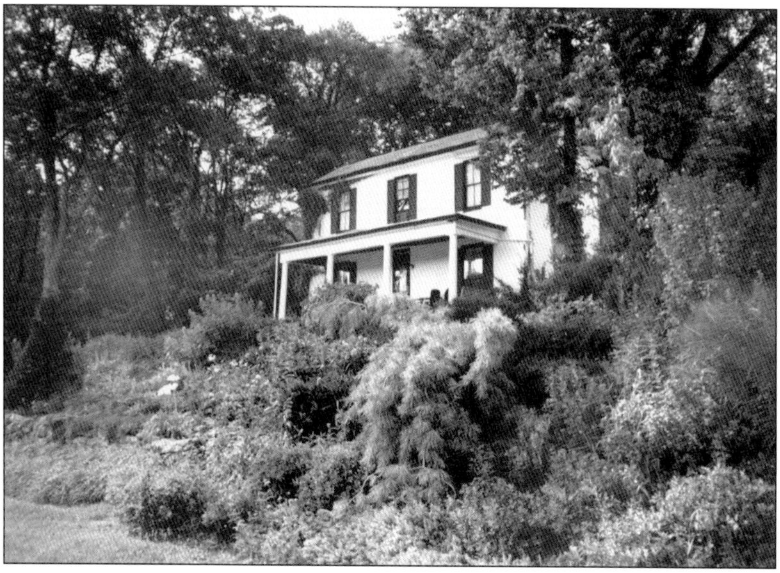

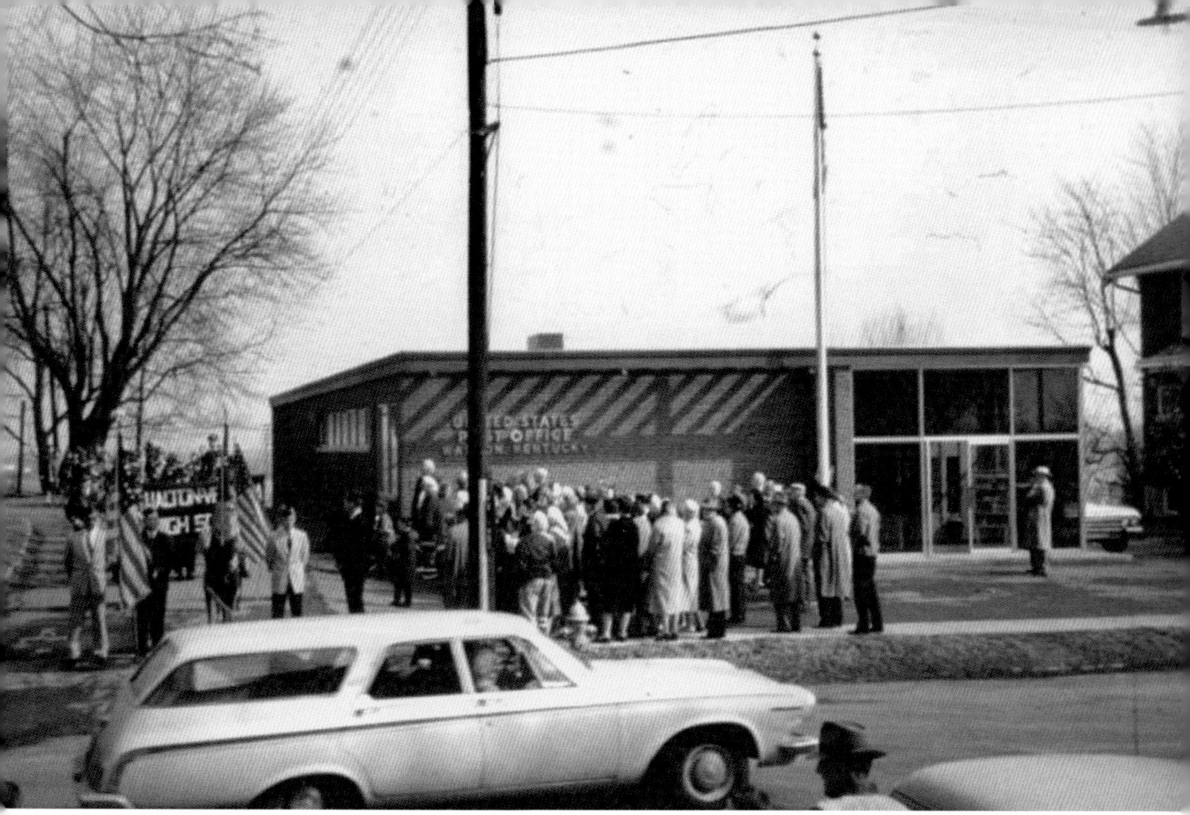

DEDICATION OF THE WALTON POST OFFICE. The current Walton Post Office was dedicated in March 1963 and is located on South Main Street. The dedication ceremony included the Walton Verona High School Band, postmasters from around the region, and many dignitaries. The post office building has changed very little since the dedication. The flag is lowered in the recent photograph to mourn the passing of Chief Justice William Rehnquist in 2005.

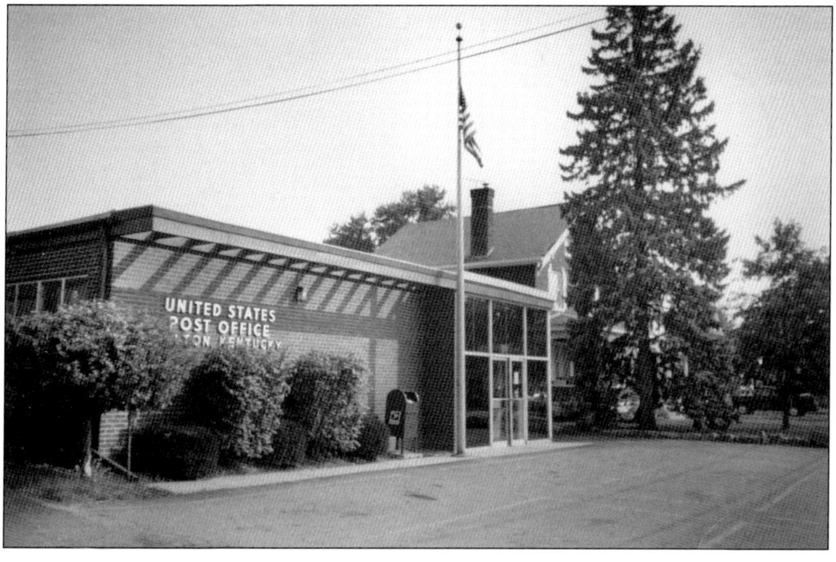

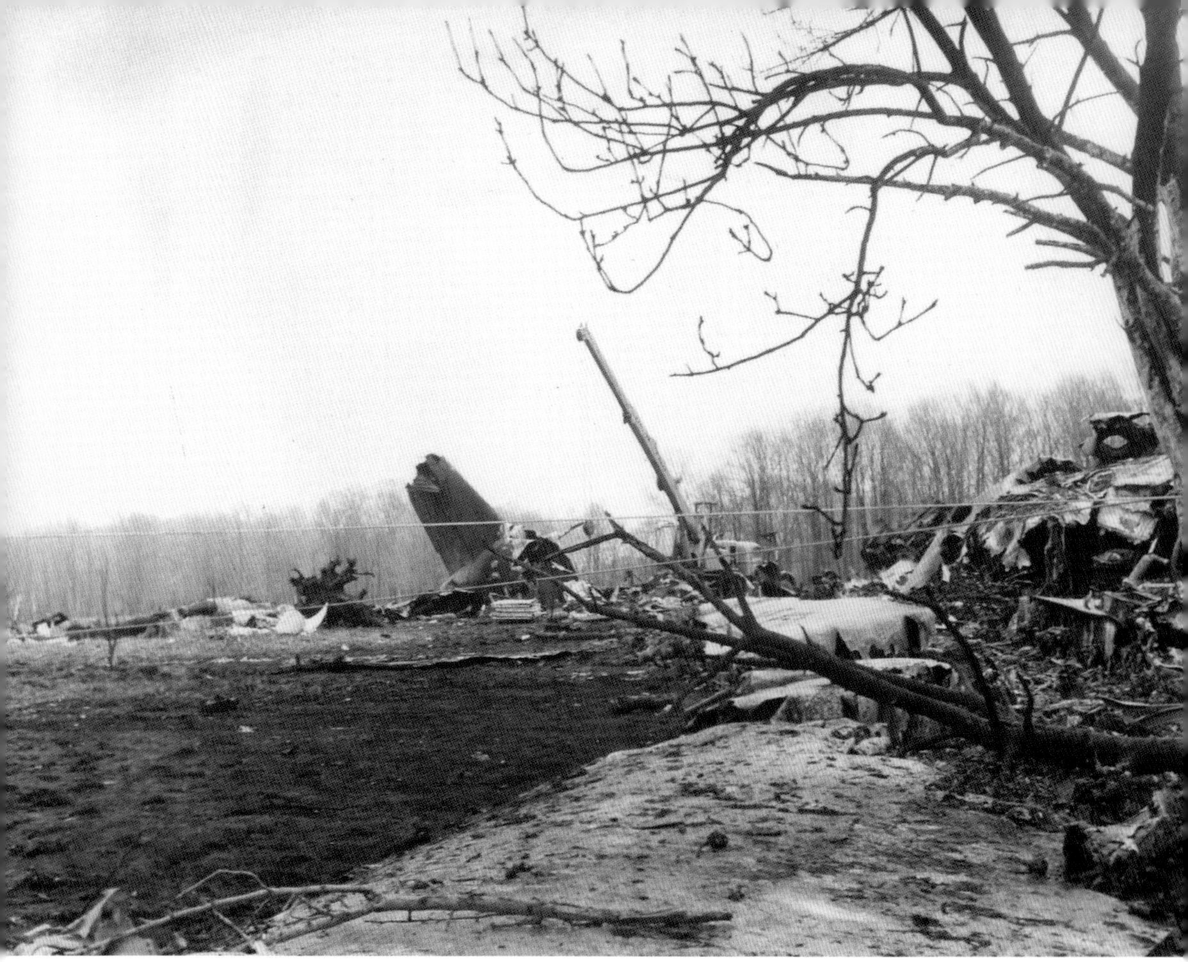

TWA ACCIDENT. On November 20, 1967, the worst aid disaster in Cincinnati's history happened when Flight 128 from Los Angeles crashed in an apple orchard near the airport. Seventy crew members and passengers died. The site today is just after the turn onto Aviation Boulevard off Kentucky Route 20. Debris was scattered all over the orchard, which included the roadway and building seen in the picture. (©*The Kentucky Post.*)

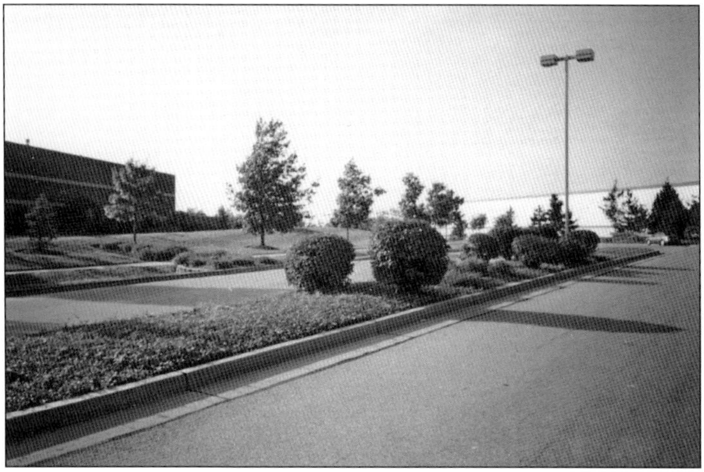

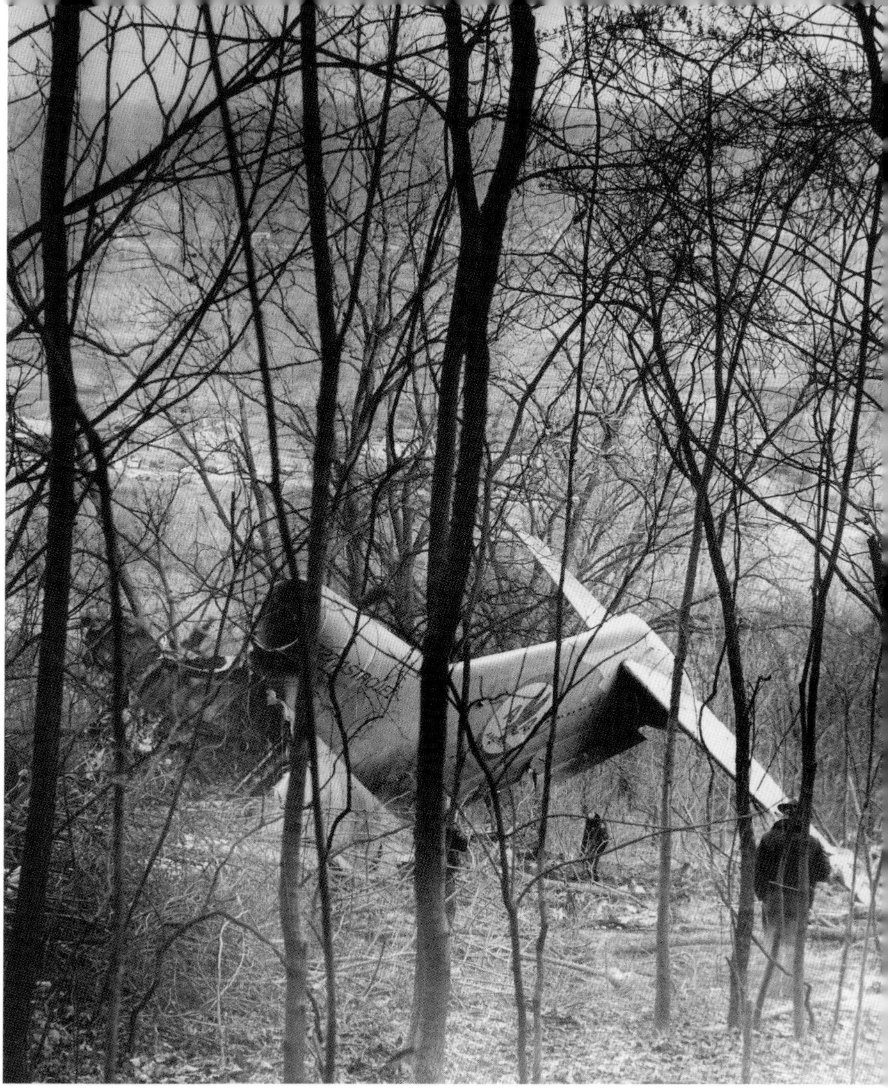

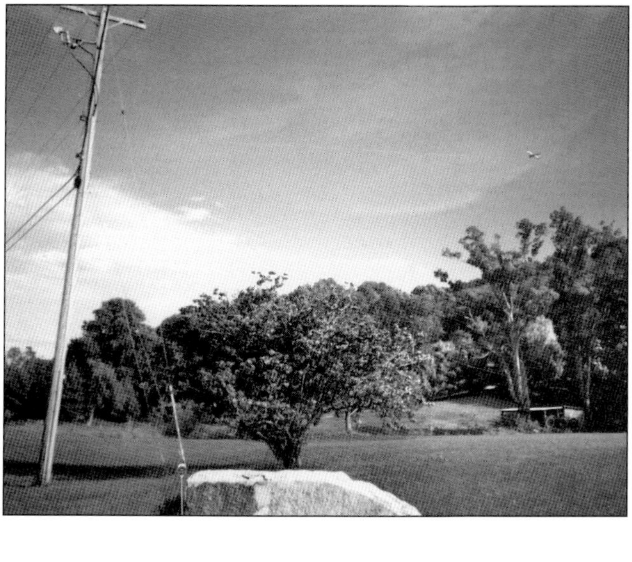

AMERICAN AIRLINES CRASH. On November 8, 1965, an American Airlines Boeing 727 crashed into a hill after crossing the Ohio River. Fifty-eight people were killed and four survived. The plane traveling from New York's LaGuardia airport crashed 6,878 feet from the runway toward the top of the hill. The site is approximately two miles down Route 8 from Constance and almost directly across the river from the College of Mount St. Joseph. The recent photograph of the hill is taken from Route 8. (©*The Kentucky Post*.)

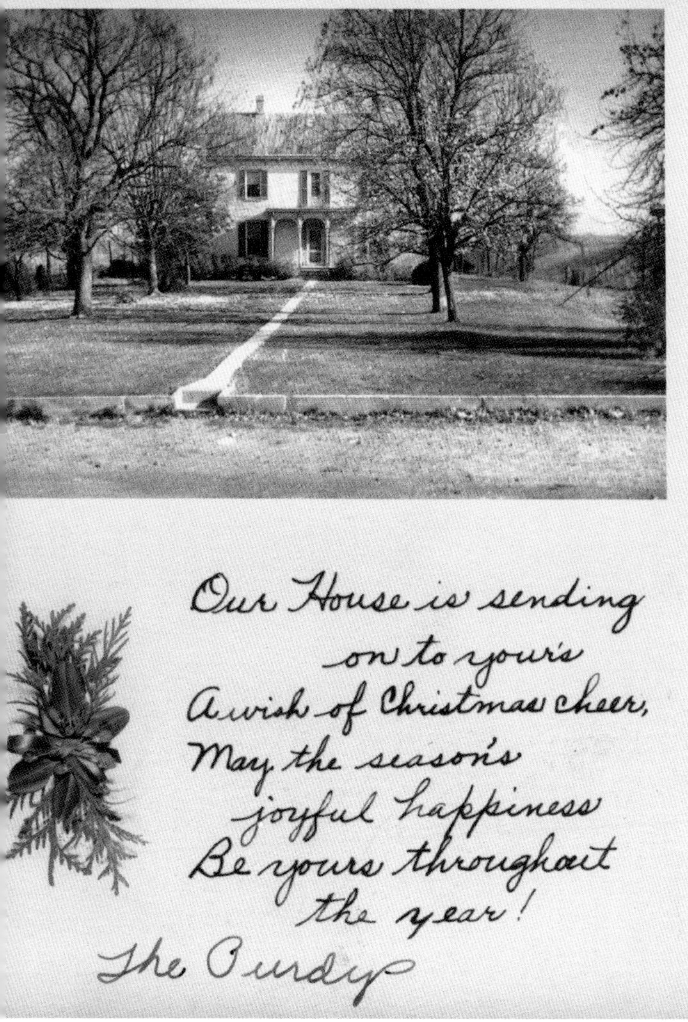

PURDY CHRISTMAS CARD. This early-1900s Christmas card was used by the Purdy family, who lived in this house on East Bend Road. Previous owner William Kite operated a grocery store next door. The home was demolished in 2005, but the old Kite (Waterloo) Grocery still stands. In this recent image, the store, built in 1872, stands next to the road at the top of Waterloo Road. The front porch of the store was removed when East Bend Road was widened. The home stood farther back and to the right.

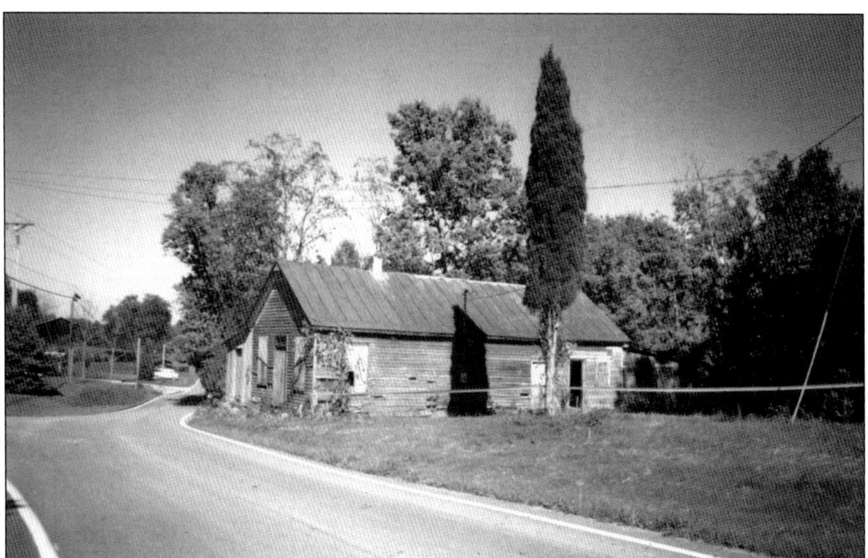

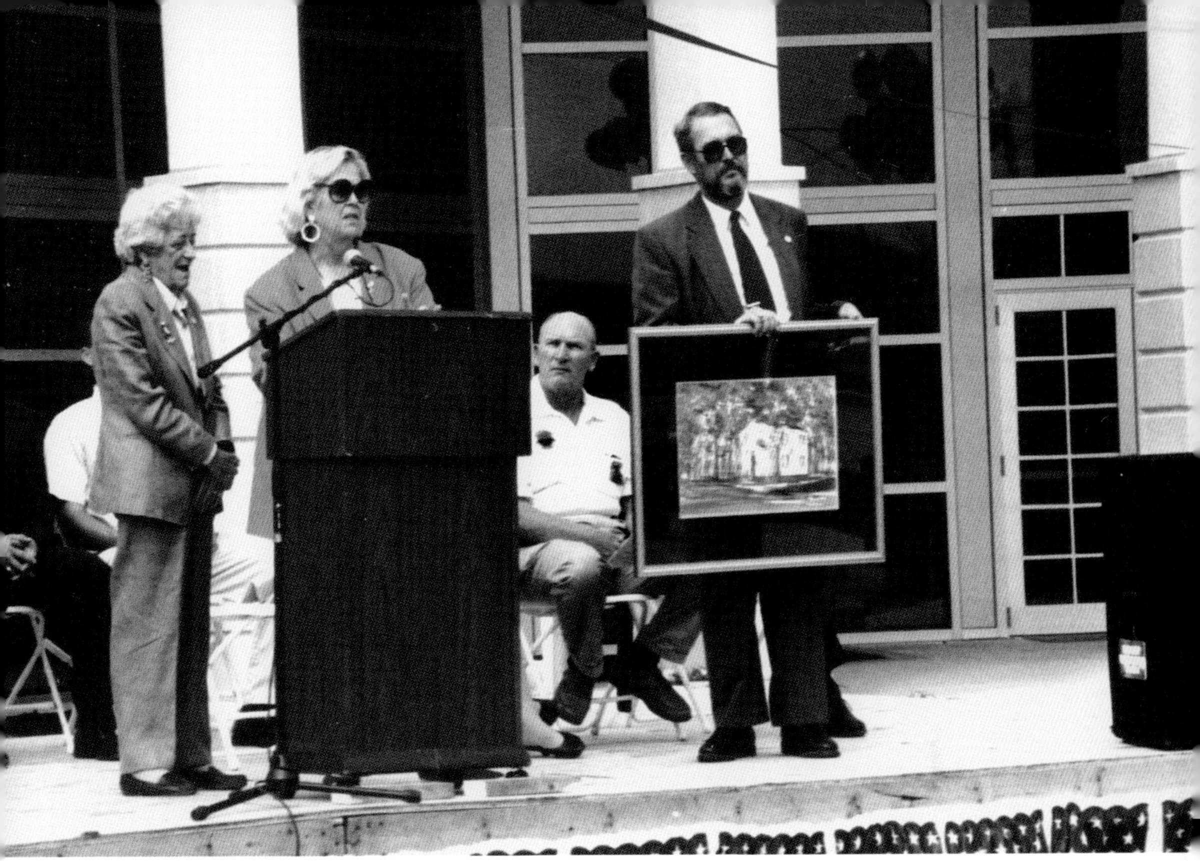

Dedication of the Florence Government Center. The new Florence Government Center was dedicated in 1998, replacing the one on U.S. 42. In this image from the dedication ceremony, Hannah Baird (at the podium) presents to the city a framed print of a previous city building. Former-mayor Roger Rolfes holds the print as Mayor Evelyn Kalb looks on. The print is on display in the city building. Mayor Kalb passed away in 2001.

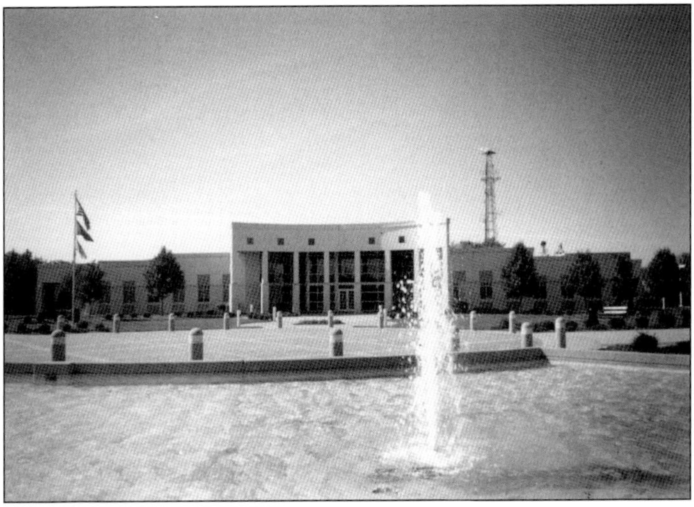

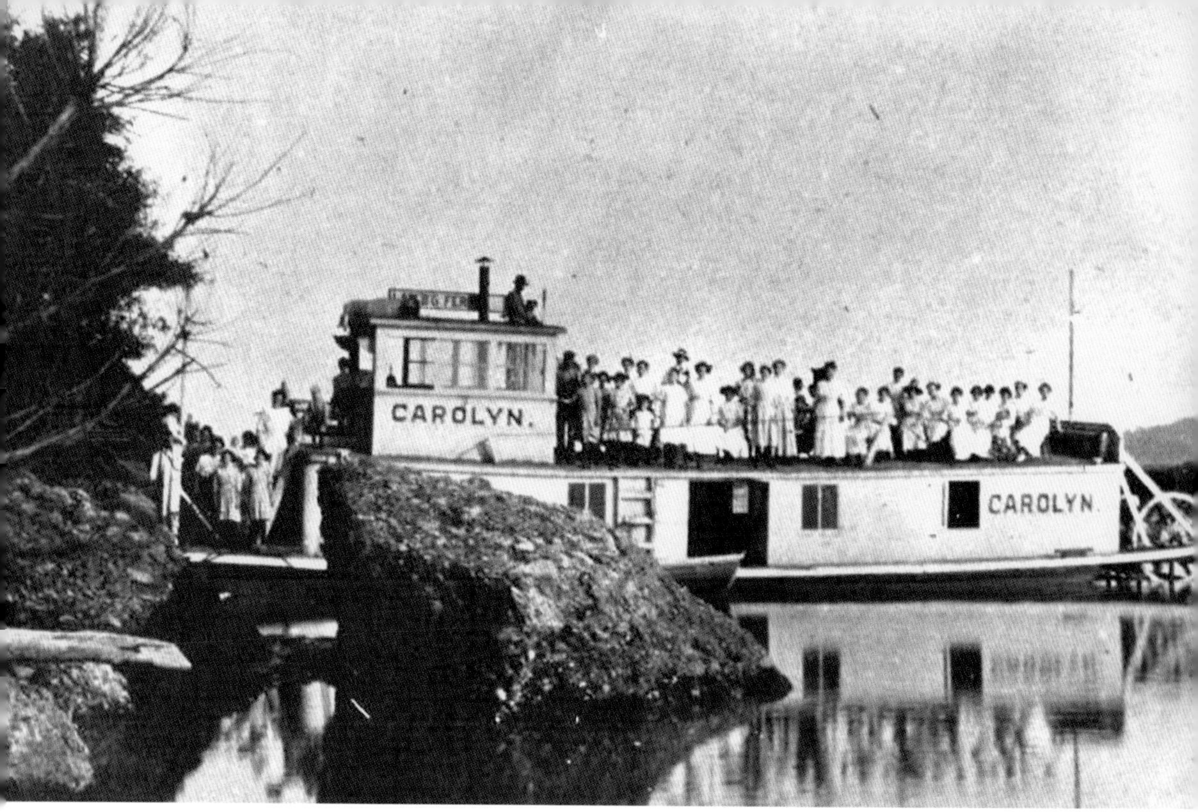

SPLIT ROCK. A passenger ferry called the *Carolyn* visits Split Rock. Split Rock is a very unique glacial formation thousands of years in the making. It is one of the most beautiful places in Boone County and was once a destination for a leisurely day by the Ohio River. Today Split Rock Conservation District is set aside to provide education on conservation and biodiversity. It is located on Kentucky Route 20, about three miles outside Petersburg.

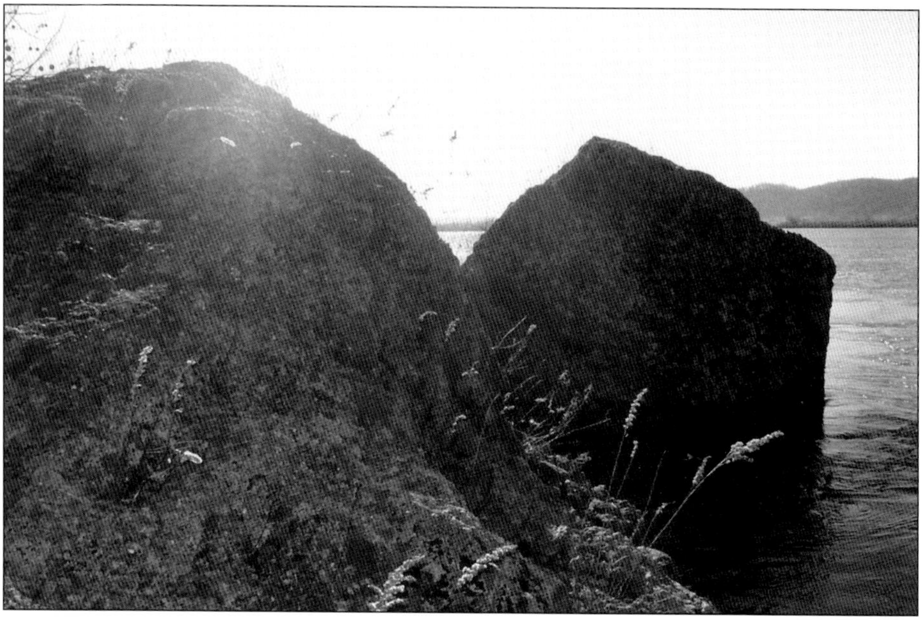

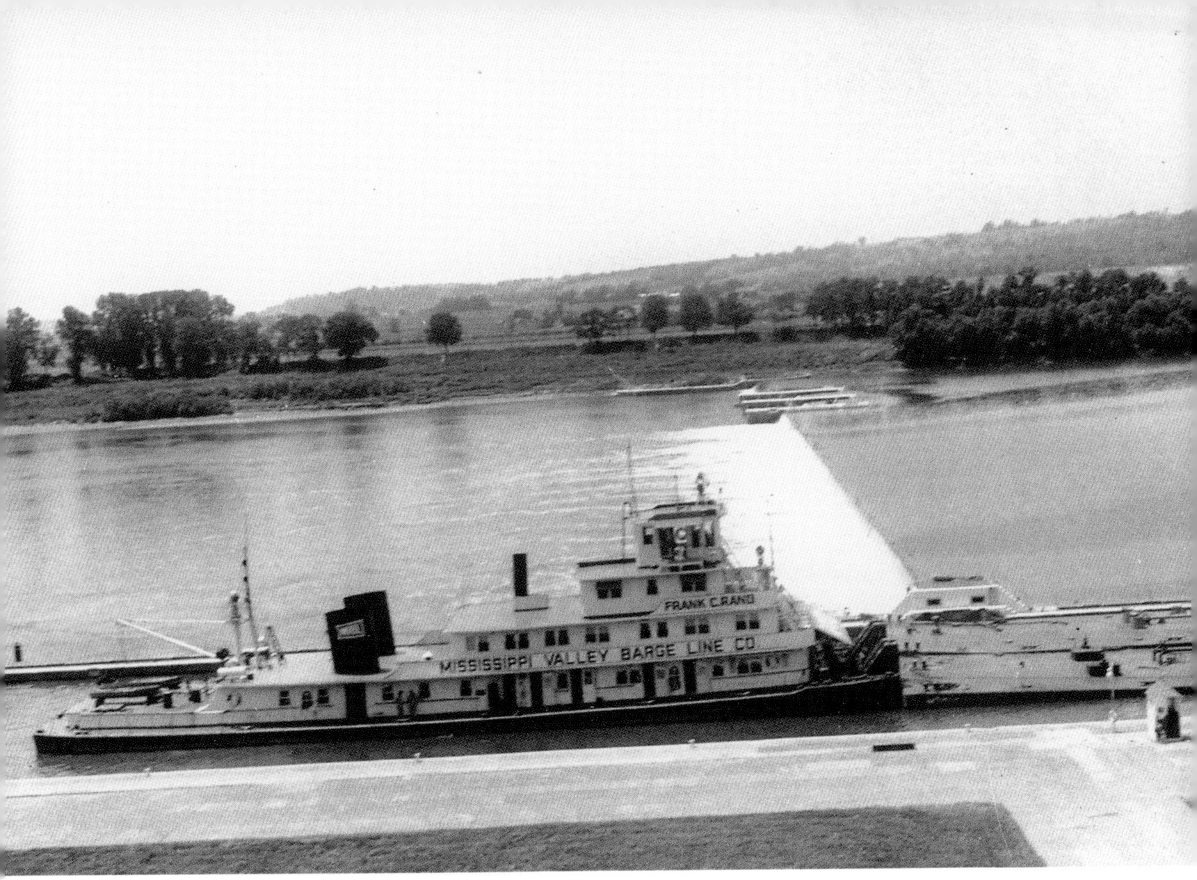

BELLEVIEW/MCVILLE DAM. Not long after the turn of the last century, the Army Corp of Engineers built a series of small dams along the Ohio River. One such dam (38) was started in McVille in 1926. Also constructed were some small homes for workers. The homes and water tower still exist. This *c.* 1950 image shows a barge passing through the locks. A set of steps behind the worker homes still exist leading down to the location of the old dam and lock. The dam was demolished in 1966.

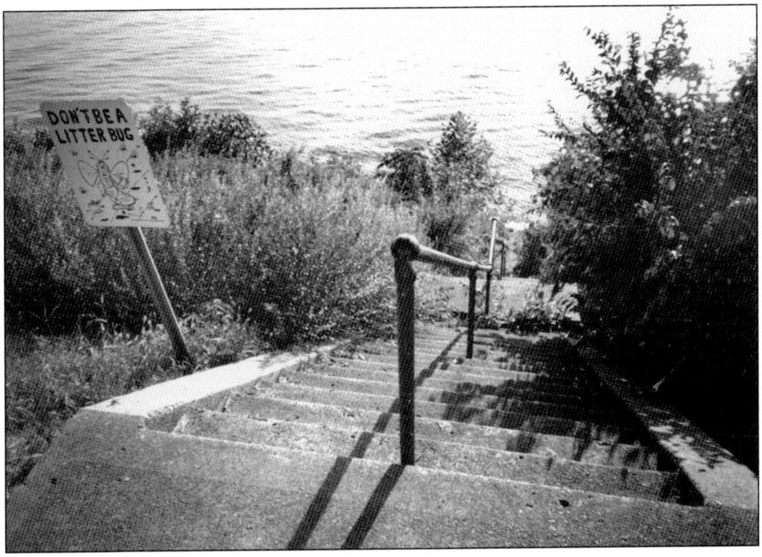

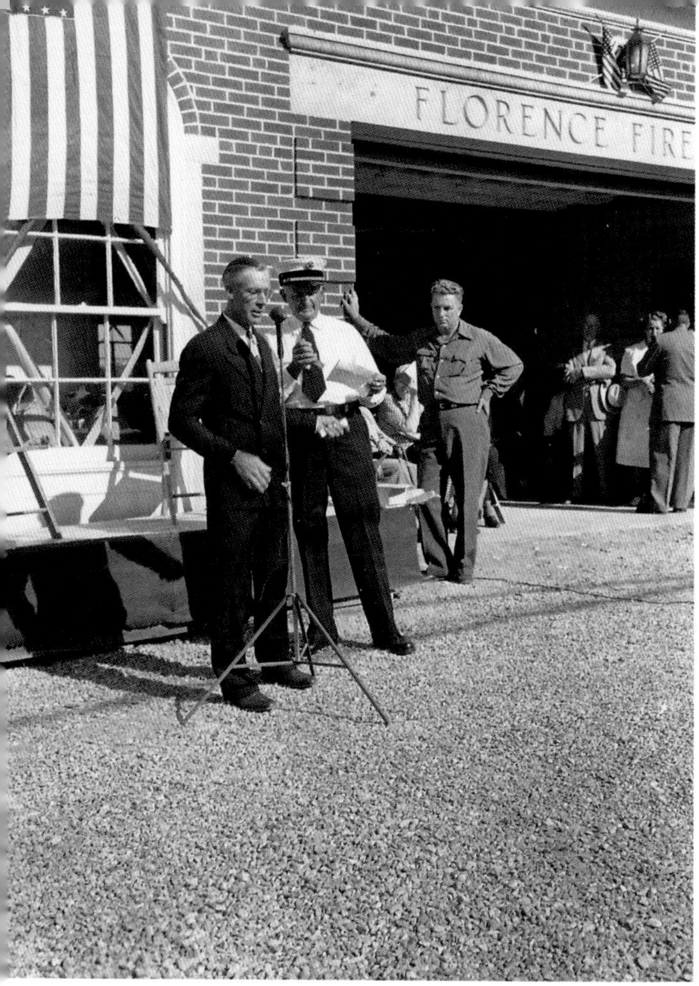

FLORENCE FIRE DEPARTMENT DEDICATION. Albert Hue organized a fire unit in Florence in 1934, which led to the modern department in 1936. Hue served as the first chief until 1952 when he died of a heart attack on the way to a fire. Fire Station #1 was dedicated in 1947, and Chief Hue can be seen in his uniform, including a white cap. Fire Station #2 on Industrial Road is named after him.

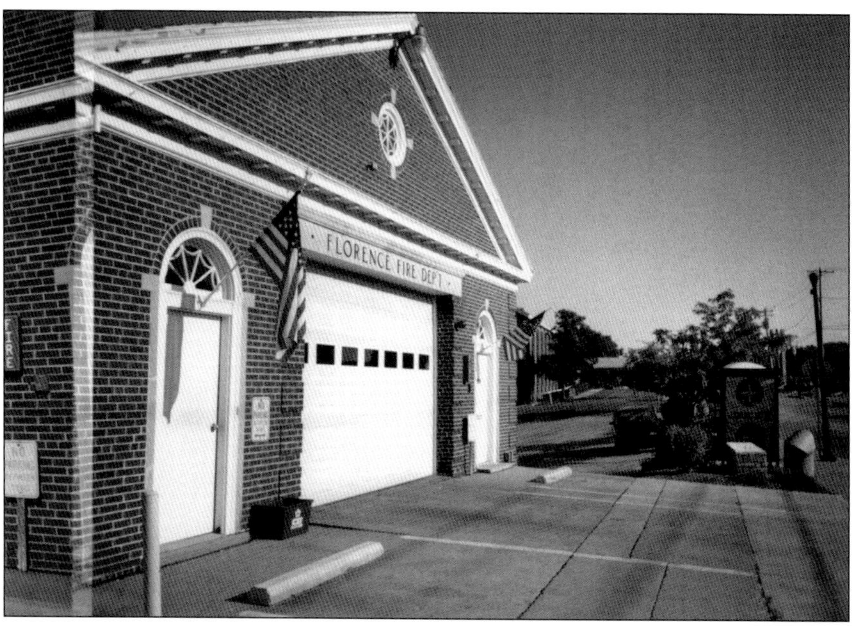

Chapter 5
BUSINESSES

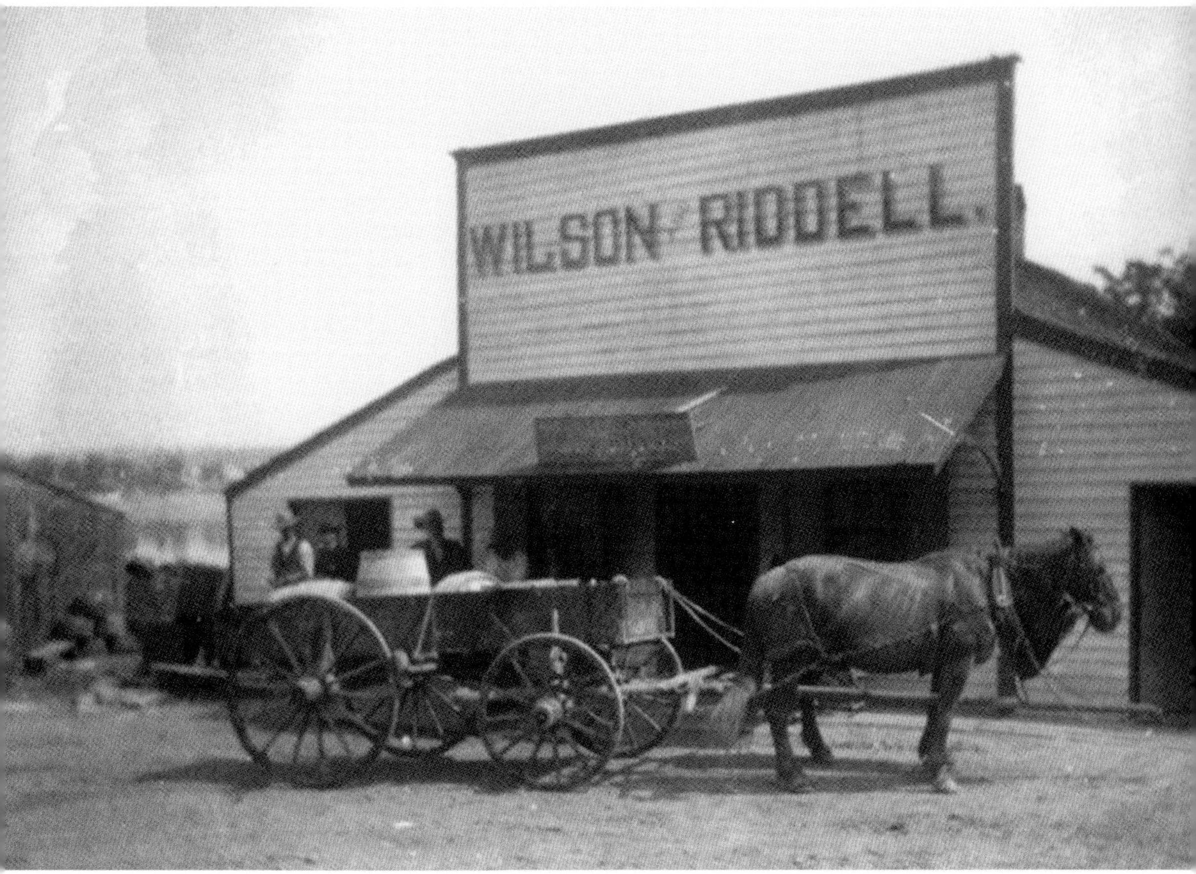

RABBIT HASH GENERAL STORE. The Rabbit Hash General Store was constructed in 1831. Located on the Ohio River, it is one of Boone County's most famous buildings. Photographed in 1894 as the Wilson and Riddell Store, it was reached by horse and buggy. The structure to the left is long gone, and today the spot is a favorite hangout for visitors and locals. The store remains in operation and serves as the focal point of the community of Rabbit Hash.

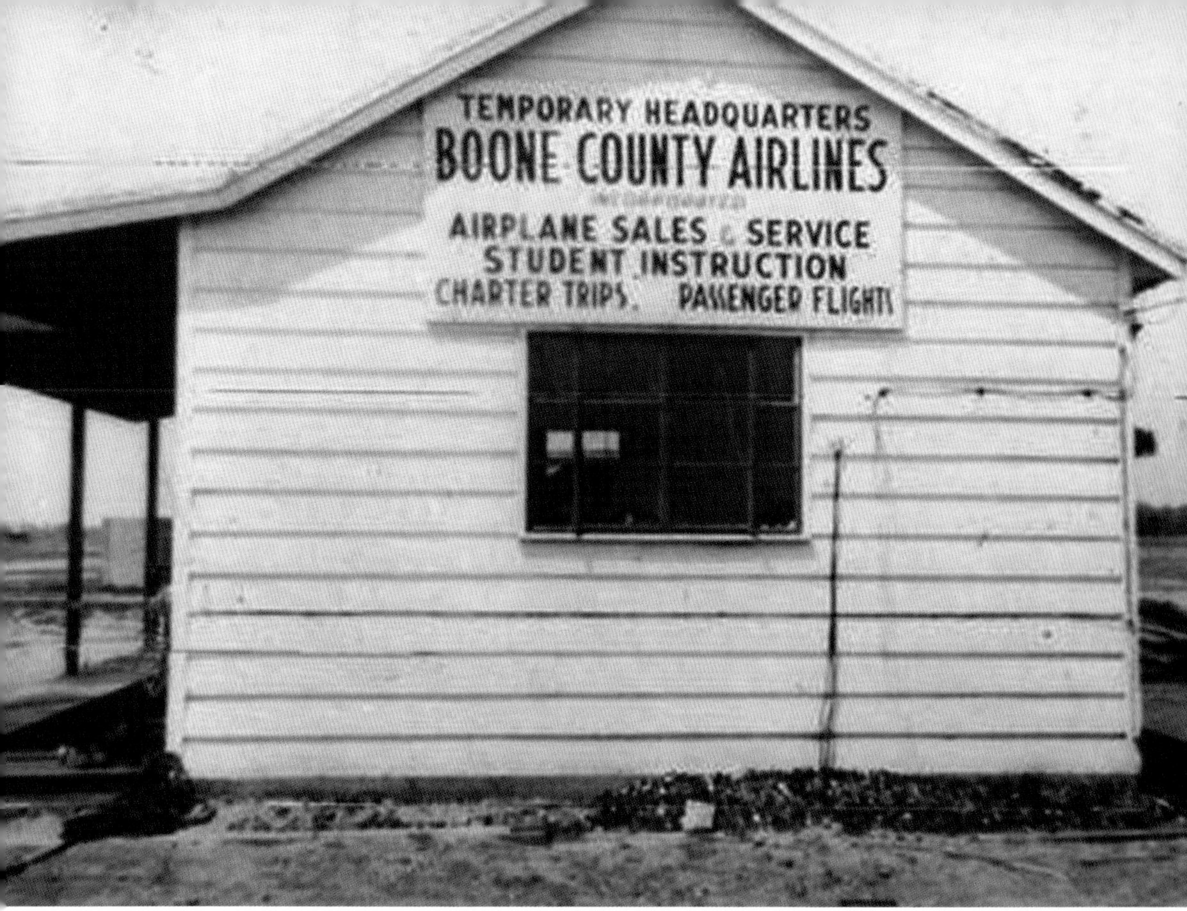

GREATER CINCINNATI/NORTHERN KENTUCKY INTERNATIONAL AIRPORT. The airport was started in the early 1940s to train military pilots and became a civilian airport after the war. In 1946, the airport's first terminal was dedicated. The first airline for passenger flights was Boone County Airlines, which operated out of the wooden building pictured here. The airport has grown rapidly over the years and is considered the economic engine that drives Northern Kentucky.

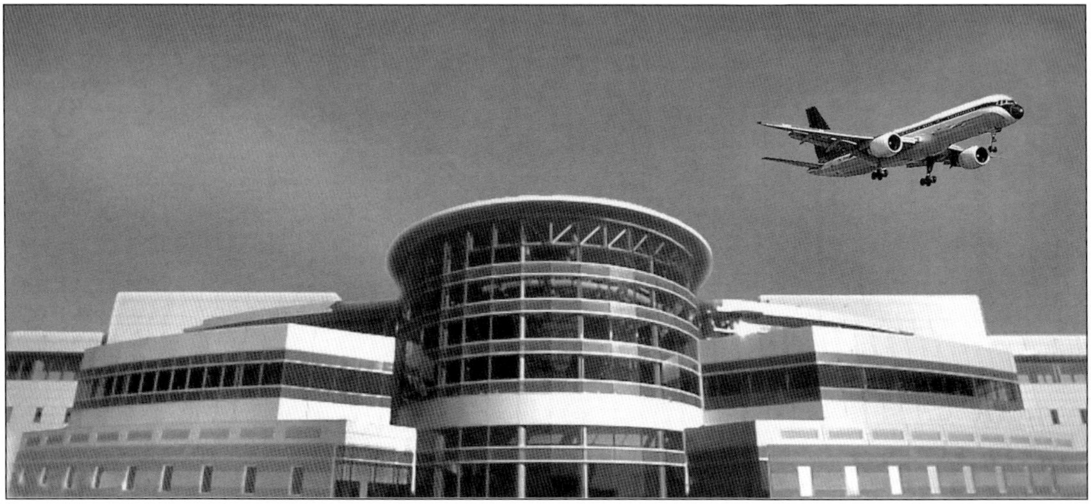

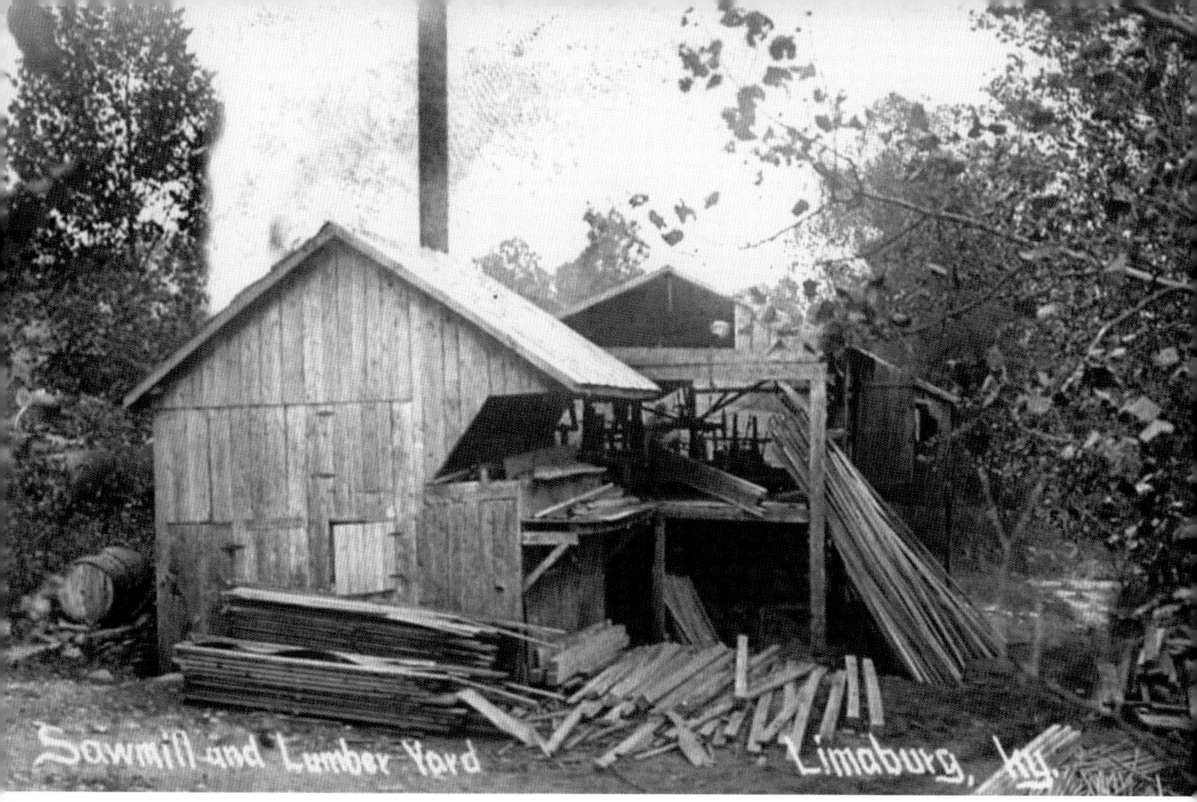

LIMABURG MILL. The Limaburg Sawmill and Lumber Yard was located in an area just off the heavily traveled Burlington Pike. The mill sat between old Burlington Pike and the new pike at Gunpowder Creek. Today the creek runs underneath Burlington Pike via a culvert. The specific location of the mill was on the north side of Burlington Pike, in the area now covered by trees immediately before the Pike meets Limaburg Road.

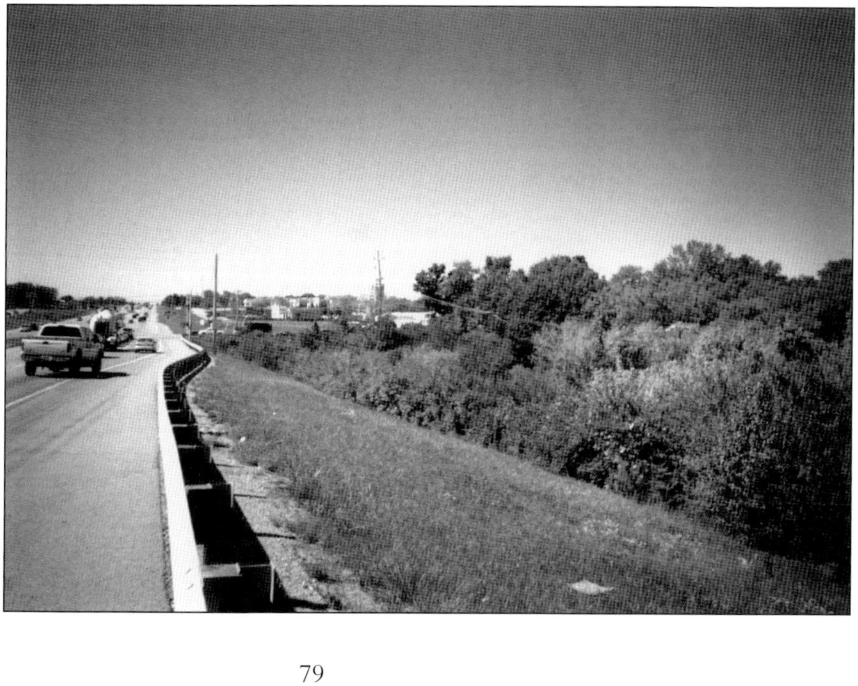

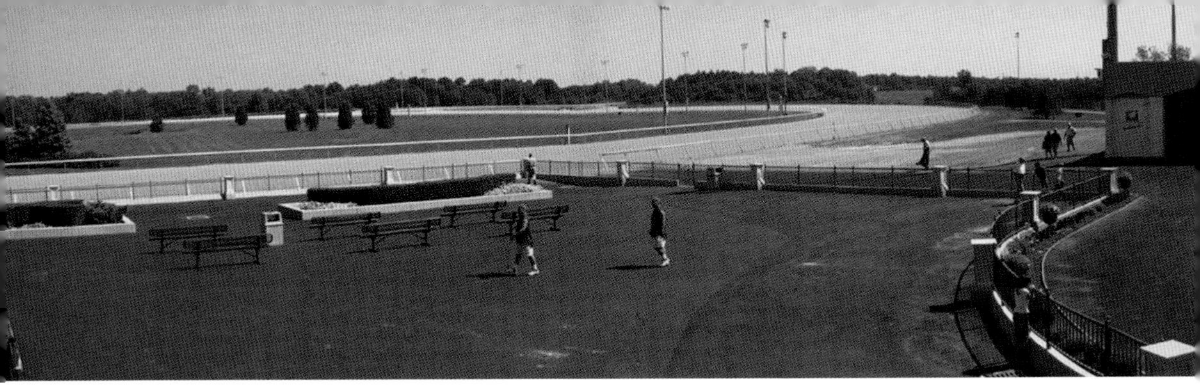

TURFWAY RACE COURSE. Latonia Race Course opened in Florence and was named after the old track in Kenton County. The first race at new Latonia was August 27, 1959. Later the track was greatly expanded and the name was changed to Turfway. The panoramic view shows the modern paddock.

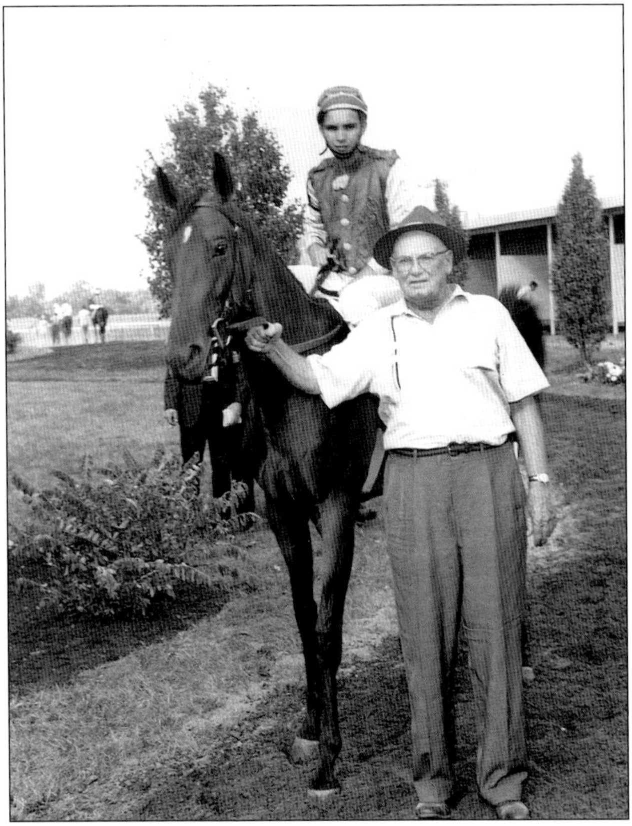

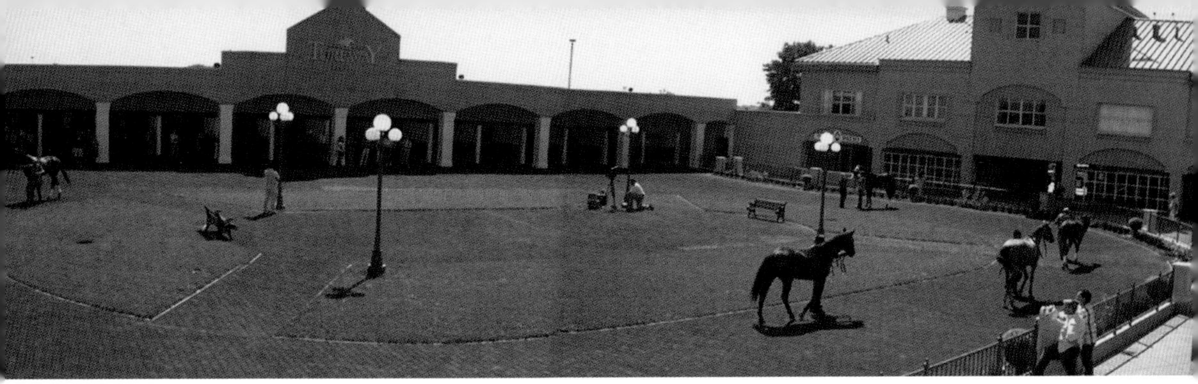

Pictured on the left is the first horse to enter the track at the new Latonia Course in 1959. The other photograph shows Big Dot, the winner of the first Spiral Stakes, which has evolved over the years into the Lane's End Stakes. This shot was taken April 1, 1972.

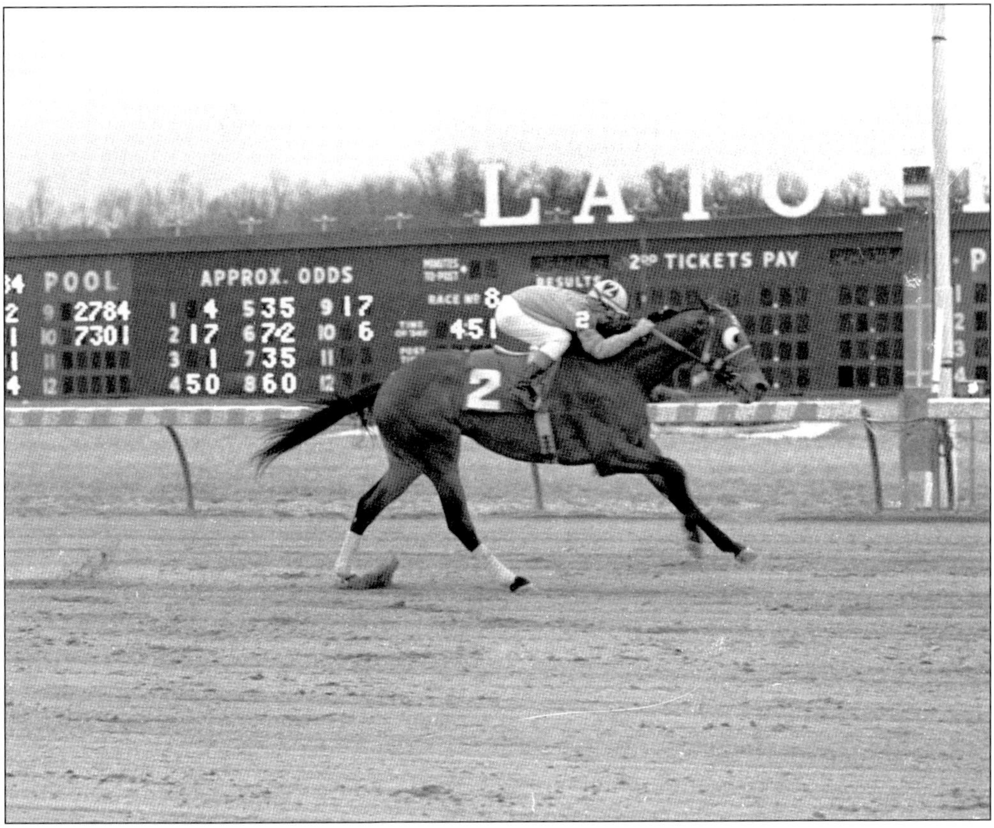

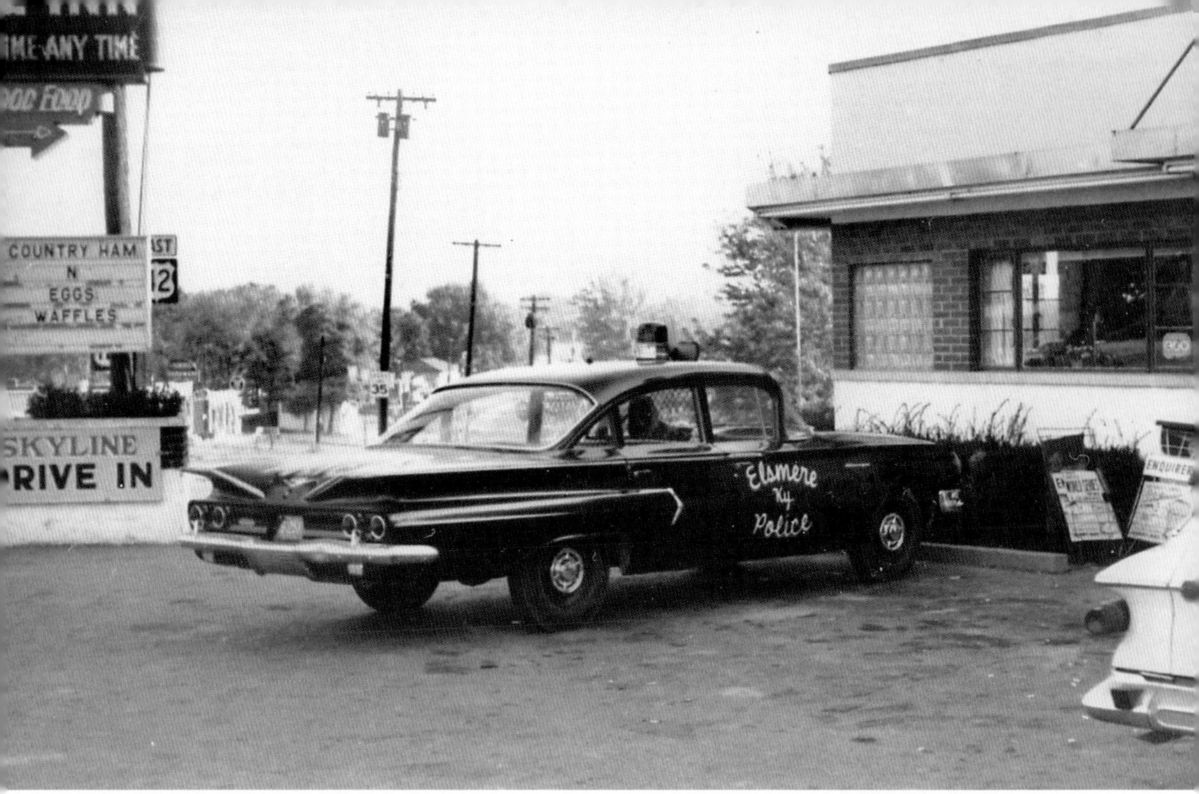

SKYLINE **DRIVE-IN.** The old Ackely's Skyline Drive-In was located in Florence on the northeast corner of U.S. 25 and 42. The popular restaurant was open 24 hours a day. In the picture, an old Elsmere police car is parked at the restaurant and the *Cincinnati Enquirer* newspaper rack predates the large metal boxes of today. Currently, the site is home to CALCARS Used Auto Sales.

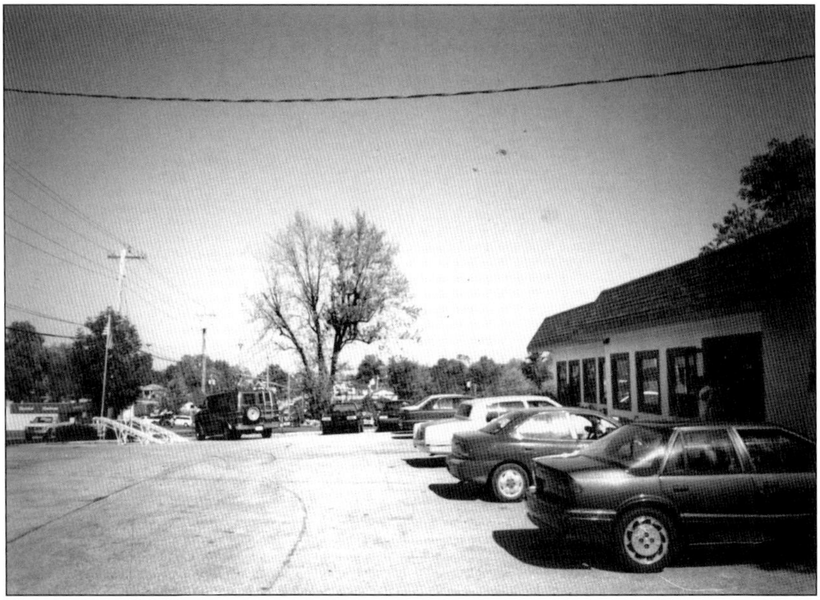

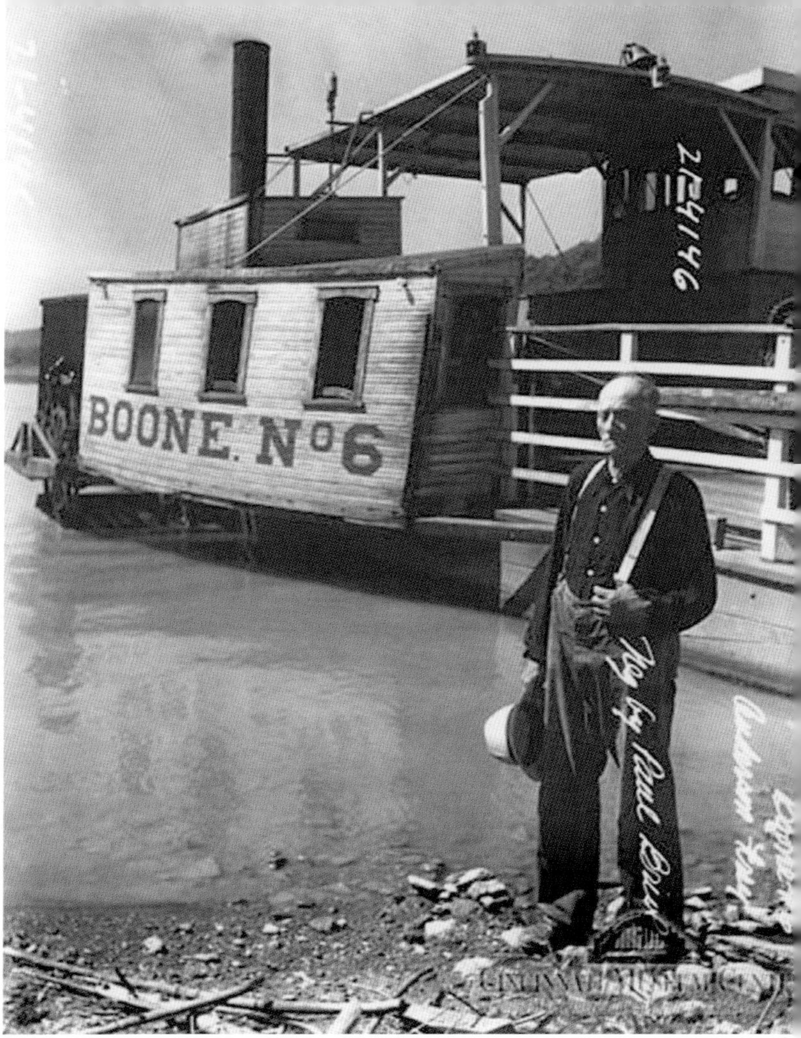

ANDERSON FERRY STILL CROSSES THE OHIO. The Anderson Ferry has been crossing the Ohio River at Constance since 1817 and is the only ferry still operating in the area. Started by George Anderson, it was later bought by German immigrant Charles Kottmeyer, a Constance landowner. This 1940 image shows Boone No. 6, the predecessor to No. 7, in the same spot near the ferry landing.

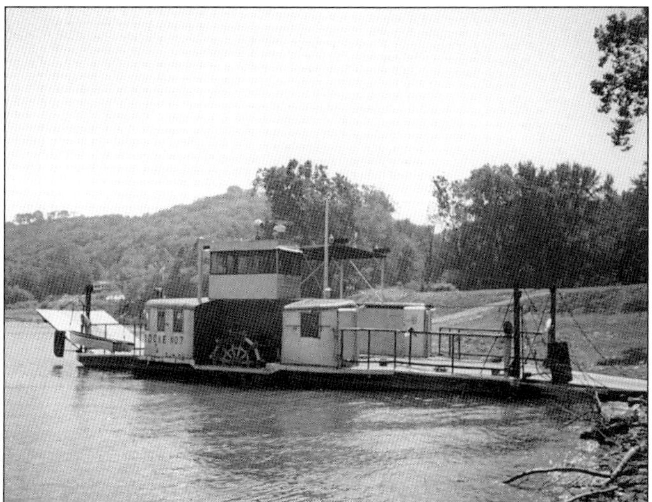

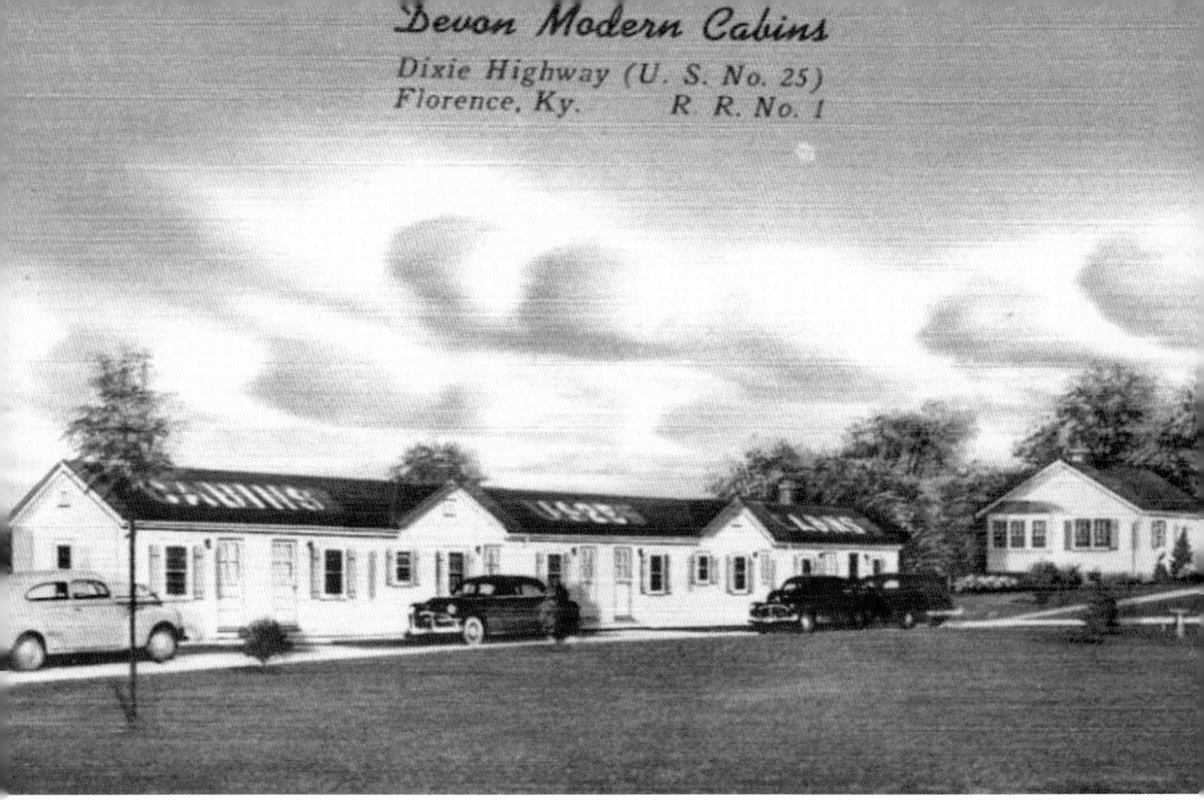

DEVON MODERN CABINS. The Devon Modern Cabins was one of many vintage motels dotting the landscape on the roads to Louisville and Lexington through Northern Kentucky. Located on U.S. 25, this postcard from the motel's heyday seems very similar today. The building on the right of the postcard still exists as a home, and the hotel serves as an apartment building.

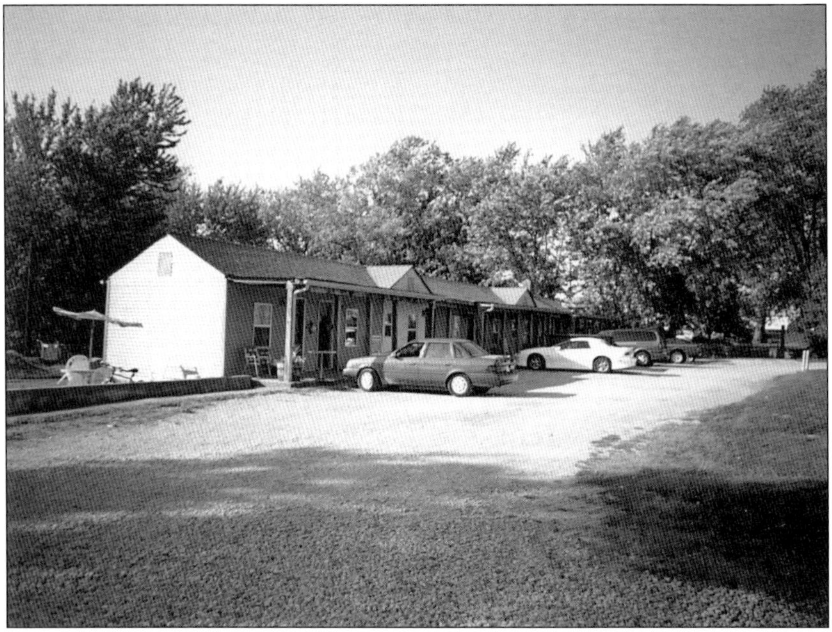

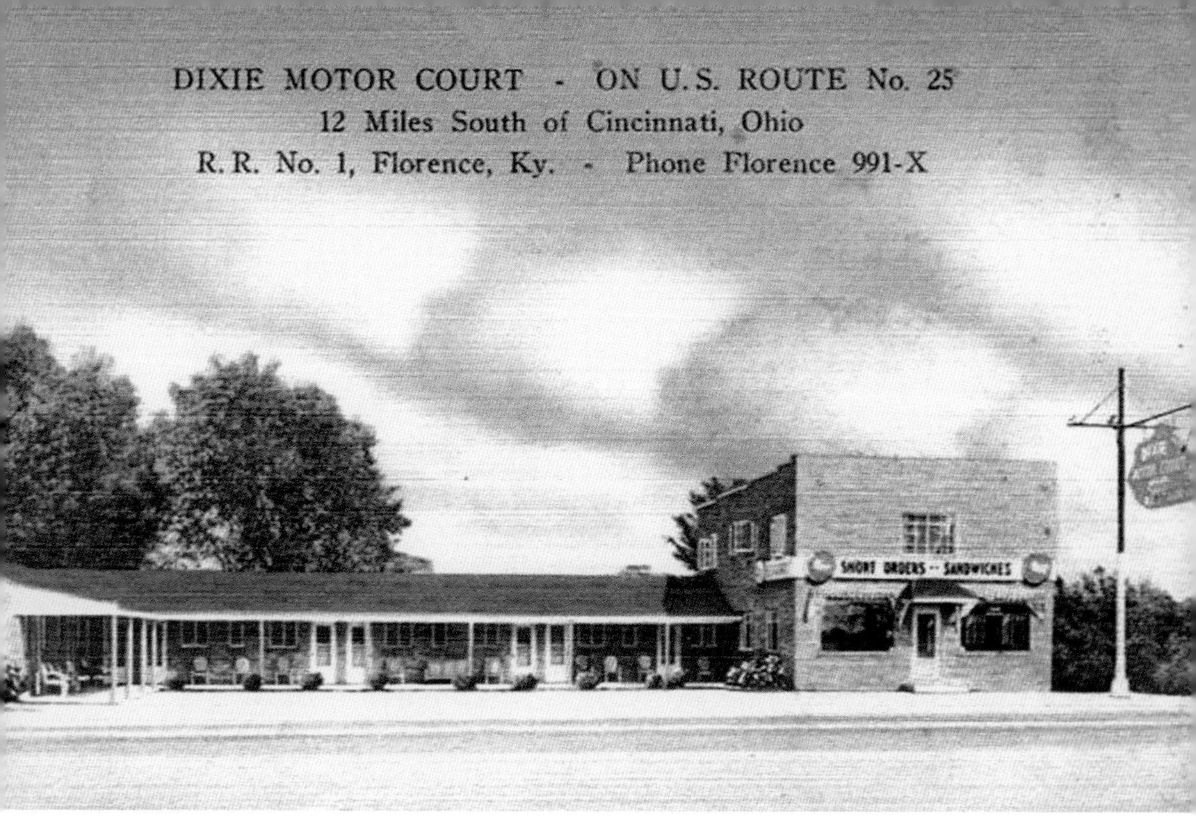

DIXIE MOTOR COURT. Another example of Northern Kentucky motels is the Dixie Motor Court located on U.S. 25, 12 miles south of Cincinnati. The Dixie had a restaurant for the weary traveler that advertised "Short Orders" and "Sandwiches" on the building front, as seen in this vintage postcard. The Dixie also had other features, including "mattresses by Beautyrest, tile baths, and steam heat." Today the Dixie serves as an apartment building.

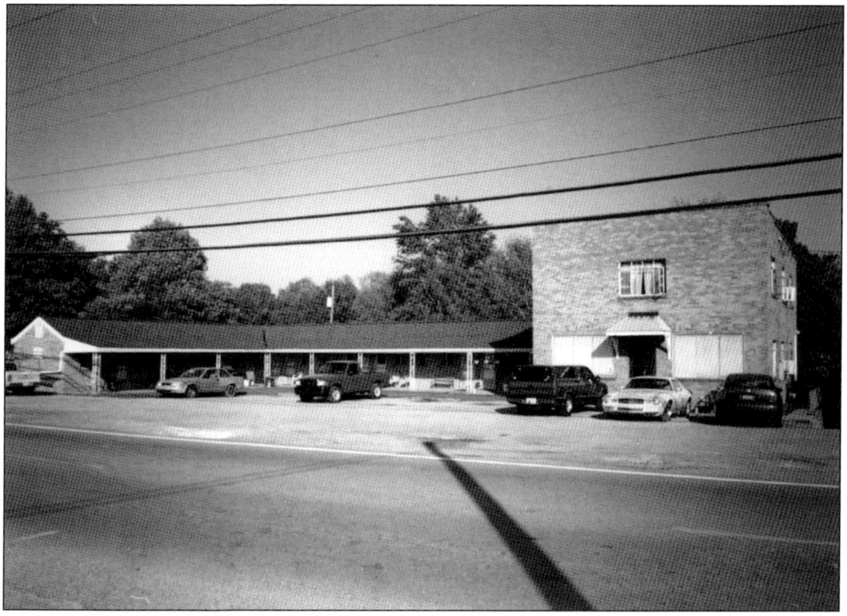

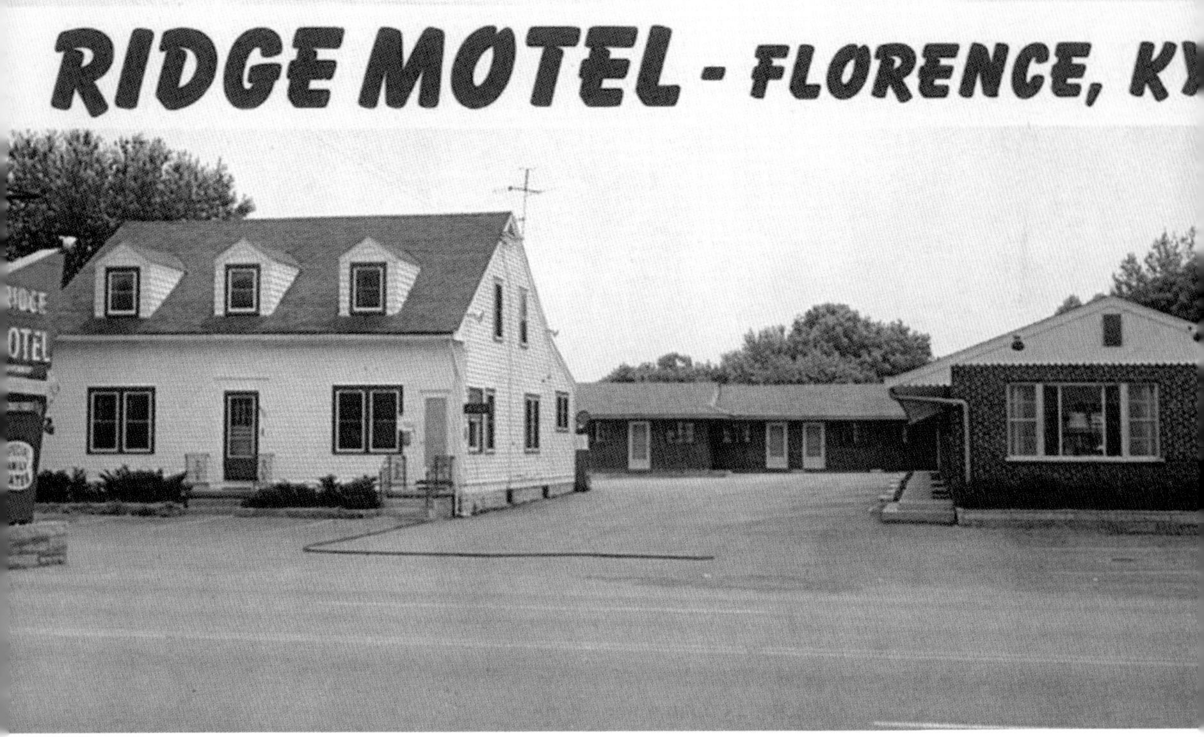

RIDGE MOTEL. The old Ridge Motel was located at 6501 Dixie Highway in Florence. It was one of many Boone County motels on the road to Lexington or Louisville. Today it is the Turfside Motel on a very different Dixie Highway. Both the Ridge and Turfside have vintage signs outside, which are classics of the American highway.

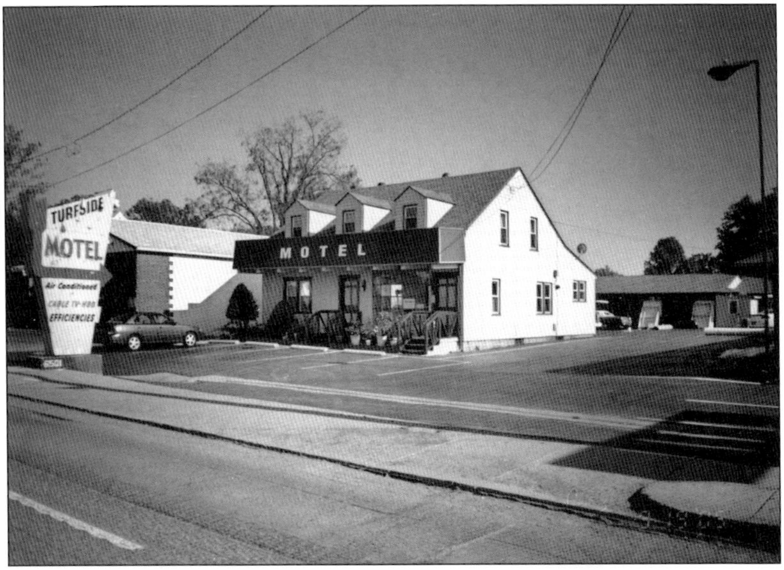

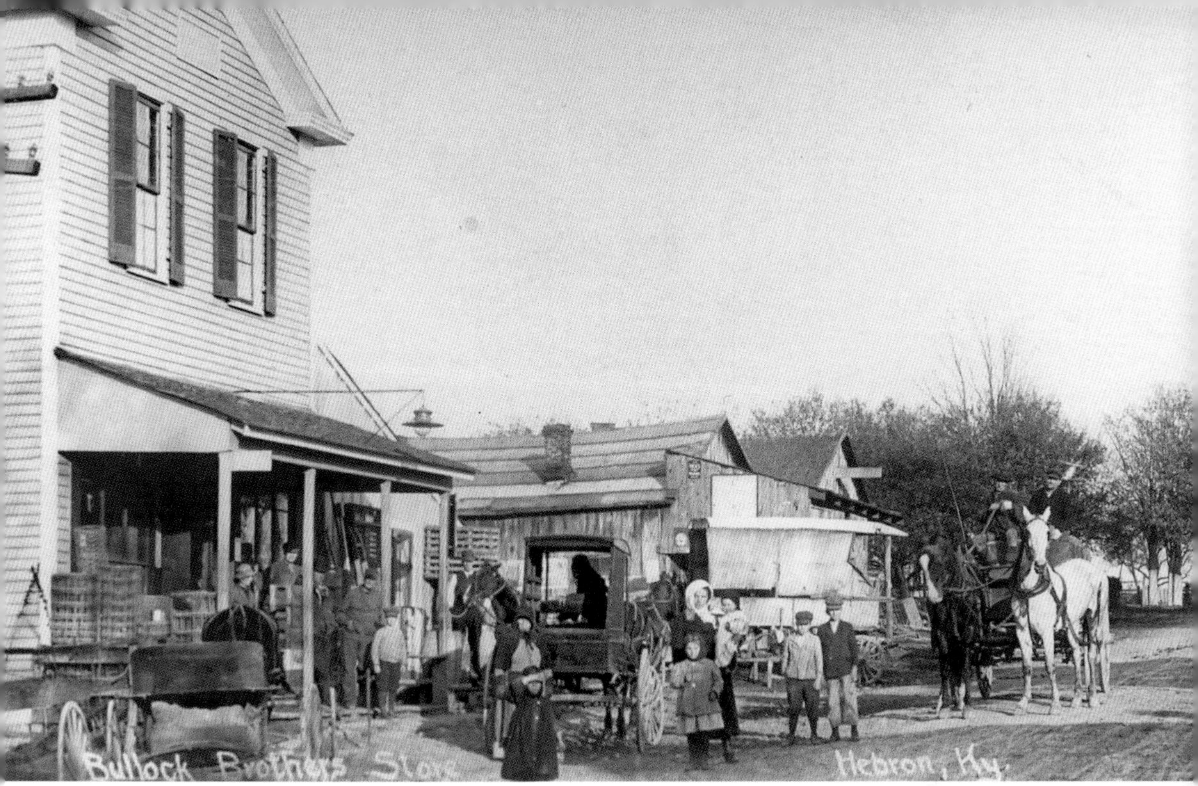

BULLOCK BROTHERS STORE. Located in Hebron, the Bullock Brother Store also served as the post office. It was located on one of the oldest roads in the county, Petersburg Road (Kentucky 20), which dates back to 1799. Today the Hebron area is expanding with new single-family homes and businesses; however, most of this development is not near the old business district. Few historic structures in the old Hebron business district exist today.

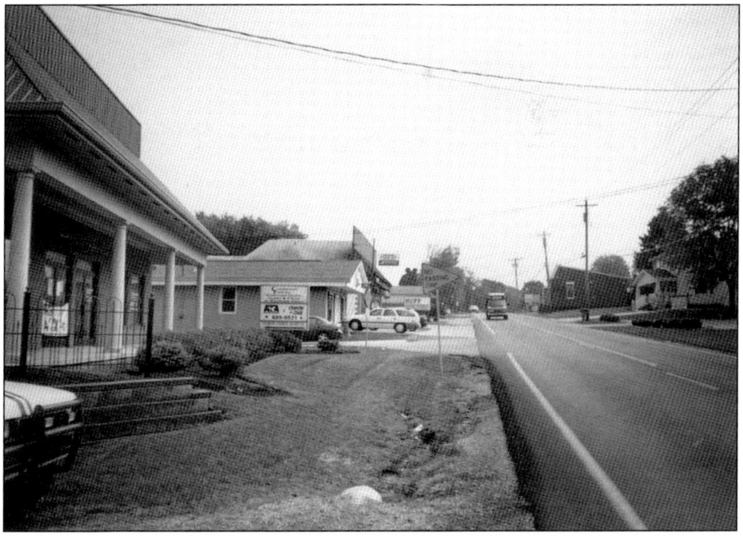

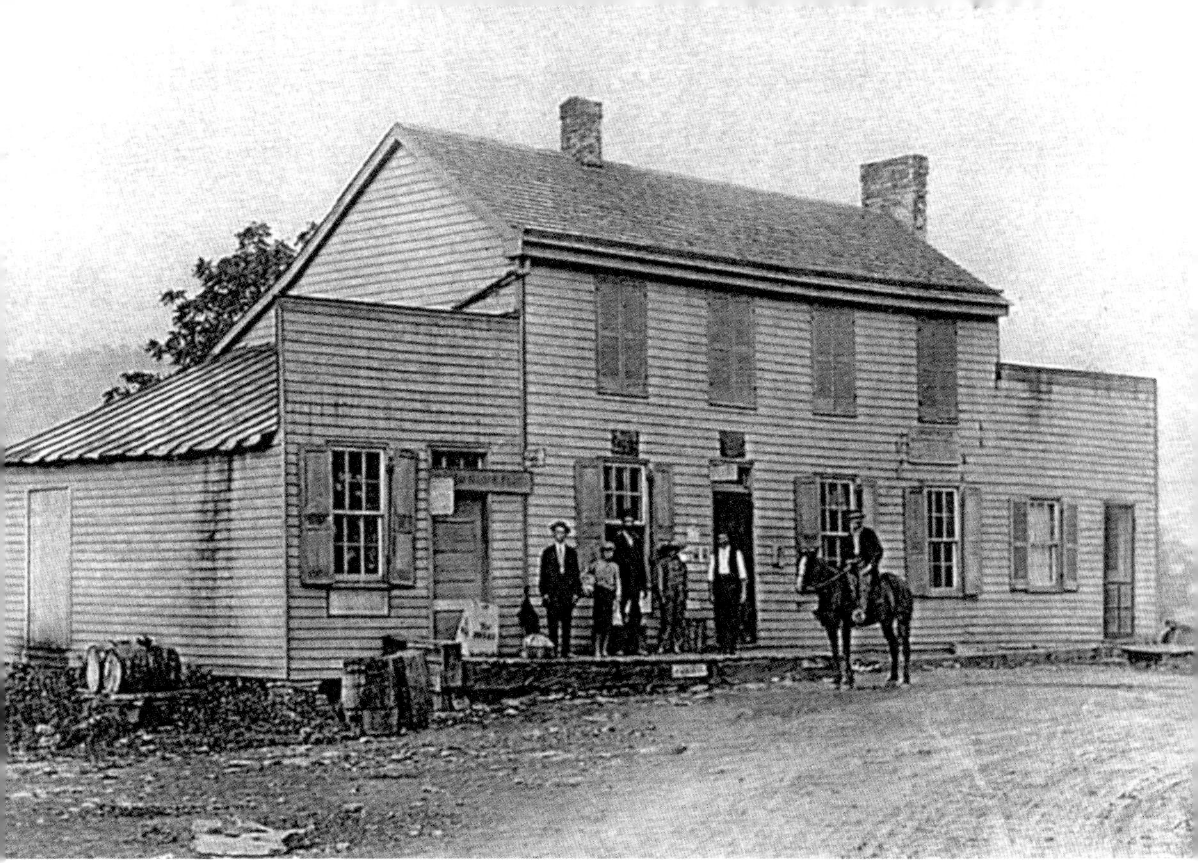

Posing at the Store. In this undated image, a man on horseback poses with three other adults and two children at the old Constance Store. The once-lively store still stands, lonely, hidden behind trees and brush on Route 8. Even though run-down and abandoned for years, many of its original features remain, such as the upper-left window as it appears today.

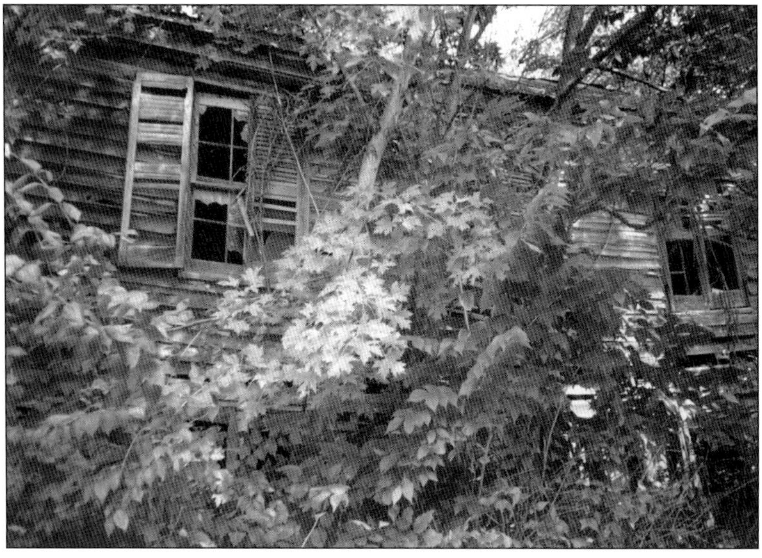

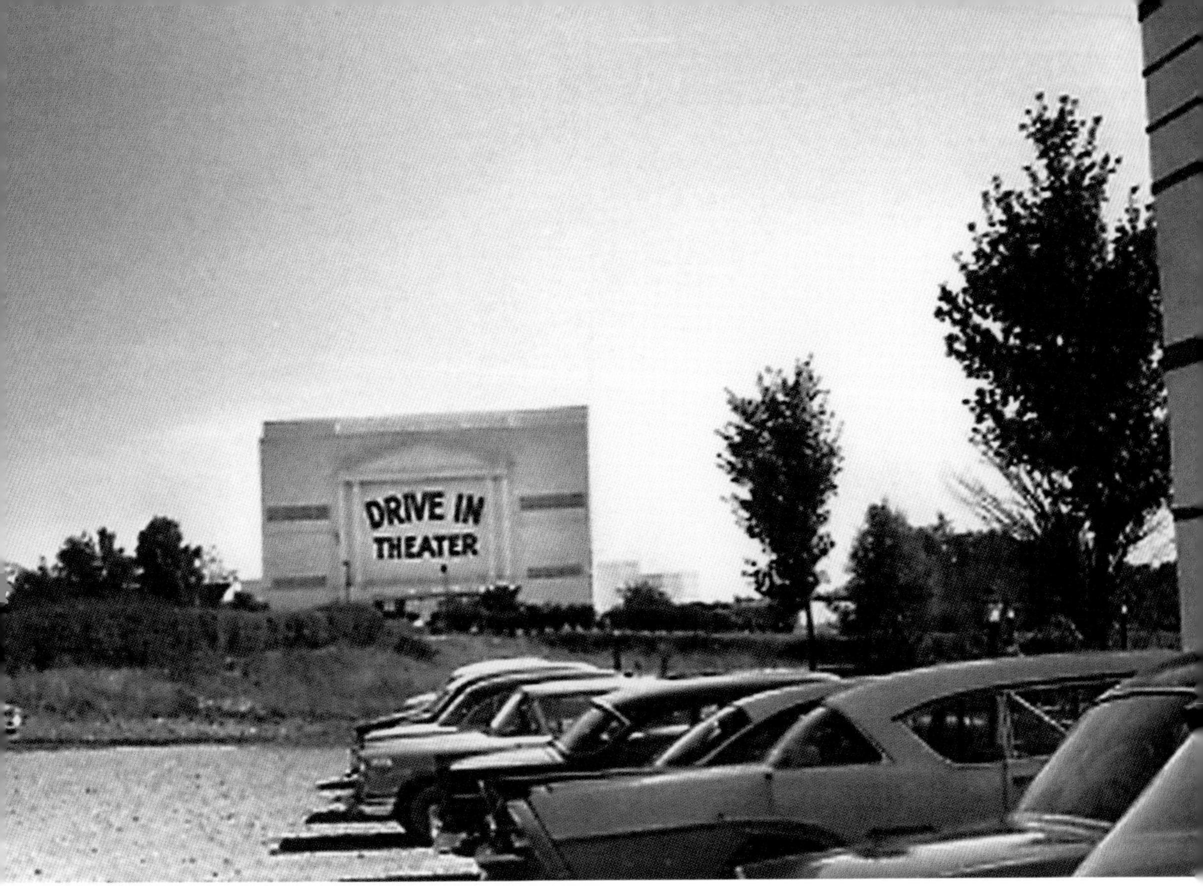

FLORENCE DRIVE-IN THEATER. The Florence Drive-in Theater was located on Dixie Highway on a site now developed as the Village Parke Condominiums. It opened in the 1940s and closed about 25 years ago. The drive-in sat vacant for years before being developed into the condominiums. The screen sat approximately in the middle of the road seen in the village photograph but well back from Dixie Highway.

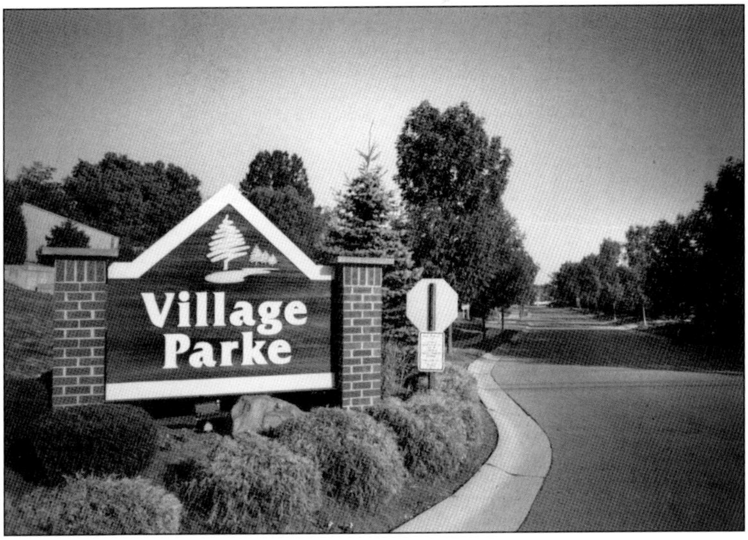

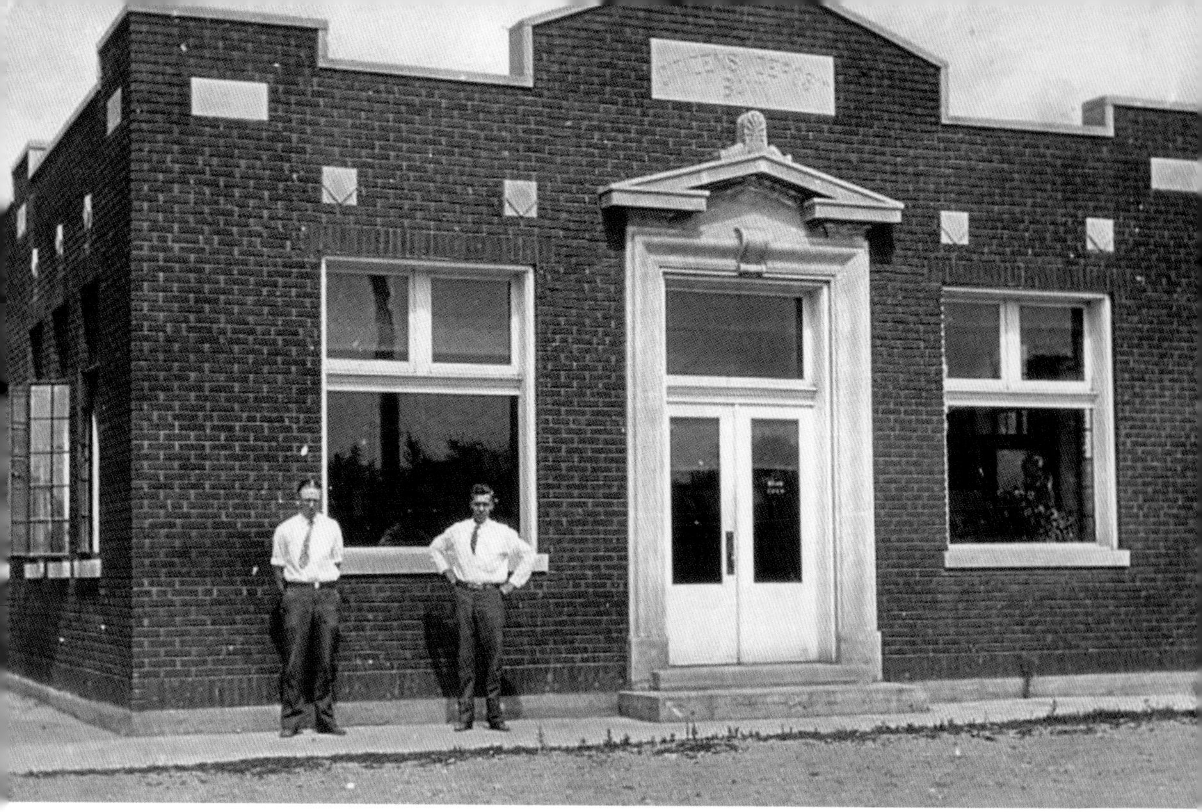

Citizens Deposit Bank. The Citizens Deposit Bank in Belleview was built in 1926 and is a beautiful example of a small rural institution. The picture of the bank is from *c.* 1930. The building today is occupied by the Bank of Kentucky and has been very well preserved. It sits on Route 18 and adds tremendously to the rural charm of Belleview.

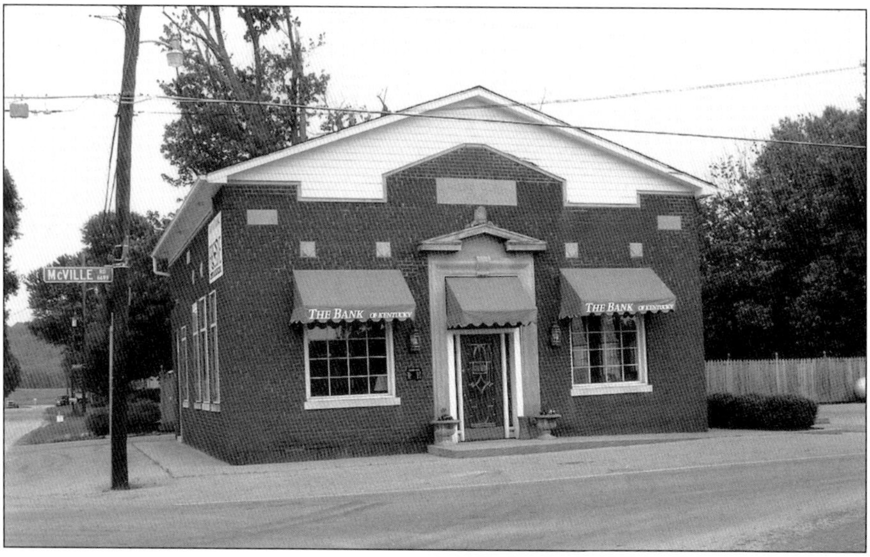

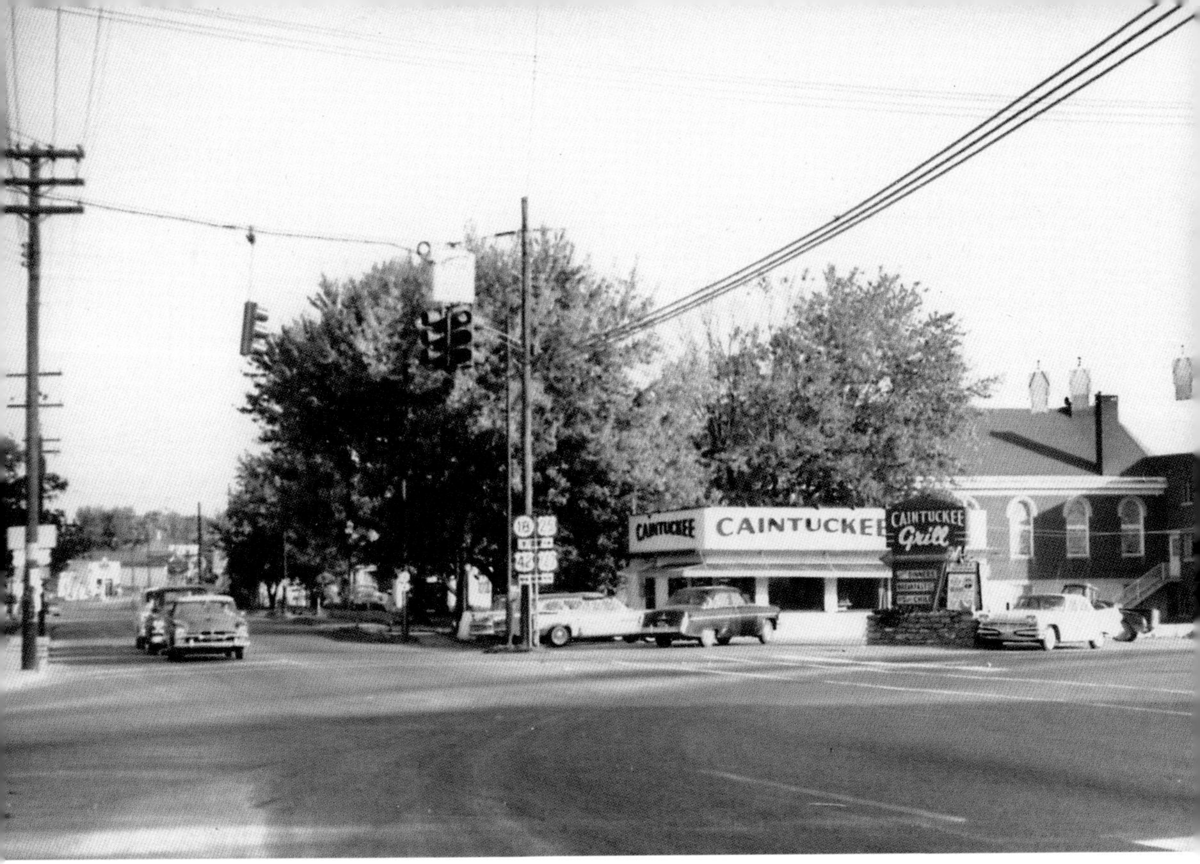

CAINTUCKEE GRILL. Perhaps one of the most famous restaurants ever in Northern Kentucky, the Caintuckee Grill, was located on the corner of U.S. 25 and Main Street in Florence. Started in 1953 by Hilda Ramler, it was truly a family business. The home cooking was said to be the best and attracted everybody who was anybody. Ms. Ramler closed the restaurant in 1984 when she retired. She died in August 2004. The restaurant building is gone, and a parking lot remains.

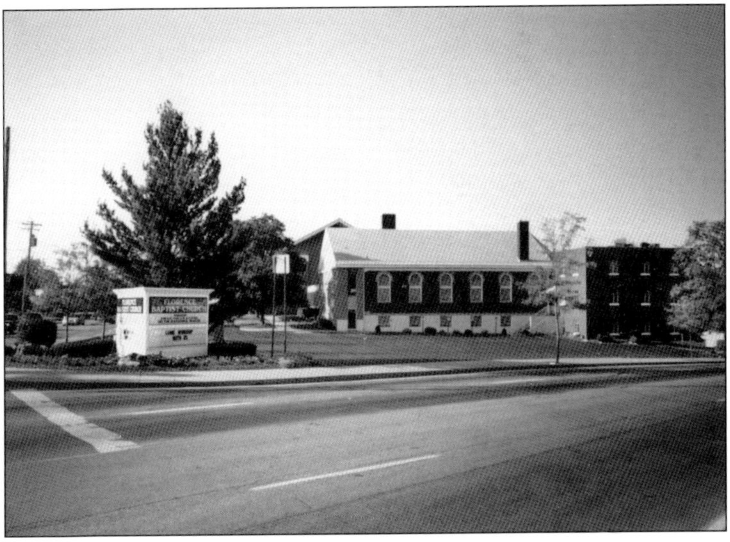

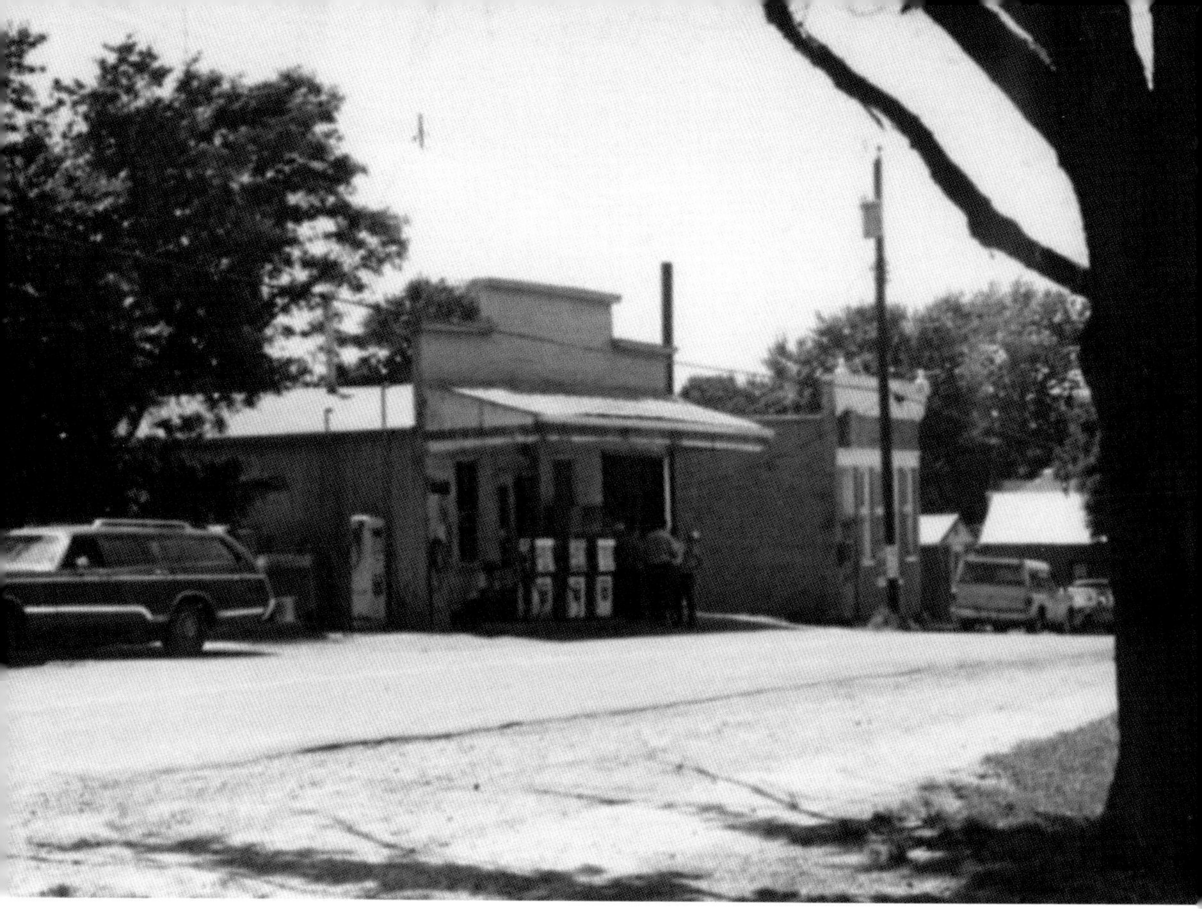

AN **EARLY GARAGE.** Garages can be historic, as seen in this photograph of the Verona Garage built in the early 20th century. This building is a great example of the transformation to automobiles. It served as Verona's informal "city hall" for many years before it was destroyed by fire several years ago. Today the lot remains empty, bordered only by the old Verona Deposit Bank built in 1903.

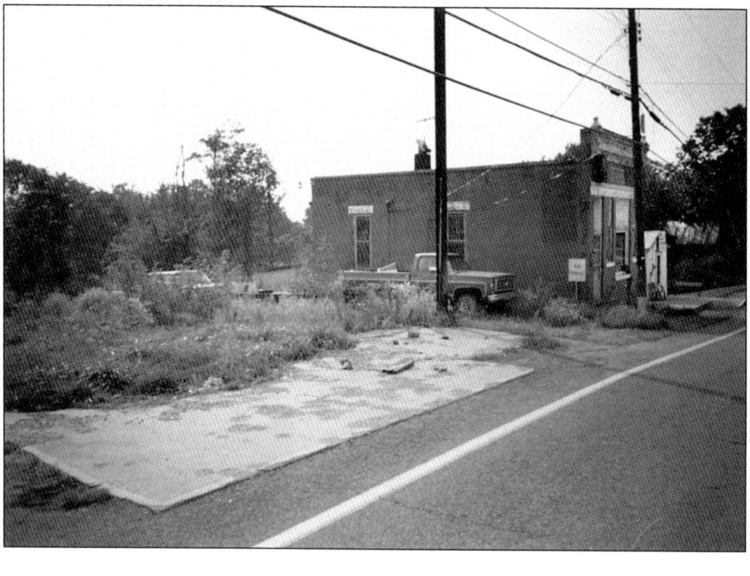

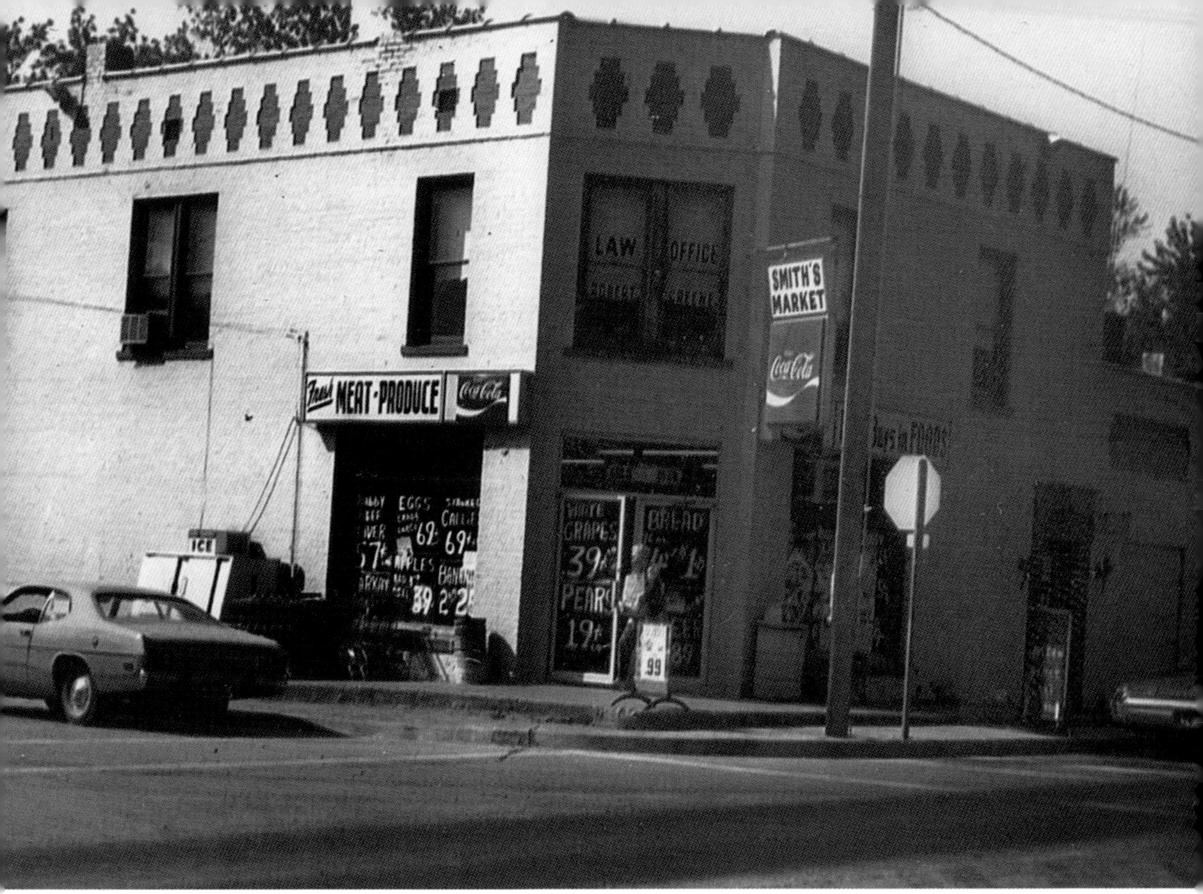

STORE NO MORE. The southwest corner in Burlington at the four-way stop had housed a general store since almost the Civil War. Originally a wood structure, the last store shown in this image was demolished in 2002. It was one of Burlington's most visible buildings and today serves as a parking lot and landscaped area for the Burlington Baptist Church. The upstairs served many uses including a law office. The old clerk's building stood next to the store.

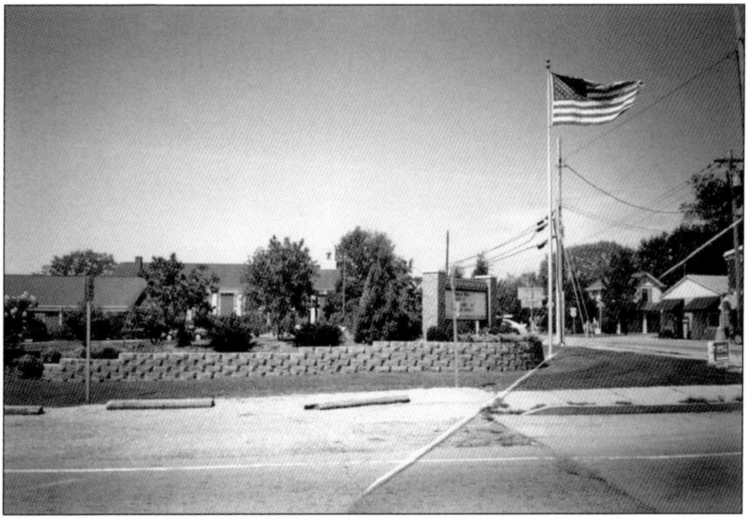

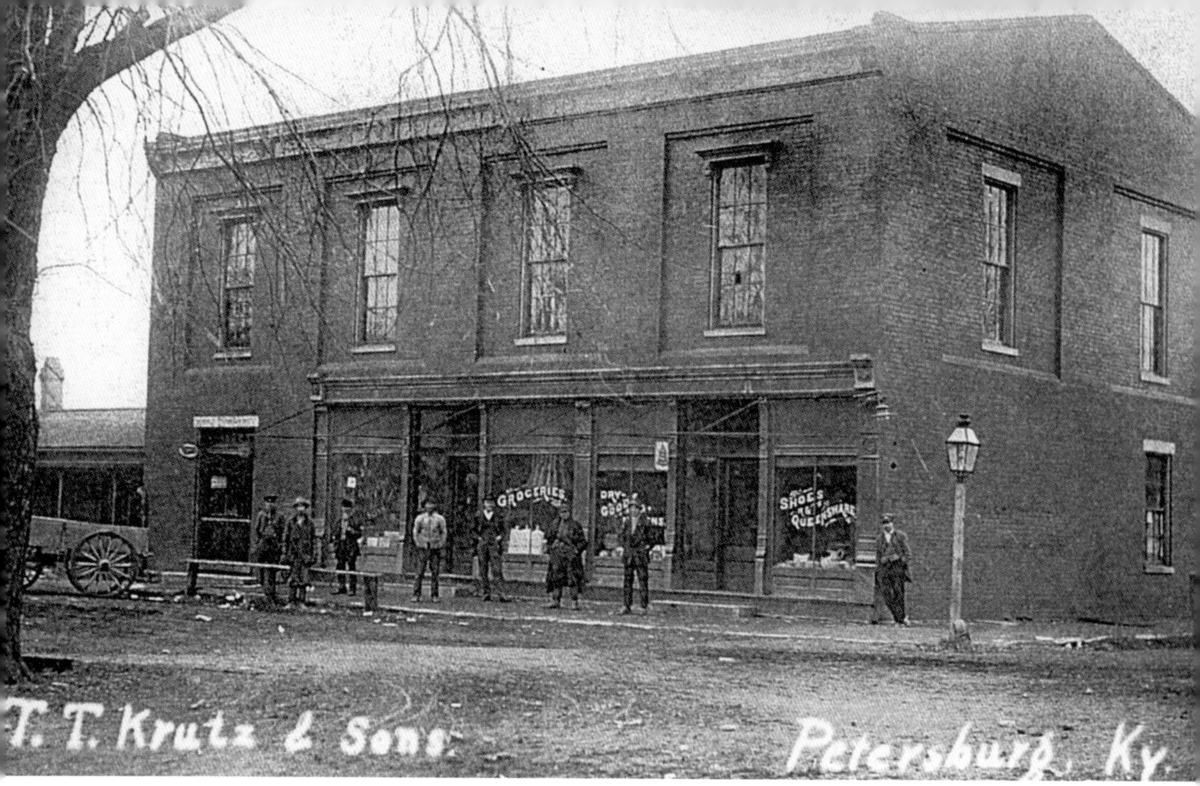

PETERSBURG OPERA HOUSE. The Petersburg Opera House was built in 1892 and has been used as a dance hall, movie theatre, and a place for musical entertainment. As can be seen in the photograph, it also housed the T. T. Krutz and Sons store, selling groceries, dry goods, shoes, and Queensware. The building is well preserved and today houses a successful business.

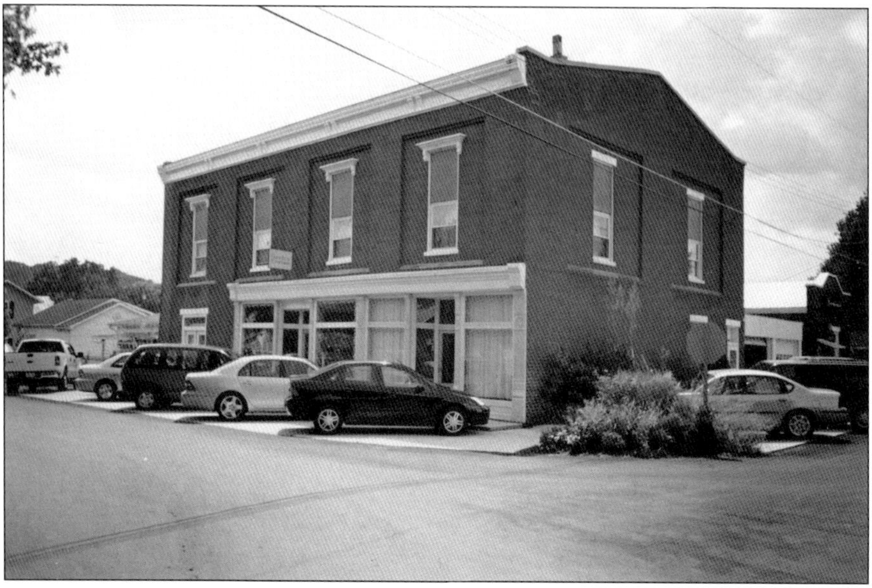

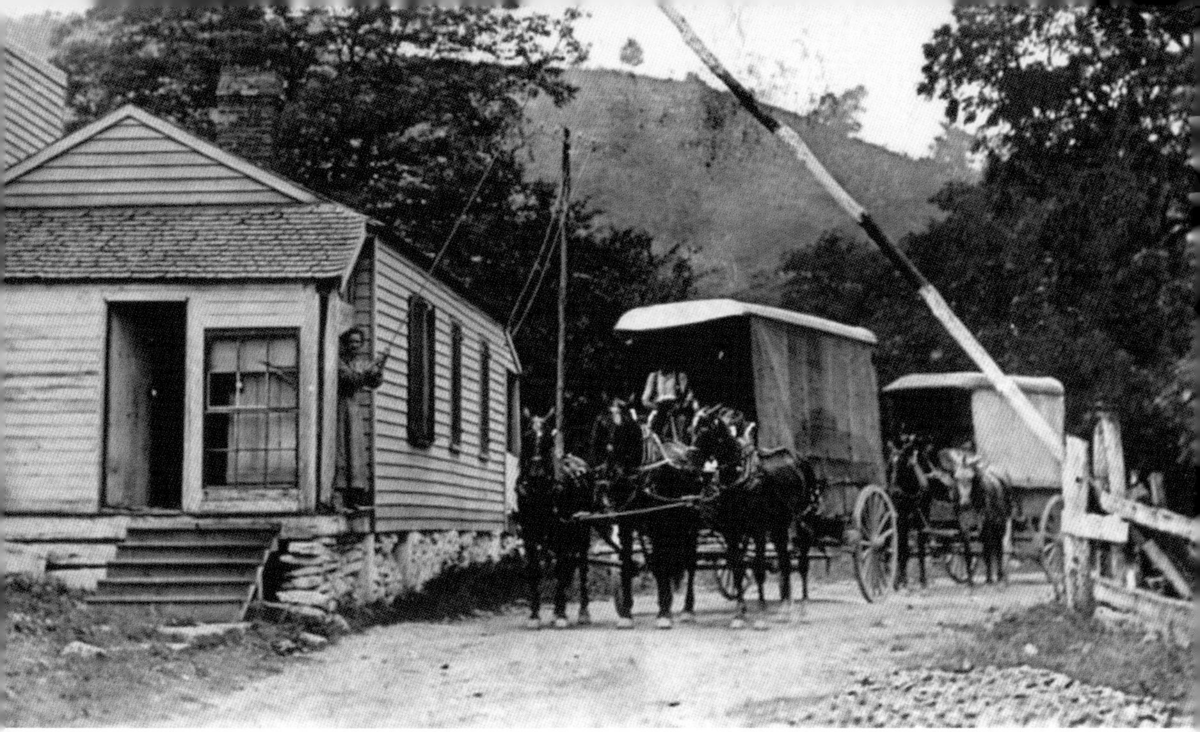

TOLLHOUSES. Boone County had many tollhouses around the turn of the last century. Usually built almost on top of the road, they were spots where tolls were collected in order for a traveler to use the road. A family lived in the house so tolls could be collected around the clock. The older image shows the Constance Toll House. A more common tollhouse design is in this recent picture taken near Pleasant Valley Road and U.S. 42 in Florence.

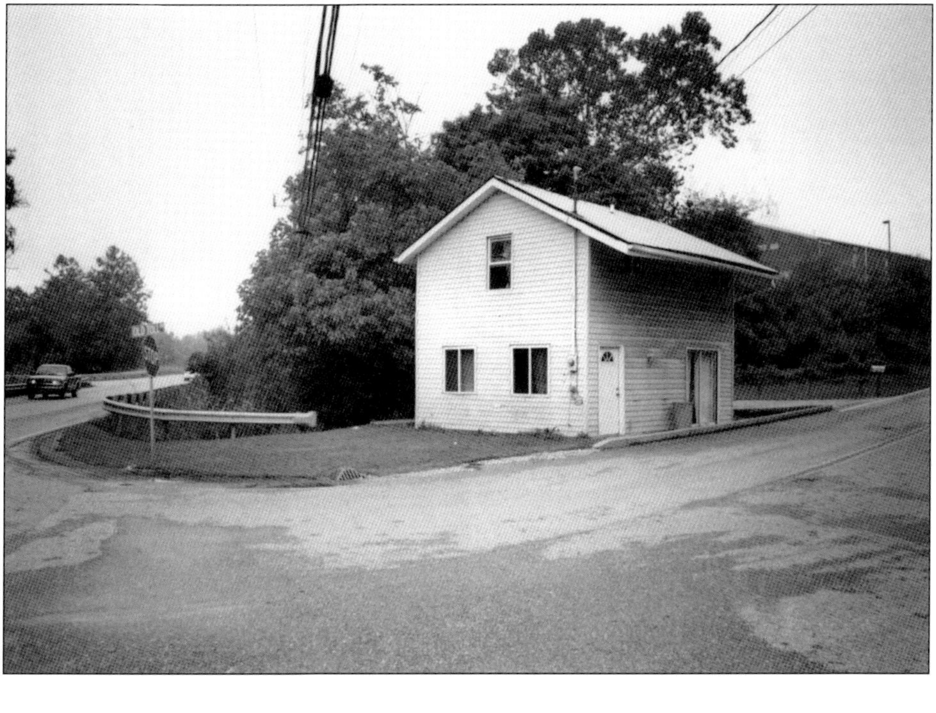

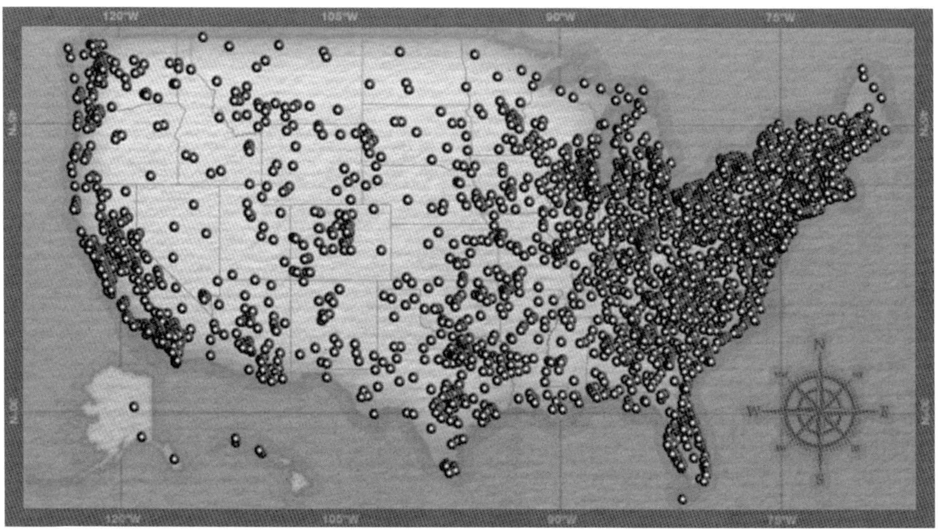